CONSTRUCTION WORKERS, U.S.A.

Recent Titles in
Contributions in Labor Studies

CONSTRUCTION WORKERS, U.S.A.

Herbert Applebaum

Contributions in Labor Studies, Number 54

GREENWOOD PRESS
Westport, Connecticut • London

Library of Congress Cataloging-in-Publication Data

Applebaum, Herbert A.
    Construction workers, U.S.A. / Herbert Applebaum.
        p.   cm.—(Contributions in labor studies, ISSN 0886–8239 ;
  no. 54)
    Includes bibliographical references and index.
    ISBN 0–313–30937–X (alk. paper)
    1. Construction workers—United States. 2. Building trades—
  United States. I. Title. II. Title: Construction workers, USA.
  III. Series.
  HD8039.B92U539   1999
  331.7′624′0973—dc21   99–22093

British Library Cataloguing in Publication Data is available.

Library of Congress Catalog Card Number: 99–22093
ISBN: 0–313–30937–X
ISSN: 0886–8239

First published in 1999

Greenwood Press, 88 Post Road West, Westport, CT 06881
An imprint of Greenwood Publishing Group, Inc.
www.greenwood.com

Printed in the United States of America

The paper used in this book complies with the
Permanent Paper Standard issued by the National
Information Standards Organization (Z39.48–1984).

10 9 8 7 6 5 4 3 2 1

Photos by Frank Zimmermann Photography, 917-804-3223. © Frank Zimmermann Photography.

To Mika, my wife
To Earl Kostak and my constuction buddies

CONTENTS

Photo essay follows p. 128

Illustrations

1

Preface

This book is dedicated to the U.S. construction industry, where I have spent 42 years of my working life and where I continue to work as of today. The content of this book is based on my work experiences in this industry and traces a time line of changes from 1956 to 1998. This volume also contains material taken from the writings of other men and women who have worked in construction and written about their experiences. In addition, findings of social scientists who have researched the construction industry and its workers are examined and utilized for insights and analysis to supplement my own findings and viewpoint.

My credentials as a full participant in the industry include the following jobs and positions—laborer, mason, estimator, engineer, project manager, contracts administrator, construction consultant, construction manager, vice president, and president of my own construction company. In my present job I am the director of commercial construction for Hartz Mountain Industries. I have worked in many areas of the United States including New York, Chicago, Michigan, Louisville, Florida, New Jersey, Massachusetts, Connecticut, Washington, D.C., Rhode Island, and Pennsylvania.

I have been involved in a diverse range of projects including housing, office buildings, dams, bridges, roads, shopping centers, power plants, hotels, convention centers, sewage treatment plants, newspaper plants, hospitals, factories, car agencies, banks, police and fire stations, warehouses, television and radio stations, and many renovations of existing offices, factories, housing, and warehouses. I have participated in a number of unique projects, such as shutting off the U.S. side of Niagara Falls, capping the Love Canal and building a leachate removal plant to carry off the contaminants, and building airstrips for Marine fighter planes with the Seabees on Okinawa during World War II.

My academic credentials include a Ph.D. in anthropology, with a specialty on work, teaching adult education courses for 13 years, and as author of six previous books on the subject of work.

This book focuses on construction workers, and on their culture and behavior as I have observed and participated in for over 42 years. I have known and worked with thousands of construction workers in every trade, sometimes with a thousand workers on a single project. Like all construction workers, I have experienced many hardships and every kind of weather from the broiling heat of Florida to the freezing winters in Buffalo.

My love for the industry and my love and respect for the men and women who build has never faltered. I hope this book conveys to the reader the feel, touch, and smell of the good sweat that lubricates the minds and bodies of workers who are discussed in *Construction Workers, U.S.A.*

PROLOGUE:
THE THOUSAND-YARD POUR

The day of the thousand-yard pour arrived.

On the morning of the pour, everyone was up and out on the job early. It was going to be a long day and Pat, the project superintendent, wanted to get started at the crack of dawn. In fact, we were on the job before dawn. It was still dark. The immense and timeless sky bent over us in its blackness. We couldn't tell what kind of a day it was going to be. Everyone's face lifted skyward, sharing a collective hope for a good day, one without rain. The resident engineer for the town was there, frowning importantly.

A mysterious silence fills the air at that time of the morning, as if the world hovers in restless anticipation. The workers talked in quiet tones and smoked cigarettes that glowed like fireflies. Despite the uncertainty, they waited patiently. Some talked about the pour; others joked; some exchanged news about yesterday's baseball scores; a few discussed food; and others talked politics.

As the first sign of light cracked the horizon, cobblestone clouds, the color of gray slate, appeared. Their foreboding shape and color augured a stormy day that did little to raise our spirits. But we had no time to dwell on dark clouds as we heard the first concrete truck muttering down Tonawanda Creek Road, about a quarter mile away.

Pat yelled, "Here it comes!"

The pour was under way.

Before continuing let me explain what it means to pour a thousand yards of concrete in a single day, a prodigious feat involving weeks of planning and solving many difficult problems.

It was the summer of 1976. In the summer, construction reaches its peak. Rain and bad weather are less frequent so work can proceed with less interruption. Each day structures become taller and alter their shape. The project site changes—hills disappear, new embankments arise, brush and weedy growth are swept away, streams and creeks are bridged, temporary roads are constructed, and electric and telephone poles go hopping across the site on one leg. Everywhere dust is blown, swirled by noisy, lumbering construction machines and trucks that criss-cross the site in seemingly chaotic patterns. Change takes place as if by magic. But there is no magic—only the palpable efforts of men working and planning together.

That summer we were working on a new sewage treatment plant for the town of Amherst, New York, outside Buffalo. We had 13 different structures to build: a pump station; a chlorine holding tank; several clarifiers to oxygenate sewage; a grit chamber to remove solid particles; an equalization tank to remove sludge; an incinerator to burn the sludge; and several collection tanks.

The equalization tank was as long as a football field and about half as wide. It had a floor slab that was four feet thick, containing 1,000 cubic yards of concrete. The men on the job decided they could pour that floor in one day. It was the men who made that decision, not the boss, because it was a challenge they dared to undertake. I was project manager. When the men told me what they had in mind the idea seemed awesome. I had never taken part in such a feat and had little knowledge of the details and problems involved. I discovered that weeks of careful planning were necessary to account for innumerable maddening details. We prayed that weather would be on our side the day of the pour in spite of "Murphy's Law"—what can go wrong, will.

Pat was the first to tell me what he and the men decided. Pat was the best superintendent in the company. He was an honest, straight, no-nonsense guy, with an unswerving gaze that looked directly into your eyes as he talked to you; if he was mad he could stare you down into silence. A carpenter by trade, Pat learned about every other trade and could give leadership to almost all construction operations. He always sought the advice and consent of the men he directed. He would discuss the various ways of performing a job and get the craftsmen to agree on the best method. He had an uncanny memory. If someone told him something and then tried to change or deny it, he would catch that man in a flash, repeat to his face, word for word, exactly what he said, when he said it, and under what conditions. Pat wasn't removed from the men he led. He drank and kidded with them, lived near them, and went hunting and to sporting events with them. He spent most of his social life with other construction workers and their families, becoming their friends through years of association on and off the job.

One day, in the shanty, I listened as Pat was discussing preparations for the pour with Carl, his labor foreman, and Cliff, one of our surveyors. They were considering the alternative of a pump or a crane to place the concrete.

"The pump works fast," Carl said, "but it's always breaking down. Don't matter if it's old or new. I never seen one go through a whole pour without something happening."

One of the ironworkers setting reinforcing steel in forms that would hold the concrete, came to see Pat to review and clarify a steel drawing. Pat interrupted his conversation with Carl to answer the ironworker's questions. Returning to Carl, he said, "I know pumps break down. But we've only got ten hours to make that pour.

And the pump can put out more than a crane. Just make sure the pump is checked and serviced at the supplier's yard before it gets to the job."

Carl was a realist. He knew no concrete pour ever comes off without a hitch and he wanted to emphasize that point with Pat. Pat always used him as a foreman because he knew Carl would never ignore a potential problem and would address it before it was too late to do something about it. Carl was also a fatalist. His two favorite words were chance and fate, which he believed determined our lives. He did his work each day based on the experience and knowledge he gained during his 20 years in construction. Whenever an accident took place or a man was hurt through some mishap, Carl would remark on how man was only a small atom in the gigantic "web" (another favorite word of his) of life.

Pat continued the discussion about the pump and the crane, saying, "Why can't we use both? We can have a crane on one side and a concrete pump on the other. That way, if the pumps breaks down we'll still have the crane to finish the pour."

Carl agreed at once. "We can have two separate crews. Let 'em fight it out on which crew gets done on their half of the pour first. Maybe we can even take bets on it."

Construction men will gamble on anything. They love to bet on sports teams, and they enjoy card playing during lunchtime. They are big customers for Las Vegas and Atlantic City junkets. Many come to work each day with fistfuls of horse racing tickets. One of the foremen owned a racehorse called "Green Gertrude," that got its name from a green-painted bulldozer nicknamed "Gertrude." A number of men bet on the horse whenever it ran. The horse had one of the worst records, but the men were loyal to their workmate and kept betting on it despite their losses. They kidded the horse's owner but never failed to bet on Green Gertrude. Finally, the horse won a race and there was great joy on the project.

A week after the decision to proceed with the large pour, the field representative for the concrete supplier was told to come to our field office. Pat gave him his usual steely stare, saying, "Look Stan, we're gonna pour the equalization tank in one day, and it's gonna take one thousand yards of concrete. I figure about ten hours to do the pour. Your trucks hold 12 yards. That means we're gonna need 84 trucks for the day, or eight trucks an hour. That means we'll be using one truck every seven minutes. Here's my question, can you give us all the trucks and all the concrete we need for the pour? No bullshit now."

"It will tie up our entire plant for the day, Pat."

"So what? That's the idea. Look at the business you're getting. Call your boss, Stan. I've got to have a definite yes. Otherwise, I'll find another supplier. You know some guys would die for this kind of order."

"Okay, okay, Pat. There's no problem. We can do it. I'll just need enough advance notice so I can tell our other customers they get no concrete that day. But you gotta tell me what day. And what about our trucks? Will they be able to get in and out quickly, and without getting stuck?"

"Yeah, don't worry about that. I've got a turnaround area. The trucks will be able to dump concrete and get right out. I'll be building a new haul road soon. As for the day, figure about three weeks. But I'll give you the day in a week."

The next day, Pat and I picked out two separate routes to either side of the equalization tank and laid out two turnaround areas for the trucks. When Carl came into the shanty at lunchtime, Pat told him,

"Herbie and me picked out two roads and two staging areas for the pour. After lunch I'll show 'em to you. Herbie agreed to spend the money for two good haul roads so we don't get screwed in case it rains. I want slag and brick brought in. Track it in good with the dozer. Then I want both roads graded and rolled so the water will run off. Get on it tomorrow."

About a week later, Carmine, the concrete finisher foreman, was called to the shanty. Carmine is a dark-skinned Sicilian-American who turns black in the summer. He has too many teeth for his mouth and they are always visible. His bared teeth, black visage, and powerful body give him a menacing appearance. Even his laugh, that borders on a sneer, does not lessen the fury that sweeps his intimidating face. He once walked in on a card game at night, wearing a black cape, white gloves, and a black hat, looking like Dracula, and scared everyone in the room out of their seats.

Pat told Carmine, "Look, we got a big pour coming up. In three weeks I'll need two crews—finishers, spreaders, laborers. I figure 14 in each crew. I'll give you the exact day in about a week."

"I'll call the union hall today."

"No screw-ups. Tell 'em what we need."

"Whadda ya want me to say, Pat? When I tell my men to come, they come. J-e-e-e-zus, it's no problem, I tell ya."

"You'd better be sure, Carmine. It's a big pour and the men better be there."

"We poured bigger, Pat. Don't worry, we'll do a job for ya."

Carmine had his following of men who worked together regularly. Although he was working for a contractor, he functioned almost like an independent subcontractor. He lined up the men, instructed them beforehand about what kind of pour it would be, what tools they would need, how long the job would take, what the job conditions were, and when he expected them to be on the job—without fail.

The next week, Pat called all the jobs in town being done by our employer. He spoke to the super on each project, and told them he had a big pour coming up, and gave them a list of numbers and types of men he needed: operating engineers and oilers, carpenters and ironworkers, flagmen, laborers, and surveyors. He asked for, and received, a commitment of the men for the day that he had already picked for the pour.

Within another week, the carpenters had completed their form work and the ironworkers had set and tied the reinforcing steel that would be incorporated within the slab. Meanwhile, Pat and Carl continued to check out details and make plans.

They double-checked with the owner of the concrete plant, and they studied the condition of the haul roads. The equipment yard was called to check out the concrete pump. Carmine was questioned about his men. The surveyors were asked to check the height, width, and length dimensions of the forms. All other trades, especially plumbers and electricians, were told to make sure they had all their pipes, conduit, and sleeves in place that had to go into the slab. Drawings were looked over to make sure all items connected with the pour were accounted for. As the time for the big pour approached, the men began talking about it with anticipation and excitement.

Finally, the big day arrived. The men were up and on the job before daybreak. When they heard Pat yell, "Here it comes!", they went into action.

Some men put out their cigarettes. They all put on their gloves, gathered their tools, and adjusted their hats and boots. The men wore a variety of clothes. There were combinations of tee shirts and blue jeans; overalls over long-sleeved work shirts; overalls over bare arms; rust-colored jackets; overalls with stripes; white overalls; high boots, low boots, high leather shoes, new shoes, worn shoes; tattered clothes, new clothes; soiled hats, hard hats, and no hats. It was an army without a regulation uniform.

The first concrete truck arrived and bumped on to the job site. A flagman at the entry road directed the driver and the truck rattled and whined its way toward the forms that would enclose the concrete for the equalization tank. At the pour site, the truck was hollered and maneuvered into position under the crane. The driver creaked back the emergency brake and leaped down from the cab amidst the large throng of men waiting to go into action. As the first driver on the job, he felt the pressure of all eyes on him. The driver went to the rear of his truck, found the water hose and opened a valve that sent water into the drum to mix with the sand, cement, and stone that make up the concrete. He also sped up the drum on the concrete truck to accelerate the blending of the concrete mix.

When the concrete was well mixed, Chi Chi, a laborer and expert "bucket man," helped the driver swing the chute at the back of the concrete truck to position it over a large round concrete bucket, four feet high and six feet across. Once the concrete was deposited in the bucket it would be lifted by the crane and swung to men waiting to empty it and shove the concrete into place.

As was his habit, Chi Chi was wearing his hat sideways. I've never found out how he was nicknamed Chi Chi or what it means. Nicknaming is prevalent among construction workers. Many of the names are terms of insult, but when used among workmates or friends they are considered terms of familiarity. Let an outsider use the same nickname and he may find himself in a fistfight.

Chi Chi loved horseplay and was constantly thinking up new ways to amuse the men. One time he brought a mannequin to the job and positioned it on a small knoll on the job site and crossed its legs. From far away it looked like a nude woman. Some of the men approached cautiously with curiosity to see what was going on and as soon as they realized what it was they howled. Whenever Chi Chi cleaned out a concrete bucket with a water hose, anyone who came within range received a good dousing. He had white hair and a white beard. His grizzled face was usually deadpan, but his eyes sparkled as he contemplated his next surprise for the men. His reputation as a tireless and efficient bucket man made him sought after whenever any sizable concrete pour was planned.

As bucket man, Chi Chi was responsible for giving signals to the concrete truck driver and to the crane man. When he wanted the truck driver to fill the bucket, he showed him a fist with his thumb down. Then a lever was thrown and the concrete whooshed into the bucket. As the concrete neared the top, Chi Chi signaled the driver by holding his fist with his thumb straight out, which meant shut off the flow. Then, he attached the crane hook to the top of the bucket and signaled the crane operator to lift by twirling his forefinger in a circular motion.

The crane operator then swung the bucket toward a gang of men who seized it from all sides as if apprehending a criminal. They pushed and pulled it to where they needed it over the forms. Then a laborer yanked a lever at the bottom of the bucket and the concrete cascaded down, making a slapping and plopping sound as it hit.

On the other side of the equalization tank, another truck was backed up to the concrete pump and discharging its contents into a large, square tub attached to the back of the pump chassis. Inside the tub, two large screws pushed the concrete into the discharge cylinders where it was slammed through into the discharge hoses by means of two piston heads operated by the pump. Two lines of hose stretched hundreds of feet away, with two men at the end directing the flow of the concrete as it pushed its way out of the hoses.

When concrete arrives on a big job, a slump test is taken. A tapered steel cone, open at both ends, is filled to the top. The cone is lifted and the concrete slumps from its own weight. The difference in height between the cone and the slumped concrete is recorded. Concrete is too stiff if its slump is less than two inches and too loose if the slump exceeds six inches. Inches of slump and strength of concrete are related. Thus, every batch of concrete gets a slump test.

The full light of day was now upon the men without their awareness. The smoke-gray light had stolen almost imperceptibly through the darkness. The gray-blue of the sky was faintly luminous with the coming of daylight and the long field that stretched away from the equalization tank looked solemn and lonely.

The pour was going smoothly, and as early morning passed into mid-morning the men became more vocal. They were soon exchanging insults and jokes and feeling comfortable with the day, the work, and each other. They walked on the raised platform of reinforcing bars with graceful assurance, their legs, arms, and backs displaying power, coordination, and skill. They were joyful. They were masters of their tools and materials. They could not control the weather, but that would not stop them this day.

About 11:00 A.M., a commotion took place at the concrete pump. I saw Pat and Carl running in that direction and I followed them. When I got there I heard the man running the pump say, "The pump is turning over, but it's not pushing any concrete out the other end."

Pat shouted, "Get Greg! Fast!" Greg was our master mechanic.

The situation was serious. The concrete was hardening in the hose lines. If the pump did not get fixed in 30 minutes, the concrete would solidify and that would be the end of the hoses and one half of the pour. Pat and Carl had to decide how long to wait before uncoupling hundreds of feet of hose and emptying them of their concrete. They were bolted together in seven-foot sections. It was a lot of connections to undo.

Many pairs of hands and eyes were busy at the concrete pump. Pat ordered the piston head off and the gear mechanism checked. Greg had half his body twisted down under the motor, calling for tools like a surgeon at an operation. It was taking too long. Pat hollered to Carl, "Pass the word. Break the connections on the hoses. Get the concrete out. I want everyone on it. Tell Monkey [a laborer] to round up as many men as he can and get them over here to help."

The equalization tank work area exploded into action, with men pushing, uncoupling, shouting, cursing and puffing with effort. The couplings on the connections were hammered free. The hose was lifted on the shoulders of one man while the concrete was pushed out by another. Some, like Pat, seized a section of hose filled with concrete alone, and with enormous strength, lifted it over their shoulders and shook out the concrete by themselves. Everyone was splattered with concrete, their faces grayed from the cement and their hands cold and bruised. The relaxed chatter of an hour ago, the proud, self-confident ring of voices, gave way to hard, angry, frustrated shouts and curses at the necessity of undoing the hoses.

Greg found the trouble. A new part was needed. He jumped into his pickup truck and headed for the supply house to get it.

Pat told Carl and Carmine, "Get all the hoses recoupled and connected to the concrete pump. By the time we get that done, Greg should be back."

When Greg returned, he went right to work fixing the pump. As I watched him I was struck by the power and massiveness of his hands. His knuckles were huge, his fingers were thick and broad. His hands looked twice the size of an ordinary man's hands. He worked on the pump parts with incredible sureness, even though he knew dozens of men were waiting and watching him and that the continuation of the pour depended on him. When he was done, he nodded to Pat who gave the word to restart the pump.

We were all filled with uneasiness. If the pump started, would it push out the concrete? If it pushed the concrete, would it crap out again with the concrete in the hoses? Would the men have to go through the whole frustrating breakdown of the operation again?

The pump started and concrete began to fill the hoses. We could see the sections jump and stretch full as the concrete entered each section. Suddenly, the pump failed. Greg went to work on the motor again while the rest of us checked our watches to see how long he was taking. Once more we were thinking of concrete hardening in the hoses.

I heard the pump going again, then Pat shouted, "Hold it!"

Off to one side, a wet stream of cement was crazily looping gray pellets that were hitting and sticking to the men. A connection had loosened. Carl and two others were on the faulty joint in an instant, hammering home the lugs that held the hose in place. As soon as they were done, they signaled Pat, who gave the word to restart the pump.

On Pat's command a lever was thrown and the whirring of the motor crescendoed into the air that seemed thick with the anger of men.

When the pump started, one of the laborers rushed to the end of the pipeline and scooped out the semi-hardened concrete. This permitted the new, fresh concrete to come pouring through. But another loose joint popped its connection. It jumped concrete into the air and the pump had to be stopped. The joint was retightened and the pump restarted. This sequence of events took place over and over. Each stopping and starting related to a loosened joint closer and closer to the end of the hose line.

Finally, after an hour of adjusting, hammering, hollering, and cursing, all joints were solid. The concrete was now flowing out at the end of the two lines that looked like two overfilled mouths gulping up gray, mealy concrete cereal that fed the forms the carpenters made.

The pour progressed steadily through the lunch hour, through the early afternoon, and then about 4:00 P.M., it began to rain—a hard, pounding, saturating rain. With a downward rush, a blanket of rain picked a million points into the freshly troweled concrete.

I was in the shanty with Pat and Greg as the rain slapped at the shanty window glass. Pat slammed his palm on the plan table and bellowed, "Goddamn it! Wouldn't ya know! Phil, [the construction clerk] get the rain gear out of the storeroom and get your ass out there with suits for the men. Get Brian to help you."

Carmine came charging in.

"Whadda ya wanna do, Pat?"

"Go ahead with the pour. Keep the finishers working."

Carmine said with a toothy smile, "I already told 'em that."

The rain intensified—it pounded, rushed, and flooded the site.

Chi Chi came in, hat cocked to one side, hair soaked and clinging to his head, water dripping off his nose, his coat one big concrete splat. He was singing "Singing in the Rain." It splintered the tension and we all had a good laugh.

Then, Bob Meyer, the resident engineer for the town, showed up. He asked, "What are you going to do, Pat?"

Pat replied, "The men have been told to complete the pour."

Raising his voice, Meyer said, "The concrete will be pockmarked. I'm not going to accept that kind of finish."

"That's up to you."

"I'm warning you, Pat."

"I've never taken kindly to threats, Mr. Meyer."

"Okay, Pat, everything you do from now on is rejected."

"Put it in writing."

"If I were you, I'd call off the pour."

"Up yours."

It rained all afternoon and into the night. Carmine and his finishers stayed until 9:00 P.M. to complete the troweling of the concrete. Meyer went home at 6:00 P.M. His inspectors stayed until the end.

The next morning the slab looked diseased. After thousands of pounds of flash patch cement were purchased, the slab was troweled as smooth as polished wax. As we walked on it our legs reflected on the shining surface. Later, the slab was covered with dirt and dust from the saws of carpenters cutting wall forms. Still later, the floor was coated with a black asphalt waterproofing. Finally, it was under water as sewage passed through the equalization tank. Nothing more was heard from Meyer about the finish. He did not want to make himself look foolish. He knew that the slab would eventually be covered, but the specifications called for a smoothly troweled surface and that's what he insisted on.

A week after the pour, these men walked on the solid evidence of their labors. Construction workers get satisfaction from seeing the physical evidence of their work. I marveled that men, left alone to work and plan independently, can produce with intelligence and skill, such creative results.

1

INTRODUCTION

The thousand-yard pour illustrates many characteristics of construction work and workers. The rest of this book analyzes these features, with the main emphasis on the culture of workers in their work environment.

As anthropologists increasingly study complex, modern society, they will inevitably investigate work and occupations that link individuals to social institutions that provide social identities. The world of work is vital for the study of (1) socialization, (2) status and prestige, (3) social role, (4) cultural values, (5) quality of life, (6) economic role, (7) family relationships, (8) leisure and play, and (9) life cycle. In short, work relates to and interpenetrates all aspects of the lives of individuals as well as influences the collective experiences of communities.

This book deals with the construction industry. In August 1997, the construction industry employed 6,885,000 persons, of which 4,190,000 were tradesmen and tradeswomen; 1,480,000 were self-employed workers; and the rest were in administration and management (U.S. Department of Commerce, 1997, p. ii). Construction is a basic industry with a large number of products that feed into construction activity, such as steel, masonry products, windows, roofing materials, lumber, concrete, acoustical and insulation products, drywall, millwork wood, tile, asphalt, and a large number of construction vehicles, hoists, cranes, and equipment. The yearly value of construction projects is one of the leading economic indicators that economists and government agencies use to evaluate and predict the state of the U.S. economy. Construction is responsible for a major percentage of our capital growth. For these reasons, it is a crucial part of our society.

The main focus of this book is on the social organization of the construction industry that fosters a particular pattern of worker behavior. The culture of construction work stresses the independence and autonomy of construction craftsmen. Many tradesmen and tradeswomen in various trades like carpentry, electrical, plumbing, pipe fitting, and sheetmetal own their own tools and control the manner in which they perform their work. Construction workers enjoy job satisfaction based on their autonomy, high wages, the physical evidence of their labor, and performing work in teams and gangs where they enjoy personalized, collaborative efforts with fellow workers.

The social organization of construction is based on a number of unique features. One such feature is the localized nature of the industry. Every structure is fixed to a local site, therefore, all construction work is decentralized. Second, each structure, especially commercial and industrial buildings, has a particular configuration on a specific site that precludes the utilization of mass production technology. Third, the long-term nature of the construction process that can last from one to three years, or longer for very large projects, reduces the degree of control that can be imposed on the construction process. Fourth, construction is subjected to the necessities and unpredictability of weather that also prevents a rigid, unbroken path to efficient production. Fifth, deliveries of materials are often imprecise as to time, quantity, quality, and distribution, which increases the uncertainty that is an industry norm in construction.

The work culture of a construction site is characterized by informality, face-to-face relationships, and loose, personalized supervision. Construction work relies largely on hand technology and craft skills to create its products. The social organization of construction work and its consequent behavioral patterns among construction workers leads to a distinctive occupational subculture. It is a craft culture based on the mastery of a skill that is one among many other skills, all necessary and crucial for the erection of a variety of structures and engineering projects. Construction work has a cultural orientation similar to that found among other roughneck, independent occupations among the blue-collar trades, where physical prowess and maleness are prominent. We will examine how these traits have been impacted through the entry of women into the construction field.

The dominant culture in the United States is strongly influenced by the bureaucratic mode of organization, as exhibited by large corporations, sprawling factories, and huge office complexes. This bureaucratic environment, especially in government and corporate entities is being challenged, but it is still predominant. Construction workers are not part of this type of work environment. However, they are not divorced from the culture of the larger society. Construction workers are influenced by the mass media, live in urban areas, and, in part, are a product of their ethnicity, religion, race, gender, education, and geographical region. They are part of an integrated economic structure with other Americans as consumers, home owners, and taxpayers. Yet, they are a discrete entity within the framework of the larger society. They are bound to one another in work, and often in family networks that interlace with their work. Construction workers project relationships, values, and norms from their work into their nonwork lives.

To summarize the culture of construction workers, I list the following traits:

1. The culture of construction workers is based on their control of their own work process through their ownership of their tools and their knowledge of their craft.

2. Construction proceeds through an informal, face-to-face organization of work.

3. Construction technology is largely a handicraft technology. This is modified somewhat by the use of machines like cranes and hoists for heavy lifting, and excavation, grading, and loading machines for site work, foundations, on-grade slabs, street utilities, and roadwork.

4. Construction work is dangerous and arduous. Construction has one of the highest accident and death rates of any industry in the United States.

5. Uncertainty is the norm in the construction industry. Construction workers are employed for the limited time of a project and most do not work a full year. Uncertainty is also the result of weather conditions that can suspend construction.

6. Field management of construction work is loose, informal, and nonbureaucratic.

7. Job satisfaction among construction workers is relatively high because of high wages, worker autonomy, loose supervision, and pride in craft and product.

8. Construction workers can be said to constitute an occupational community through their lifelong commitment to craft, merging of their work and nonwork lives, and their sense of identity and self-image stemming from their work.

Construction workers can be viewed as an occupational group, in that they identify more with their occupation than with a specific employer or specific job. Many if not most workers in the United States identify with their job or the corporation or company that employs them. Even professionals often identify with employers (law firms, hospitals, and universities). Construction workers have a history of strong identification with craft and trade as they are constantly changing employment with contractors and shifting from project to project.

Every new project in construction is a new challenge. The design, shape, and technology of construction is constantly producing new concepts, new materials, and new methods of construction. The satisfying thing about construction is the social contacts between construction workers, because no matter how large or small the project, there is always a sense of camaraderie among trades on any project. In the course of one's career in construction one meets many familiar faces on the various projects, especially in the localized areas where construction work takes place. Men, like myself, who have worked all over the country, are constantly running into others with whom they have worked before. Having been in construction for 42 years, and still at it, I have had the pleasure of many lasting friendships among workmates.

There is probably no greater satisfaction from work than seeing the physical evidence of your efforts—hence, the joy of building. Artisans who create paintings, sculpture, and pottery must share the same feeling.

I have been a full participant in the construction industry, which has given me an advantage in studying construction workers at their work. I have been able to find them each day in one workplace from seven to eight hours and as a result I have been able to use my own direct observation of these men and women working and relating to one another. I did not have to rely on the semantically booby-trapped analysis of interviews while manipulating regression equations (Chapple, 1953, p. 830; Kluckhohn, 1940, p. 331; Bruyn, 1966, p. 15). I have shared the work, circumstances, life activities, and interests that have affected construction workers. In this book I try to register, interpret, and conceptualize what I have observed over a 42-year-period. I hope to present these men and women as they are, not as I think they ought to be. Through the social involvement with construction workers, I believe I have come to understand and know their behavior, thoughts, and values.

The term "construction worker" in this book refers to men and women who work in the field building structures—houses, industrial and commercial buildings, office buildings, hotels, religious and educational buildings, hospitals, public utility facilities, highways, roads, military facilities, sewer and water systems, dams and bridges, conservation projects, shopping centers, warehouses, banks, sewage treatment plants, and many others. I have participated in the building of every one of these kinds of buildings. The trades involved include carpenters, plumbers, steam fitters, operating engineers, bricklayers, masons, concrete finishers, electricians, painters and paperhangers, plasterers, laborers, tile setters, drywall installers, insulation installers, carpet installers, sheetmetal workers, structural and reinforcing ironworkers, roofers, glaziers, acoustic tile installers, telephone installers, kitchen installers, millwork carpenters, boilermakers, marble and granite setters, temperature control installers, surveyors, elevator constructors, truck drivers, concrete curb and sidewalk installers, blacktop installers, landscapers, and rock blasters. I have had contact with every one of these trades on projects I have participated in and managed. As you can see from the list, putting a building or structure together is a complex undertaking. The industry also includes (and I have had to deal with) architects, engineers, building inspectors, contractors, subcontractors, material suppliers, resident engineers, and owners.

The construction workers I have worked with, both union and nonunion, the skill requirements for various trades, the types of contractors, and the types of projects, are characteristic of the construction industry nationwide. I have worked mostly in metropolitan areas, where building codes are enforced and which ensures that buildings constructed under these conditions are typical for similar structures built throughout the country. All construction must adhere to regulations regarding health and safety, as well as designs that are structurally sound and contain all the safeguards against fire and collapse.

Finally, I have changed the names of the construction workers I have worked with and who are discussed in this book.

2

The Construction Industry:
Brief Review

NATURE OF THE INDUSTRY

Construction, with 5.4 million wage and salary workers and 1.5 million self-employed nongovernment jobs in 1996 (U.S. Bureau of the Census, 1997), is the single largest industry in the United States. The products of the construction industry include houses, apartment buildings, factories, office buildings, schools, roads, bridges, power plants, shopping centers, warehouses, gas stations, convention centers, ballparks, tunnels, government buildings, courthouses, and others. The industry's activities include not only work on new structures, but additions, alterations, and repairs.

The construction industry is divided into three major segments: general building contractors, heavy construction contractors, and specialty trade contractors. General building contractors build residential, industrial, commercial, and other buildings. Heavy construction contractors build sewer systems, roads, highways, bridges, tunnels, dams, and other projects. Specialty trade contractors are engaged in specialized work activities such as carpentry, masonry, plumbing, electrical, painting, heating and air-conditioning work, and all other trades that go into the building of a structure.

Construction work is performed and coordinated by general contractors (or construction managers who serve the same function representing owners), who often specialize in either residential or commercial and industrial building. They take full responsibility for the complete job, but sometimes an owner will omit certain portions of the work and have them performed by others, like fitting up a hotel with beds, furniture, drapes, pictures, lamps, and so on, installing the special conveyor systems in a factory, or installing the racking systems for clothing in a warehouse. Although general contractors may do a portion of the work with their own crews, like carpentry, concrete, and masonry, they often subcontract most of the construction work to heavy construction contractors and to the specialty trade subcontractors.

Specialty trade contractors usually work at only one trade, such as painting, carpentry, electrical work, or two or more closely related trades, such as plumbing, sprinkler work, and heating and air conditioning. Beyond fitting their work to that of other trades, specialty contractors do not have the responsibility for the building of the structure as a whole. Specialty contractors get contracts or purchase orders for their work from general contractors, architects, engineers, construction managers, or owners. Specialty contractors also do repair work, which is normally given to them by owners, occupants, architects, or rental agents.

WORKING CONDITIONS

Construction workers need sufficient physical stamina because work frequently requires prolonged standing, bending, stooping, and working in cramped quarters. Exposure to weather is common because much of the work is done outside or in partially enclosed structures. Construction workers often work with potentially dangerous tools and equipment amidst a clutter of building materials; some work in high places on temporary scaffolding. Thus, they are more prone to injuries than workers in other jobs. In 1995, cases of work-related injury and illness were 10.6 per 100 full-time workers, which is significantly higher than the 8.1-rate for the entire private sector (U.S. Bureau of Labor Statistics, 1998, p. 16). Workers who do roofing, masonry, and stonework experienced the highest injury rates. In response, employers emphasize safe working conditions and work habits to reduce the risk of injuries. They often hold monthly meetings in the office among management to discuss various topics regarding safety. General contractors also have safety manuals and require that safety meetings be conducted on all their projects. They also ask subcontractors to conduct toolbox safety talks among their workers in the field and supply them with topics and materials to hand out.

EMPLOYMENT

About 6 out of 10 jobs in construction are with specialty trade contractors. Almost 1 out of 4 jobs are with general building contractors. The rest are with road and heavy construction contractors. Employment in construction is distributed geographically in much the same way as the nation's population, with concentration of employment in industrialized and highly populated areas. There are about 621,000 construction companies in the United States, of which there are 187,000 general contractors; 34,000 heavy/highway contractors; and 399,000 specialty trade contractors. Most of these establishments tend to be small, the majority employing fewer than 10 workers. About 8 out of 10 workers are employed by small contractors (U.S. Bureau of Labor Statistics, 1998, p. 17).

Construction offers more opportunities than most other industries for individuals who desire to own and run their own business. There are 1.5 million self-employed and unpaid family workers in construction as of 1996 (U.S. Bureau of the

Census, 1997), who perform work directly for property owners or act as contractors on small jobs, such as additions, remodeling, and maintenance projects. Self-employed workers represent 19 percent of construction employment, with the high rates of self-employment among carpet installers, tile setters, painters, carpenters, drywall installers, roofers, and brick masons.

Going into business in construction may be easy, but staying in it and making it a success is a struggle. You have to get the work, perform the work, finance the labor and supplies, get paid, and then get more work. If you hire others you've got to make sure you make payroll every week. It sounds easy but those who have tried it know that you need lots of energy, skills, and luck. The best way to succeed is to bid public work where you know the money is good and you'll get paid. But competition for public work is brutal and there can be 12 or 15 bidders for every job, many of whom are willing to drop their price to the point where there's no profit and you're lucky if you can do the work at cost.

OCCUPATIONS IN THE INDUSTRY

Work in construction offers a great variety of career opportunities. People with many different talents and educational backgrounds—managers, clerical workers, skilled craftsworkers, semiskilled workers, and laborers—find job opportunities in construction.

Most workers in construction are either skilled craftsworkers, or laborers, helpers, and apprentices who assist the more skilled workers. These groups represent 75 percent of the industry's employment; over 50 percent are construction craftsworkers. Construction craftsworkers are generally classified as either structural, finishing, or mechanical workers. Structural workers include carpenters, operating engineers who operating construction machinery, bricklayers, cement masons, stonemasons, roofers, and iron workers who erect structural steel. Finishing workers include lathers, plasterers, marble setters, terrazzo workers, carpenters, ceiling installers, drywall workers, painters, glaziers, roofers, floor covering installers, and insulation workers. Mechanical workers include plumbers, sprinkler fitters, pipefitters, electricians, sheetmetal workers, and heating, air conditioning, and refrigeration technicians.

The greatest number of construction craftsworkers work as carpenters, electricians, plumbers, pipefitters, painters, concrete and terrazzo workers, bricklayers, and drywall installers. The construction industry employs nearly all workers in some construction craft occupations such as plasterers, roofers, structural iron workers, and drywall installers. In other construction crafts occupations, like electricians, painters, paperhangers, plumbers, and carpet installers, large numbers also work in other industries. Other industries employing large numbers of construction craftsworkers include transportation equipment manufacturing, transportation, public utilities, wholesale and retail trade, educational services, and state and local government.

Many people enter the construction crafts through apprenticeship programs. These programs offer on-the-job training under the close supervision of a craftsperson, as well as some formal classroom instruction. Depending on the trade, apprentices learn a variety of skills, ranging from welding to laying brick, and learning to fit pipes together to putting steel beams together.

A number of aspiring construction workers advance to construction craft occupations from related, less skilled jobs as helpers or laborers. Many men (women rarely have the contacts to get in without going through apprenticeship training) start as helpers or laborers and perform a variety of unskilled, physical tasks needed on a construction project. They erect and dismantle scaffolding, clean up debris, help unload and carry materials and machinery, and operate simple equipment. They work alongside experienced craftsworkers and learn from them the basic skills of a particular craft. A mason's helper may spend his time mixing mortar, but he also observes the journeyman laying block and brick and he learns how to apply mortar, place the block and brick, and strike the joints. After acquiring experience and skill in various phases of the craft, helpers and apprentices may apply to become skilled journey-level craftworkers by either getting into the union or by being hired by a nonunion specialty contractor.

To develop their skills further after training, construction craftsworkers may work on many different projects, such as housing, office and industrial buildings, shopping centers, stores, highways and roads, bridges and dams, or in renovation work. Flexibility and a willingness to learn new techniques and use new power tools, as well as the ability to get along with people in one's own and other trades, are essential for working in construction. Those skilled in all facets of the trade and who show good leadership qualify for promotion to foreman. As foremen, craftsworkers oversee journeymen and helpers and make sure that all the work is done properly and on time. They also plan the work and solve problems as they arise. Those with good organizational skills and supervisory ability may become superintendents when openings arise. Superintendents are responsible for getting a project complete on schedule by working with the architect's plans, making sure materials are delivered on time, assigning work, overseeing craft supers, and making sure every phase of the project is completed according to schedule and in accordance with the architect's plans and specifications. Supers also resolve problems and see to it that all work proceeds without interruptions as much as possible. There are always unforeseen problems like strikes, bad weather, and a failure of suppliers to deliver materials on time, that delay a project. It is up to the superintendent to overcome these problems. With approval of the managers in the contractor's office, they may have to order overtime or ask the specialty subcontractors to put more men on a job in order to make up for lost time. Planning and use of such techniques like CPM (Critical Path Method is a method using matrix networks to relate one construction task to another with duration times for each activity) and bar charts help coordinate the work, but since construction is such a long-term process, it is hard to foresee all problems and many unanticipated situations arise that require special measures. Good superintendents can sometimes advance to large projects as general managers, and even enter the home office as executives. Those who believe they are capable may decide to become their own bosses and go into business for themselves as contractors.

TRAINING AND ADVANCEMENT

Many men (and a few women) may enter jobs in the construction industry without any formal classroom training after high school. Laborers can learn their jobs in days, weeks, or months, but they need to have the physical stamina to perform the work. A laborer may not think there is much to shoveling, but let him try to do it all day long and see how long he lasts on the job. For most of the trades the skills required are substantial even if they can be learned on the job. Skilled workers such as carpenters, bricklayers, plumbers, and other construction trade specialists either need several years of informal on-the-job experience or apprenticeship training. Workers pick up skills by working alongside more experienced workers and through instruction provided by their employers or in an apprenticeship program. As workers and apprentices demonstrate their ability to perform tasks to which they are assigned, they move to progressively more challenging work. As they broaden their skills they are allowed to work independently and given more responsibility, which results in a rise in their earnings.

Apprenticeships administered by local employers, trade associations, and trade unions provide the most thorough training. Apprenticeships usually last between three and five years and consist of on-the-job training and a certain number of hours of related classroom instruction. Those who enroll in apprenticeship programs usually are high school graduates, at least 18 years old, and in good physical condition.

Individuals can enter the construction industry with a variety of educational backgrounds. Those entering construction right out of high school start as laborers, helpers, or apprentices. Those who enter construction from technical or vocational schools may also go through apprenticeship training; however, they progress at a somewhat faster pace because they have had courses in mathematics, mechanical drawing, and woodworking. Skilled craftsworkers may advance to superintendent or foreman positions, or they may transfer to jobs such as a construction building inspector, purchasing agent, sales representative for building supply companies, or technical or vocational school instructor.

Executive, administrative, and managerial personnel usually have a college degree or considerable experience in their specialty. Individuals who enter construction with college degrees usually start as management trainees or construction managers' assistants. Those who receive degrees in construction science often start as field engineers, schedulers, or cost estimators. College graduates may advance to positions as assistant manager, construction manager, general superintendent, cost estimator, construction building inspector, general manager and top executive, contractor, or consultant. Although a college education is not always required, administrative jobs are usually filled by people with degrees in business administration, finance, accounting, or similar fields.

Opportunities for construction workers to become contractors who form their own firms are better in construction than in many other industries. Only a moderate financial investment is needed, and it is possible to run the business from one's home, hiring construction workers only as needed for specific projects. The contract construction field, however, is very competitive, and the rate of business failure is high. Starting one's own construction contracting business sometimes only requires a contract and financing to meet payroll for one month. After that, payments from the general contractor or owner can keep a small contractor going. It is touch-and-go but many individuals manage to survive and complete a number of projects. They often run the business from their home, but eventually they rent an office, and hire a secretary, engineer, and superintendent.

EARNINGS

Earnings in construction are significantly higher than the average for all industries. In 1996 average earnings for craftsworkers was $15.43 an hour, with higher earnings for unionized construction workers. Union electricians average more than $20.00 an hour, as do carpenters, pipefitters, and masons. Average earnings of workers in the specialty trade contractors segment are somewhat higher than those working for building or heavy construction contractors. Earnings of workers in the construction industry vary depending on education and experience of the workers, type of work, size and nature of the construction project, geographic location, and economic conditions. Earnings of construction trade workers are often affected by poor weather. Traditionally, winter is the slack period for construction activity, especially in colder parts of the country. Some workers may not work for several months. Heavy rain may also slow or even stop work on a construction project. Because construction trades are dependent on one another, especially on large projects, work delays in one trade delay or stop work in another.

About 21 percent of all construction workers are union members or covered by union contracts, compared to 16.2 percent of workers throughout private industry (U.S. Bureau of Labor Statistics, 1998, p. 19). Many different unions represent the various construction trades.

OUTLOOK FOR CONSTRUCTION IN THE FUTURE

Employment in the construction industry is expected to grow about 9 percent through the year 2006, slower than the average for all industries. Over the 1996 to 2006 period, employment growth is projected to add about 500,000 new jobs in construction. Many openings will also result each year from the need to replace experienced workers who leave jobs in the industry (U.S. Bureau of Labor Statistics, 1998, p. 19).

Employment in the construction industry depends primarily on the level of building activity and new investment in plant and commercial buildings. New construction is usually cut back during periods when the economy is not expanding. The number of job openings in construction fluctuates from year to year.

Employment in residential construction is expected to grow slowly because the anticipated slowing of population growth and household formation will reduce the demand for new housing units. Slow employment growth is also expected in nonresidential construction because existing vacant office and commercial space, resulting from the commercial building boom of the 1980s, will meet demand for years in some areas. Demand for commercial buildings will be lessened by technological trends favoring telecommuting, electronic shopping, home offices, teleconferencing, and the globalization of information services, as well as business management practices in downsizing, temporary workforces, and inventory reduction. Industrial construction, however, is expected to be stronger because exports by the manufacturing sector of the economy are expected to increase. Replacement of many industrial plants has been delayed for years, and a large number of structures will have to be replaced or remodeled. Construction of nursing, convalescent homes, and other extended care institutions will also increase for several reasons—the aging of the population, the increasing use of high technology medical treatment facilities, and the need for more drug treatment clinics. Construction of schools will also increase to accommodate the children of the baby-boom generation (U.S. Bureau of Labor Statistics, 1998, p. 20).

Employment in heavy construction is projected to increase about as fast as the industry average. Growth is expected in highway, bridge, and street construction, as well as repairs to prevent further deterioration of the nation's highways and bridges. Bridge construction is expected to increase the fastest due to the serious need to repair or replace structures before they become unsafe. Poor highway conditions will also result in increased demand for highway maintenance and repair.

Employment in specialty trades contracting, the largest segment of the industry, should grow a little faster than the entire construction industry. Demand for specialty trades subcontractors in building and heavy construction is rising, and at the same time more workers will be needed to repair and remodel existing homes. Home improvement and repair construction is expected to continue to grow faster than new home construction. Remodeling should be the fastest growing sector of the housing industry because of a growing stock of old residential and nonresidential buildings. Many starter units will be remodeled to appeal to more affluent, space and amenity-hungry buyers. Also, some of the trade-up market may result in remodeling and additions rather than new larger homes. Remodeling tends to be more labor-intensive than new construction. (U.S. Bureau of Labor Statistics, 1998, p. 20).

Employment growth will differ among various occupations in the construction industry. Employment of construction managers is expected to grow as a result of advances in building materials and construction methods, as well as a proliferation of laws dealing with building construction, workers safety, and environmental issues. Construction managers with a bachelor's degree in construction science will be in demand. Administrative support occupations are expected to decline due to increased office automation.

Although employment in the construction trades is expected to grow about as fast the industry average, the rate of growth will vary among the various trades. Employment of bricklayers, electricians, sheetmetal workers and duct installers, painters, tapers and spacklers, and heating, air conditioning, and refrigeration technicians should grow faster than the industry average because technological changes are not expected to offset employment demand as construction activity grows. Employment of carpenters, concrete and terrazzo workers, drywall installers, plumbers, roofers, and structural iron workers is expected to grow more slowly than average because the demand for these workers is expected to be offset by a greater use of new materials and equipment. Increasing use of prefabricated components in residential construction is expected to reduce the demand for carpenters. Most industry sources feel job opportunities will be excellent in most construction crafts because there is a shortage of skilled workers and adequate training programs (U.S. Bureau of Labor Statistics, 1998, p. 20).

3

CONSTRUCTION WORKERS

Construction workers are mainly high paid skilled craftsmen. They enjoy good working conditions and they occupy a top-level position among U.S. blue-collar workers. The physical and social conditions of their work give rise to an occupational culture that stresses directness, concreteness, and having to look at reality honestly and with confidence that problems can be solved. Construction workers view the fruits of manual labor as just as worthy as intellectual labor. Construction work takes place in a milieu in which human beings are placed before machines and social solidarity is placed before occupational rank.

ENTRY INTO THE INDUSTRY

I got into the construction industry in 1956 because I knew someone. That's the way it was in construction in 1956 and that's the way it is today. It's a given that the way to get a construction job or to get into the union is to know someone, a relative, or a friend. This is true for all industries, but it is especially true in construction. I learned three things from my first job in construction:

1. You had to know someone to get in the industry.
2. It was dangerous.
3. There was camaraderie and satisfaction to be gained from the work.

With work in construction you see the results. It's what Hannah Arendt, the philosopher, called work, as differentiated from labor. Work is the human-made world that is interposed between humans and nature. It is this human-made world that we interact with to make sense of nature and our own social world (Arendt, 1958, pp. 7, 136–138). Building is basic to this idea. It creates what Heidegger called dwelling in the world, that is, building that fulfills the needs of dwelling. He says that the erecting of edifices and works and the production of tools is a consequence of the nature of dwelling by human beings. Man is capable of dwelling only if he is building (Heidegger, 1971, p. 217). Today, analysts and others talk about computers as if they perform work. Computers do not work (unless of course they are robots); they assist work. The terms CAD and CAM stand for "computer-assisted-design" and "computer-assisted-manufacture." Computers do not design or make things, they assist. A computer may help to design a toilet bowl or a sink, it might even be programmed to turn on a sink or a urinal valve automatically, but it does not carry off the waste products. A piping system and an underground waste system discharging into sanitary mains is needed. Furthermore, workers are needed to install these systems. Men and women who know what they are doing and who perform work to make your sinks and toilets work are needed. Next time plumbing goes wrong in your house, don't call a computer expert, call a plumber.

Individuals learn by doing and by repetition on the job. No matter how much training someone may have in a trade school or an apprenticeship program, he or she must have on-the-job training. There are too many small tricks of the trade that one needs to master before the daily problem of what to do and how to do it can be confronted. Then, the boss or foreman only has to say, "Take care of this job, figure out what materials you need, and how you are going to perform the work." No one can take that away from a craftsperson, that is, the tools and the knowledge. To get satisfaction from work, knowledge is needed, a picture of the total work process and control over an individuals's own labor, and the instruments of work. John Locke said that one's own labor was the basis of property and was something that no one had the right to take away from individuals if they are to preserve their freedom (Locke, 1967, pp. 32, 35).

To illustrate some aspects of construction work and its dangers, I describe a job I worked on at the Graybar Building on 43rd Street and Lexington Avenue in New York City. At the Graybar Building, one of our tasks was to install 72-inch riser lines in a shaft that extended through the entire building—20 stories high. The strategy was to bring each 20-foot length of pipe to the top of the shaft and work our way down. We had to install a hoist at the top of the shaft to lift the pipe, then drop a welder inside the shaft, hanging in a bosun chair, to weld each length of pipe as it was raised into position. There were two lines, one supply and one return. The lines ran from the top of the building down to the basement, where they were brought into the building through a dock on Lexington Avenue. On top, the lines were brought out to the roof and connected to a cooling tower. The hoist was attached to a structural beam at the top of the shaft. The task was to create a platform at the top of the shaft on which the men could work, chipping the concrete off the structural beam to attach the hoist. But someone had to lay down that first plank and walk on it, over the shaft that went straight down for 20 stories. I stood next to our foreman, Chuck, when he dropped that first plank, and looked down into the snarling blackness of that shaft that seemed to descend into the heart of darkness. I could not look down into that scary shaft without feeling queasy. I watched Chuck calmly step on to that plank, which he carefully laid across the shaft, and call for the other workers. Then he and three men attached the hoist to an overhead structural steel beam. I never asked him what it felt like, but I had to admire his courage and that of thousands of men I've watched risk their lives in construction while working in high places.

Later, when we started to hoist up the pipe and we had the first two lengths in position we had to send our champion welder, Tim, down into that shaft, sitting in a bosun chair, hanging from steel cables in a housing attached to the overhead structural beam. Tim had to work with a battery light attached to his hard hat and maneuver himself around the pipe as he welded one length of pipe to another. We used a Miller electric arc welder so Tim had to contend with the cables and the electrodes. Tim was an older man, a drinker, with an anonymous weather-beaten face, but what he did was heroic. Tim was a man of few words who never balked at any assignment, and none of his welds in that shaft ever failed. What he did defies description—it was a death-defying act that he performed every day, worthy of Houdini. When it was over, no one hoisted Tim on their shoulders, like a team does when it wins the Super Bowl or the NCAA basketball championship. But he deserved it and I hope these few words will serve to preserve his memory. That was 40 years ago and unless Tim is in his nineties, he is probably gone by now, but his welds are still holding those pipe lines together.

A large percentage of construction workers enter the industry by following in the footsteps of fathers, grandfathers, uncles, brothers, cousins, and other relatives. When I first got into union construction in New York City, many of the members of the local carpenters and steamfitters union were German, Irish, and Italian. At that time, in the 1950s, the Irish were very strong in the piping trades and the Germans were strong in carpentry. At one time, in Brooklyn, during the 1930s, Jews were strong in carpentry and in construction contracting, and they hired people they knew, mostly relatives and friends. Italians were strong in the concrete, laboring, and excavating trades.

In the cities . . . the Italian immigrant became a common laborer. In New York he replaced the Irish and Poles on the work gangs, building streets, sky-scrapers and subways. . . . Everywhere in the states of the Northeast, starting at the turn of the century, he [the Italian] contributed the lion's share of toil to the building of roads, dams, canals, tunnels, bridges and subways. (Lopreato, 1970, pp. 143–144)

Many of the construction workers I have known over the years lived in working-class neighborhoods along with many other families in the construction industry. Family and ethnic affiliation are important elements in bringing men into construction. A man's relative can get him into the union and into a job with a contractor. Marc Silver, commenting on entry into construction stated, "Close relatives of contractors, union officials, and journeymen have a distinct advantage in this context" (1986, p. 113). Some start as truck drivers, while others learn by working during summer vacation. Most work as helpers or laborers. This was true in the 1950s when I started and it is still true today to some extent, though getting a college education and a nonmanual job certainly competes with construction work in the minds of youngsters. Still, a high percentage of the young men that I see in my work today have a friend or relative in the construction industry.

Seidman et al.'s profile of plumbers in the 1950s was as follows:

With few exceptions the plumbers had been reared in an urban environment; about a fourth of them . . . had followed their fathers' trade and many others had plumbers among their relatives. . . . . There were some among the plumbers who find the occupation a family tradition, followed it with as little conscious choice as the young man in a mining community gives to his entrance into the mines. As one plumber said: "My whole family are plumbers and I just followed along . . . my oldest brother was in it at the time and I don't know why, but I had a craving for it." (Seidman, et al., 1958, p. 50)

George Strauss states that among the trade unions in construction that he studied in the 1950s there was a period when "the union was only accepting sons of members" (Strauss, 1958, p. 95). This is no longer true but having a relative in the union is still one of the best ways of getting into the union and into construction. There is a young man on one of my projects today (1998). He was an excellent laborer. All of a sudden, he is installing studs and drywall. I asked him, "How did you get into the union?" His answer was simple, his brother has been a carpenter for 16 years. Is this young man a full-fledged carpenter? No. He is learning, but he is already in the union, and he's getting the full wage, not apprentice wages. I asked his journeyman, who has been a union carpenter for 20 years, "Sid, how did you get in?" He answered, "I was an apprentice, working for my father. He paid me first-year apprenticeship wages for six years before I made journeyman." So the rules are loose and enforced in different ways. I got two of my own children jobs in construction in the summertime. I got my son a job as an assistant to the master mechanic on a road job for one summer. He made very good wages, but I could not get him into the Operating Engineer's Union. The union would not take him, even into their apprenticeship program, and I had plenty of connections. As for my daughter, I was able to get a summer job for her on a large project as a laborer, and I was able to get her into the union. It all depends on the union, the area, the situation, and the kind of contacts possessed by a young recruit.

APPRENTICESHIP TRAINING

The traditional method of becoming a union member and thereby gaining entry into construction is through apprenticeship training. Apprenticeship is the most widespread of the formal methods of getting into construction. Many men enter by informal means, provided they can show proof of qualification. This proof ranges from answering questions asked by the business agent to appearing before a union examining board. Sometimes a man has to put in a few hours of work on a project to the satisfaction of the foreman or the steward. Direct admission outside the apprenticeship program usually takes place when all regular members are working and there is a labor shortage in the region, and it is difficult to bring members in from other districts.

During the past four decades, training methods have substantially improved in the construction industry. Before that, apprenticeship involved informal on-the-job training. Modern apprenticeship training entails a systematic program of instruction, including the following elements:

1. A formal course of classroom instruction.
2. On-the-job training.
3. Related instruction off the job site.
4. Satisfying a joint labor-management committee responsible for the apprentice's progress.

In 1937, the National Apprenticeship Act established a federal apprenticeship policy in the United States. The Bureau of Apprenticeship and Training was created in the Department of Labor to administer this act. Minimum standards were established, including: (1) a minimum starting age, (2) a schedule of work processes to be learned, (3) the number of hours per year of organized instruction in technical subjects, (4) a wage schedule, (5) the method of supervision of the program, (6) evaluation of the apprentice's progress, (7) role of employers and employees, and (8) equal opportunity without regard to race, creed, or national origin. State apprenticeship councils were formed throughout the nation.

The administration of apprenticeship programs is done by local joint apprenticeship committees (JAC), composed of equal representatives from union and management. Apprenticeship programs are financed by assessing employers a few cents per hour for the number of man-hours employed. Applicants must meet minimum standards that vary in different states and crafts. Most building trades require a high school education; some have residence and citizenship requirements. Age requirements range from 17 to 30, with exceptions for veterans. Applicants are interviewed by the JAC and ranked according to criteria the JAC consider relevant.

After selection, apprentices enter a program, typically from three to five years, that includes classroom instruction and on-the-job training. Starting pay is usually half the journeyman's wage and increases over the term of the apprenticeship to the full wage. In some cases, building trades unions and employers contract with the federal or state government to provide training for a certain number of youths. On one of my road projects that was financed in part by state and federal funds, we contracted to train 11 youths in various trades—ironworker, teamster, carpenter, operating engineer, and labor foreman.

In 1997, unions claimed that because of their apprenticeship and training programs, union hiring halls, and screening methods, union labor was more productive than nonunion labor in the construction industry (Allen, 1997). The Associated Builders and Contractors—the nonunion sector of the industry—admitted that they do not have proper and consistent training programs to meet the demands for skilled workers among their contractors (Steiger, 1997, p. 9).

When a business agent or employer takes a personal interest in a young man then a sincere effort is made to give him training. A construction union business agent in Buffalo told me that he took an almost fatherly interest in the young men he placed in the apprenticeship program: "I have to look after them. I just don't sponsor anyone. A lot of people ask me to get their sons or their friends in the union, but I take a long hard look at the boy before I say yes. Once I say yes I follow what they're doing like a parent."

CONSTRUCTION WORK PROCESS

Working in the building trades is ultimately related to the social organization of the construction industry. Construction work tasks are as unique as the construction process is distinctively related to the specific project. Unlike the factory worker, a building craftsworker's job is neither narrowly defined nor performed under close supervision. The repetitive nature of manufacturing work is absent. An apprentice might be given a repetitive job, like pulling nails from form lumber, or preparing sheet metal collars for flexible duct, but it is usually for a limited time and is not something he or she would do every day, year in and year out. In construction, instructions are general, not specific. For example, during one road construction project on which I was project manager, the superintendent, Fred, gave these instructions to his general foreman:

I want Charles on the street breaker on Swan Street. Let Sam and Paul work with Harry on the water line at Seneca. Put two trucks on slag and two on stone. If Ecol [sewer subcontractor] has no truck under his backhoe, let him cast the dirt on the street and we'll pick it up later. If we get any curbing today, let Frenchie and Shorty unload it. After the brickies get done with the manhole at Sycamore, there's a catch basin pad to be poured at Genesee. Tell Clint to put heaters in the hole. Make sure you put tarps over the hole after they pour the concrete.

As you can see from Fred's instructions the men are given their work locations and told what work to carry out and what materials and equipment are available. Organization of the tasks and how the work is to be performed is left to the craftsworker and their foremen. The craftsworker is responsible for the layout of the work and completing it within a certain time.

In the 1960s I had my own general contracting company, and I was building an apartment house on Riverside Drive in Manhattan. I hired a bricklayer, Julie, who was a Jewish refugee from the Soviet Union. I agreed to pay him a good wage regardless of hours and I also agreed to pay the laborers I hired to work with him. He supplied the scaffolding and he was responsible for installing the brick and block across the front face of the building. The building was attached to party walls on either side so there was only one brick face, the front wall. Julie worked out all the coursing, made sure all the MOs (masonry openings for windows) were correct, and he installed the limestone heads, jambs, and sills for windows and the front door. He did all the math and calculations, which I checked, and he organized the work, moving scaffolds, loading brick and block with my laborers, and ordering the laborers to supply a certain amount of material for each day's work. He also called the yard to arrange for brick and block deliveries as he needed them. Since we were working on Riverside Drive in a limited space we could not load all the material at once on the job site. Julie was my employee, but he functioned as if he was an independent contractor, even though he was receiving a fixed wage. At the end of the work, he did such a good job I gave him a bonus.

Stinchcombe commented on the construction industry as follows (1959, pp. 168–169): "Administration in the construction industry depends upon a high professional manual labor force . . . and . . . is more rational than bureaucratic administration in the face of economic and technical constraints on construction projects."

Steiger and Form studied construction workers and concluded:

Construction workers demand responsibility for their work, and they typically receive it. Subcontracting in some ways debureaucratizes the industry by reducing the number of supervisory levels over the worker. . . . Unlike bureaucracy, subcontracting has minimal effect on the labor process [involving] work, workers, and work organization. These remain well within the ken of work crews where it has always been. (Steiger and Form, 1991, p. 267)

The following is an example of how work gets done in construction. On a road project on which I was project manager, I told a carpenter I needed some road signs and gave him a sketch of what I wanted. The signs had to meet certain state specifications for road building. I told the carpenter to figure out what materials he needed. After he gave me the list, I had the construction clerk order the materials and ask for immediate delivery. I told him I needed the signs in two days and he answered that there was no way he could do it unless I gave him more men. I assigned two more carpenters to the job and the signs were ready when I needed them, built according to state department of transportation standards, and I did not have to supervise the work.

Practices of the trade regulate performance, pace, and quality of work. A journey-level mechanic must not only perform under loose supervision but must supervise himself. Construction contractors often have projects at widely separated sites. Under these conditions, maintenance of close supervision with each member of the work force is prohibitively expensive. Thus, the self-administration of the construction craftsworker is the most efficient response to the peculiar circumstances of construction work. The journeyman and journeywoman is trained to perform organizational and planning functions that in other industries are the responsibilities of management. On a job which I am presently involved in, a millwork carpenter told me that he has to carry his own tools and the company's power tools in his own truck as he goes from job to job. He receives no extra compensation or mileage pay for use of his truck. But the contractor he works for keeps him working 52 weeks a year and when things get slow they let him work in the woodworking shop.

In contrast to construction, in manufacturing both product and work process are organized and planned by persons other than those in the work crew. The construction craftsman can see the total product and knows what it will be and how it will look. The mass production worker usually knows only one small part of a product, which has little significance for him. The planning is done for him.

Peter Drucker (1950) contrasts craftsmen with blue-collar workers in mass production based on three concepts:

1. *Fitting the Man to the Job:* Drucker points out that a craftsman "performs a variety of processes in the course of his work. He constantly changes tools, rhythm, speed, and posture. He is bound to find at least one phase of the work congenial to him" (1950, p. 169). In the mass production process of work,

   each job embraces only a very small number of operations . . . the productivity of the mass production plant is geared, by and large to the output of the wrongly placed workers. The "standard of performance" for any one operation is the amount of work that can be turned out by an "average person," that is by someone without obvious physical or mental handicaps but also without any pronounced ability or liking for the job (1950, p. 169).

2. *Fitting the Job to the Man:* The craft worker is the master of his tools, using them to perform an entire range of complex operations. On the manufacturing line there is "the tacit assumption that man is a badly designed, single-purpose machine tool (Drucker 1950, pp. 172–173).

3. *The Worker and the Work Team:* In construction, men work in teams or gangs. Many craftsmen have helpers. One must not only cooperate with one's immediate gang, but must coordinate with other trades. Each tradesman has a sense of the totality of a structure and the part that each trade plays in creating it. Therefore, all trades can share in the pride of creating something new. In contrast, "mass production technology tends to isolate man from man. . . . The traditional automobile assembly line provides a visible example of this social isolation" (Drucker 1950, p. 174).

Since Drucker wrote this, however, management in the auto industry have come to realize that such social isolation has had an adverse effect on worker productivity and they have tried to introduce worker teams and quality circles to give mass production workers more of a say and interest in what they are doing and in their part in the total work process. The jury is still out whether this will result in more worker involvement or the raising of productivity.

Thus, work organized on a craft basis permits a worker to perform an entire complex of operations, gives him mastery over his tools, and provides a work environment that permits social integration and cooperation. Work organized on a mass production basis tends to give workers a limited number of repetitive tasks and treats workers as though they were tools, and tends to isolate workers from the work process and workmates. More and more manufacturing work in the United States is getting away from mass production and moving toward smaller batch production that can react quickly to the changing demands of consumers, thus requiring more flexibility on the part of workers. Whether this will reduce the monotony and boredom of many manufacturing jobs remains to be seen. There are indications already that new electronic technology is leading to "electronic sweatshops," with employees doing boring, repetitive, fast-paced work that requires constant alertness and attention to detail, where the supervisor isn't even human, but an unwinking computer taskmaster. One of the biggest problems in the American workplace today is stress. In a recent survey, more than 75 percent of American workers describe their jobs as stressful and believe that the pressure is steadily increasing (Rifkin, 1995, pp. 188–189).

In the latest issue of the *Futurist* (Knowdell, 1998, pp. 19–24), in an article on the new workplace of the future, the author, Richard Knowdell, talks about ways of working in the future that have been the norm for construction workers in the past. He talks about workers making a commitment to their craft rather than their employer and working maybe three days on one job and two days on another (p. 21). For many construction workers this has been a pattern for many years. Knowdell also states that future workplaces with a flat rather than a pyramidal organization will have workers who will be more knowledgeable about their work than managers (p. 22). This too is already true in construction. Knowdell states that workers will have to learn to work independently or in teams (p. 23), and, again, this is the way construction workers have always performed their work. Perhaps theorists of the future workplace would do well to study the construction industry.

SOCIALIZATION

Occupational socialization is a process through which the recruit becomes a regular member of the work group (Hughes, 1971). Necessary skills and techniques are learned and are at least minimally internalized. Concomitantly, the recruit begins to identify himself with his occupation (Becker and Carper, 1956). This enculturation process is completed when the initiate is fully accepted into the fraternity of regular members and at the same time identifies himself as a member.

The transformation process can be conceived of as a set of stages along a career line in which the new member is evaluated regularly and given increased responsibility and wage increments as he or she progresses satisfactorily. The evaluations are typically based on two criteria: (1) the explicit mastery of skills and techniques particular to the work, and (2) an acceptable adoption of a related set of behavior patterns that the new recruit is expected to display as a member of the occupational group. In the training of apprentices, skills and techniques are usually the focus. But there are other less noticeable aspects of the socialization process as the new recruit becomes a full-fledged member of the group. I focus on three of these other aspects of socialization—tools, costume, and jargon.

Tools

The "tools of one's trade" are one of the most important possessions of the skilled craftsman. The tools themselves, how they are used, when they are used, and how they are taken care of, are important indicators of skill and expertise among construction craftsworkers (Riemer, 1979, p. 72). The tools of a craftsworker are not only crucial for carrying out work, but also reflect something about the worker. Much can be determined about a construction worker by the tools he carries, how he displays them, and how he uses them. The tools brought by a young craftsworker serve as an indicator of his ability and experience. Worn, quality tools reflect experience; specialized tools reflect ability (Riemer, 1979, pp. 73–74).

Many workers drive to work in their own pickup trucks. Some have tool boxes custom-built for their trucks that are attached to the side frame or fitted into the rear of vehicles. When a craftsworker has a tool that is rarely owned by an individual and that is borrowed by others, his name becomes associated with the tool. It becomes "Dom's bolt cutter," "Harold's banding tool," or "Chuckie's tapping machine." New apprentices often carry and display more tools than are necessary. On one of my present jobs, a new man who just made carpenter after being a laborer, carries a full complement of all the tools he can fit on his tool belt, while his journeyman partner carries just a few, essential ones. Riemer (1979, p. 74) points out that an experienced electrician carries just a few tools—a six-foot folding rule, one channel-lock pliers, one screwdriver, and a pair of side cutters. One of the electricians that regularly works on my jobs has a cart that he wheels around with neatly arranged screws and fasteners in glass jars that he needs for different kinds of jobs. On most jobs, there are gang boxes where the heavy tools are kept, along with the drawings. Foremen, who pride themselves as directors of the work, carry few, if any tools, usually only a six-foot folding rule stuck in their back pocket.

Costume

Jeffrey Riemer (1979, pp. 76–78) has identified costume as an important indicator of status and identification among construction workers. The hard hat, a safety measure, also serves to define status. Hard hats often have insignias or a particular color. Worn hard hats signify experience, while new shiny hard hats signify new recruits. Different trades used to wear different types and colors of coveralls, blue jeans, and overalls. Painters and plasterers wore white; carpenters wore blue; concrete finishers wore rust-color; plumbers and electricians wore dark blue. Nowadays, the new (and especially the younger) construction workers wear just about anything they wish and there is not much identification of trade with color or type of work clothes. For a discussion of costume as a symbol of occupations, see Harrison Trice (1993, pp. 97–99).

Jargon

Acquiring and using the jargon of one's trade so that it becomes second nature is another aspect of the socialization process among workers. Each trade has its own particular way of referring to tools and materials that are used in the work process. Often these are shorthand terms that need no further elaboration, much like jargon used by scientists, doctors, or lawyers in their professions. Thus, plumbers talk about "nipples" (short pieces of pipe threaded on both ends), and carpenters refer to "two byes" (a piece of lumber nominally two inches thick by four inches wide, but actually one and one half inches thick by three and one half inches wide). Masons refer to the mortar used to hold their bricks and blocks as "mud." Jargon sets off one craft from another, identifying those who use it as belonging to a particular group. For a glossary of construction worker argot and jargon, see Riemer (1979, pp. 181–192).

Not only does language become particular to the individual trade but sometimes part of a building site becomes part of the language argot for those working on the project. When I was project manager for the main library at SUNY, Buffalo, the central portion of the structure was called "the tower" by the men because it was four stories higher than the east or west wings of the building. Equipment also comes to have a distinct argot applied to them. On a downtown Buffalo road project, the men called one of the small bulldozers, "Gertrude." The machine used to break up the pavement was a "hog-knocker" and the demolition ball used to demolish buildings that had to be taken down was called a "headache ball."

In short, becoming a construction worker involves more than simply learning the craft. It requires a process of looking, talking, and acting like a construction worker.

PERSONAL RELATIONSHIPS IN CONSTRUCTION

Organizational principles for most construction firms are informal. Personal relationships dominate rather than the impersonal rules and procedures that are predominant among large corporations in other industries. In the construction industry the majority of contractors employ fewer than 10 workers. These are firms where workers know everyone else employed in the firm and where the working group is a familiar one based on contacts over a long period of time.

A new labor force is assembled for each project. Craftsworkers are constantly engaged in negotiations with employers or superintendents in their attempts to find desirable new employment as their current projects are completed. Employers, for their part, as they obtain new contracts, are seeking to assemble a work force and set of subcontractors to enable them to build their projects. Most of the negotiations involved in the hiring process are based on personal relationships. Construction workers in any locality rarely walk on a project without being known by their employers. If they are not known by their employers, they are usually known by other members of their trade.

The selection of the labor force for projects is usually in the hands of foremen and superintendents. Once a superintendent is selected by management to supervise a project, he starts the assembly of work crews. Foremen and superintendents use personal standards with regard to the kind of men they wish to hire. A superintendent told me what type of men he intended to hire for a project on which I served as project manager:

I'm going to choose men who know the work but who are not prima donnas. I'm not interested in superstars. Maybe they'll give you 200 feet of pipe one day. The next day maybe some dust'll blow in their face and they'll take off on you. I'd rather have guys who are steady. They don't have to be geniuses. I don't want dummies either. But guys who are not afraid to throw on some rain gear when it's pouring or who'll get into a trench full of water, or an operator who'll get down out of his cab and help push a piece of pipe home. Also, I want guys who'll come running when they're being held up and tell the truth. No cover-up guys. I don't want deathbed calls all the time from guys who should know how to get out of a jam. I want men who'll tell me when I'm screwing up but who'll listen when I holler.

Foremen and supers want to have harmonious crews on their jobs. They will not necessarily (nor are they expected to) accept men chosen by the front office. There was an instance when the front office wanted us to rehire a man on the Love Canal project who had been fired on another project. The superintendent's first reaction was negative. One of the bosses in the company came to our field shanty to argue for the man. The super said that the man was so disliked, "he had been punched more times than Muhammad Ali." Our boss could not arbitrarily override the superintendent without creating bad will, something that isn't good for any job. But he persisted and finally the superintendent relented, but he insisted that the re-hired man take a cut in pay until he proved himself. The man's wages were reduced to that of a third-year apprentice.

Foremen and superintendents often put into effect their own biases when they hire. Ethnic background is a factor in their choices. It was no accident that one company I worked for in Niagara Falls, New York, had mostly Italian-American workers, since the bosses were Italian-American. Religion can also be a factor. When I worked for a contractor in New York City and Queens, most of the construction workers were Catholic—German Catholic, Italian, and Irish. When I had my own general contracting firm doing work in uptown Manhattan, and working nonunion, most of the men were African-American and Hispanic.

Despite the racial prejudices of foremen and superintendents, when they are working on a public works contract, they must hire minorities since most public works funding is predicated on the requirement that the firms that win the contracts must have affirmative action plans. Many construction workers resent the requirement to hire minorities, especially if some of their friends or relatives are out of work. My own personal observation is that the resentment was stronger 20 years ago, and that today, after many minorities have entered the construction trades, there is less ill-will toward them. Once minority workers are employed, if they are competent and their particular skills become known, they are accepted for their work. On a road project in Buffalo, New York, we had a black foreman on our blacktop gang. His skills and prestige were so pronounced that one of our white workers, after a good day's stint of work behind the heavy roller, exclaimed, "Hey, I worked so hard and so good today, I feel like a white Sanford," using the black foreman's name.

Since supers and foremen do most of the hiring in the field they have great power. Still, a skilled, competent tradesman will act with independence, pride, and no sign of subservience before construction authority figures, not even the boss. They will give him respect, but they will not be subservient. They may even take liberties and kid with the boss, especially if they've known him for a long time. Foremen and supers are treated pretty much like other workers. Foremen and supers are frequently dependent on getting good craftsmen to work for them since it increases their own standing if they can line up competent crews who will produce. It is not unusual for a super or foreman, address book in hand, to drive around at night or on the weekend, seeking out workers in their homes as they try to round up crews for a project. These personal negotiations require mutual concessions that serve to enhance the craftsman's sense of self-esteem—sometimes the boss himself will go out to find a good man to do a certain job for him. I was working for a powerful developer in a northeastern city. My boss wanted to tear down our office building in the center of town and erect a new one, and was having trouble getting approval for the new building plans. Since the city was taking a long time granting us a permit he decided to take matters into his own hands. We moved all of our people out of the old building on a Friday, and on Friday night I accompanied my boss to a trailer park on the outskirts of town. There we tracked down a wizened older man with red hair that was turning gray. My boss asked him what he wanted to tear our building down and when he heard the price, offered him 50 percent over his number if he could do it over the weekend. Here was this man, in old clothes, frankly looking like a bum, being approached by one of the richest men in town, who had the confidence to entrust an important, and even dangerous job to him. They shook hands on the agreement, and on the following Monday morning, when people came to work in the downtown area they were surprised, and even shocked, the see our office building gone, with the lot covered over with neatly graded gravel.

The personalized system of work relationships in construction is modified to some extent by the union hiring hall that is mainly for men either not well-known or not as competent as those who are working. A laborer's union business agent in a northeastern city told me one day:

We've got 2,300 men in the local, with about 1,600 working. That's a pretty high percentage for us for men with steady jobs. The other 700 are what we call floaters. We use them to fill in short-term jobs. Most are just laborers. A laborer is not just a pick-and-shovel man the way he used to be. He has to know how to use tools; he has to run equipment sometimes. If a man can use the laser [laser beam devices are used to install ceilings level or to run pipe straight, by providing a beam of light to serve as an elevation or line marker for the journeyman], or do a little welding he's more useful to the contractor. At the hall, when we call for a certain job, the more a man knows the more he can put up his hand. We're getting a younger bunch these days, more educated; they can do more than laborers used to do. The unskilled worker is no longer around in construction. Everyone has to be skilled to some extent. Otherwise, they're floaters and maybe get a flagman job or a "gofer" [errand boy] job, but they don't work steady.

As a worker and a member of a construction union, the average foreman does not want to hold himself aloof from his fellow craftsmen or exercise autocratic power. Skilled craftsworkers suffer little from shyness or apprehension in dealing with their supervisors. Many are friends or drinking buddies with their foremen. Construction workers do not view foremen as all-powerful instruments of powerful corporations. In many cases, construction workers know their unions have more power than their employers, who may be small specialty trade contractors, or sometimes one-man operations. Dealing with supervision on a personal basis permits construction workers to maintain their independence and self-respect without feeling they are nobodies. Each foreman or superintendent tends to have a circle of friends or relatives who constitute a labor pool from which he hires. Tests for hiring are personal ones. Foremen consider personality and other attributes. I have questioned a number of superintendents who said they considered the following items important when they hire workers:

- *Availability:* Supers need to schedule work and rely on a man's availability when he is needed. We were blacktopping in December 1988, on a job in Nyack, New York, and we had to make a decision each morning on the day we blacktopped since the weather was a factor on whether we would work or not. We could call certain men on the morning we decided to work and we knew they would get dressed to come to the job. We gave those men preference in hiring for other projects.

- *Craft Skills:* Men who get hired regularly must have competence with regard to their craft skills. Foremen and supers have to feel they can depend on them to execute work that is up to the standards of workmanship in the trade. That doesn't mean that these men are perfect in all respects. Some men are excellent workers but have screwed up personal lives. Although most construction guys I've known are not angels, they do have strong work and family values that stress comradeship with workmates and responsibility to family and friends.

- *Sociability:* Construction work is based on teams and gangs and requires cooperation that depends on crews being friendly and sociable. Dissension can wreck a project and men who foment conflicts and arguments are avoided.

- *Good Judgment:* Construction workers are expected to solve problems and use good judgment. They should not cover up mistakes or try to lie their way out of a jam. That behavior exhibits bad judgment and men who do this consistently get bad reputations and are poor hires. Good judgment also means standing up for the rights and practices of one's trade.

- *Initiative:* Construction craftsworkers are expected to perform work on their own. This often requires initiative in rounding up materials, tools, and equipment and figuring out the various moves to carry out work. It also requires laying out work and figuring out blueprints as they apply to one's trade, including dimensions, geometry, angles, and math. A man who has to be told every detail about how to go about his work is not going to last long in construction.

A journeyman who expects to work steady makes himself known to a wide circle of possible fellow workers, foremen, and superintendents. He finds it advantageous to be in contact with others in the construction industry after working hours. He knows the favorite bars of men and women in his or her trade and frequents those places that workers go to after work to drink, shoot pool, bowl, play cards, dance, and relax with workmates. He may drop in to see a foreman or super who lives in his neighborhood. He visits with the business agent at the union hiring hall. The result of all this activity is the expectation that someone will put in a good word for him when supers and foremen are hiring.

The fluid nature of construction work requires adaptability by construction workers. In many cases a man does not know who he will be working with until he arrives on the job. This requires adjustment and if a craftsworker cannot adjust he is likely to be laid off. Foremen and supers do not judge a man solely on his work. Bennie Graves talks about construction work as follows (1974, p. 415):

More than other technically advanced and rationalized industries, construction work seems to depend upon informal systems of personal relations to locate skilled workers when they are needed. Consequently, the purely technical requirements of a job may be markedly modified by particularistic criteria. Mohawks, for example, are prominent in the high steel construction of the northeastern United States; various ethnic groups dominate particular building crafts in Detroit; the pipeline construction industry seems to depend largely upon groups of friends and kinsmen to recruit its work crews.

Learning skills often involves father-son relationships to a significant degree (Strauss 1971, p. 103). Journeymen have preferences about whom they wish to work with and a smart super will take those preferences into consideration. Many construction firms are small enough for employers to gather their work force through face-to-face meetings. Sometimes contractors are so small that employers work alongside their employees.

Strong emotions, pride, and personality contribute to construction work performance. On one road project, we had a crew building manholes. One January morning, the assistant superintendent in charge of masonry work challenged the men. He told them that if they produced 30 vertical feet of manhole height a day, instead of the usual 20 feet, they could leave when they finished. That day the men did 30 feet by 3:00 P.M., but they did not go home until 4:30 P.M., quitting time. When the foreman, came into the field office, the following dialogue took place:

Foreman: Don't expect 30 feet every day, Casper. We're not animals, goddamn it.

Super: How come you did 30 feet? You do it when you feel like it? Is that it?

Another bricklayer: If conditions are right we can produce.

Super: What do you mean, if conditions are right?

Foreman: It's winter. Those enclosures you're building—they suck!

Super: What the fuck you want, a cathedral?

Bricklayer: No, but it's supposed to be above freezing in the hole. Tarps are wide open. The wind's whipping our ass. The mortar is freezing on the blocks.

Super: But you still got 30 feet. What gives?

Foreman: Up your ass, Casper. Don't expect 30 feet every day. You know what a 12-inch solid block weighs?

Super: My ass bleeds for you.

Bricklayer: You try humping a hundred pound block all day.

Super: I call those blocks my birth control blocks. You lay them all day and when you get home you're no good for nothing except to sack out.

After that confrontation the men continued to produce 30 feet, complaining and cursing the super. The force of the super's personality, the men's pride, and the challenge were all personal factors that led to an increase in output. Meanwhile, the men laying block closed ranks against the super and continued to razz him.

Personal attachment and interdependence is prevalent among high steel workers. Because death is the penalty for mistakes, high steel workers are particular about whom they work with. Working relations among a crew is so finely tuned that if someone doesn't show up the entire crew may not work. Mike Cherry was so attached to his partner on his steel erection crew he had dreams of death at the hands of a faceless partner (1974, p. 132). Jack Haas comments about controlling the situation in dangerous occupations (1977, pp. 167–168):

The process of social control I have described—testing and controlling fellow workers and maintaining and enhancing individual and collective control over the work setting—are processes characteristic of occupations where danger is a perceived worker problem. The careful surveillance and testing of colleagues, particularly newcomers, the controlled actions belying any fear, and the unified effort to increase worker autonomy, are sociologically relevant outcomes in situations where workers face extreme danger.

PRIDE IN WORK

Most construction workers believe they work hard, contribute to society, and earn an honest living. They feel they produce something real and tangible as they see the physical evidence of what they accomplish. The physical stress on their bodies gives testimony to the effort that they put into their work. Tom Wicker of the *New York Times* said that among the factors lessening the quality of modern life is that people do not care about their work (Sheehan 1975, p. 191). This is not true of construction workers who care about their work and who share a code of craftsmanship that goes back to the Middle Ages. Every construction trade union agreement and every set of building specifications has phrases like "good workmanship" and "according to the good practices of the trade." This is not mere lip service. Craftsmen are proud of quality work and ashamed of shoddy work. There are men who are exceptions, but they are exceptions, not the norm. Where hand and craft methods are important, as in construction, the ethic of workmanship and quality operate as a cultural ideal. Caplow captured the idea as follows (1954, p. 131):

In the crafts, the most distinctive attitudes are those which revolve around contractual obligations, implicit or explicit, which specify the rights and duties of each in relation to all. These attitudes, which define a day's work, a fair wage, a good shop, a bad foreman, the right tools, a reasonable order, a one-man job, or the jurisdiction of a craft, are essentially moral. They contain a principle of justice drawn from two important sources: the medieval idea of the "just price" and the early modern theory that society is founded by a free contract.

SELF-RESPECT

What are some of the elements that contribute to self-respect among construction workers?

Leadership

Those who enjoy their own self-respect and that of others exercise leadership in construction. Many are leaders by example and do not occupy formal positions; others are leaders because they are willing to risk their reputations by taking charge of a difficult situation, even a dangerous one. We were doing a road job in a northern city at a major intersection. The pressure of the load of one of our heavy backhoes broke a water line below the pavement and water came gushing out with great force. The young man, Bruce, who was in charge of the crew, wasted no time in crawling below the pavement, locating the shut-off value, and turning it off before all the fill below the street washed out and collapsed the pavement. In fact, the pavement could have collapsed on him and killed him. It was a daring act of leadership that gained the unspoken admiration of everyone who witnessed it. Bruce waved it off as nothing, something he was expected to do when faced with an emergency.

Knowledge of the Work

A worker who knows his trade exudes self-confidence and self-respect. He must demonstrate his knowledge through work considered acceptable by his fellow tradesmen. "Acceptable" means that work is straight and true, level, in accordance with the dimensions on the drawings, and in the proper location. Work is also acceptable if it is performed at the correct time, that is when it is needed to be done so that other trades can continue to work. It is electrical roughing so that walls can be closed up. It is sheet metal roughing above a ceiling so the ceiling can be completed and closed up. It is a counter installed so a sink can be dropped and connected. The evaluation of a craftsworker's performance by his workmates and other trades gives the tradesman his self-respect. Respect is given to those who have mastered tools, techniques, and knowledge of materials associated with their trade. The journeyman or journeywoman would have to commit some flagrant act breaking the norms of workmanship or behavior to lose his or her standing among workmates.

Since knowledge and skill are acquired through experience, older construction workers are often treated with respect based on their years in the industry. A man with experience is assumed to have acquired many tricks of the trade. Rather than viewed as inadequate because of age, older construction workers are treated as elder statesmen. If his physical strength wanes, an older worker will be given a job suitable to his years, with no lessening of his standing among his peers.

On one of my jobs in upstate New York, we had an older bricklayer who had not finished high school, yet his knowledge of his trade was considerable and highly respected. He could look at a wall and figure out courses of brick and how many were required for each row. He was a mathematical wizard with regard to brick, knowing the dimensions of various types of brick and how they could be fitted around windows, doors, corners, and curved shapes on a building. Once he found something wrong with a blueprint and commented, "Look, I'm just a dumb bricklayer and never finished high school, but there's something screwed up here." A group of us gathered around him and while we were wrestling with the problem he came up with the solution, to our great relief.

Earning a Living

Most people in America respect workers who earn a good living. At a retirement party for one of our men, a construction laborer said to me, "My job gave me the kind of income without which I'd have no respect for myself. Look at Gary, just a laborer and he has enough to retire. And he gets a party to boot. I hope I get the same treatment when I retire."

Physical Strength and Stamina

These attributes play a large part in giving construction workers self-respect. Strength and stamina are associated with ideas about maleness and manliness; sometimes they are also associated with requirements of the job. Construction work involves hard physical labor under trying conditions. Construction workers must develop stamina to persevere through adverse conditions—extreme cold, arm-weary shoveling, leg-weary sloshing through mud, the chilling effect of high winds, and the back-straining lifting of heavy weights. Workers who do this work are proud of their physical capabilities and admire those who perform great physical feats.

Billy was admired for his physical attributes. Besides being feared for his adeptness with his fists, he had a body that looked like forged steel. When he twisted his arm, the muscles would bulge and jump like a bunch of knots. His stomach was like a rippled washboard. I had him with me on a hospital job in Florida. One night we were drinking in a local bar and he asks me (or orders me) to smash him in the face as hard as I could with my fist. I told him to get lost, but he kept after me. Finally I said, "Here it comes, Billy," and I hauled off and socked him as hard as I could on the side of his face. Billy laughed at me, saying, "Is that the best you can do, fer crissakes. Come on, you can do better than that." I refused and after he saw I was adamant in my refusal, he says, "Look, this is the way you smash someone in the face." And he start pummeling himself with his fists, with hard and ferocious blows. Some guy at the bar asked me, "What to you have to do to hurt that guy?" "Shoot him," I answered. The man observed, "The bullets would probably bounce off."

Today, many new lifting devices have been introduced in construction to lift heavy loads and lighten physical labor. Carpenters still have to raise a four foot by eight foot sheet of drywall or plywood, laborers have to pull concrete with a hoe when they are pouring a floor, and masons have to lift 60-pound blocks when they are laying up a wall. Anyone not used to hard, physical labor will find it hard to last in construction. An academic friend of mine, a rather big guy, asked me to get him a construction job for the summer so he "could have some fun" and earn extra money. I got him a job on a road gang. He lasted one day and was not up to reporting for work, physically or mentally, on the second day. Backs and knees, arms and shoulders, and legs take an awful beating in some trades. Carpet layers and concrete finishers wear pads over their knees, but still wear out their knees over the long term. Backs are one of homo sapiens weakest structures because of our erect posture, and construction workers test that hypothesis every day.

SPORTS, HORSEPLAY, KIDDING, AND STORYTELLING

Many construction men like physical sports—arm-wrestling, prize-fighting, football, weight lifting, and wrestling. On the Exxon project in Clinton, New Jersey, a $210 million project that lasted three years, during the summer months the men pitched horseshoes every day during lunchtime. Matches were spirited with betting, kidding, and insults flying through the air along with the horseshoes. Wintertime is bowling time for construction men. A large percentage of workers belong to bowling leagues. Many men drink at bars that have bowling alleys. Bowling night is a night out with friends and workmates that combines beer, competition, and no wives.

Construction workers enjoy physical horseplay. On one of our sewer treatment plant projects, a favorite game was ripping clothes. Sid, a concrete finisher, always had some tear or hole in his clothing. Being teased about it by Hank, a surveyor, Sid challenged him to a clothes-tearing fight. Each man tried to get his finger into a hole in the other man's shirt or pants. They would then pull and away would come a shirt or pants leg, revealing bare limbs and setting off peals of laughter and joshing from onlookers.

Some of the men liked to play the Italian game of "fingers" or "boom." The game is played by two men. The idea is to show a certain number of fingers and shout a number from one to ten. The one who calls the number corresponding to fingers shown wins a point, with the game played to ten points. Players love to shout and scream into each other's faces, flinging arms and hands with great gusto, leering at each other with disdain, and showing mock contempt. Challenges are thrown down by habitual rivals who bet as much as a keg of beer or $100 on a game. When the game is over, the loser slinks away in mock humiliation.

Kidding and comic stunts are regular occurrences on construction projects. On one job, a carpenter made a wooden platform in the shape of buttocks for a short-statured laborer. The platform was placed on the lunch bench and labeled "Reserved for Shortie." On another project, the men drew stars on a folding chair, labeled it, "The Chief," and presented it to the concrete foreman. Construction men are typically male chauvinists who tell sexual jokes and stories about their sexual exploits. They also regularly display nude pictures of women from *Playboy* and *Hustler* in their shanties or on their tool chests. It remains to be seen if the introduction of more women into the industry will have any effect on this behavior.

Construction workers are big eaters and like to throw feasts on the job. On one job, we had a load of rebars that came in the wrong thickness and the wrong dimensions. Rather than pay for shipping the rebars back to the supplier in the South, the company donated the bars and told us to scrap the metal and use the funds for a feast. We held a big feast after work and had enough money to give out prizes for lucky numbers. One day, on a job in upstate New York, two men were working on the sixth floor, out on a scaffold at the edge of the roof cornice, a very dangerous perch. They were having an animated conversation. I wondered what it was about and when I came within earshot, I heard them exchanging ideas about the best way to prepare pasta. On one feast the men used concrete blocks and oxy-acetylene torches to make a stove and prepare favorite dishes. Another time, the men organized a "wild meat" feed, featuring meat from animals they had hunted. The meal was accompanied by hunting stories filled with frustration, comic situations, and triumphs.

Kidding, horseplay, storytelling, and communal feeds contribute to group cohesion and produce feelings of fellowship and affinity.

ATTITUDES TOWARD THE UNION

Men who give construction unions their loyalty reflect their understanding of benefits received. Construction unions have raised wages, increased employment opportunities, reduced competition, and lessened job insecurity to some extent. Unions give workers social contacts with fellow craftsmen and keep them informed about news and trends in their trade. For all these reasons, the union occupies a central place in the life of construction workers who are organized in the building trades, mainly in urban centers. But even among nonunion workers, the unionized sector has an influence, particularly on the wages paid. Nonunion contractors will say that they don't mind paying the same wages that unionized workers earn. What they object to mainly are the rules, and sometimes the benefits.

Construction workers view a good union official as one who can settle disputes without resorting to strikes. But whatever their opinion of strike action most construction workers would agree with the statement I heard an ironworker make, "If the union tells me to go on strike, I'll have to go." Most men accept the union's power to call a strike. Construction unions and strikes have been around a long time. The carpenters formed a union in colonial times; the ironworkers formed the International Association of Bridge and Structural Iron Workers from six local unions in New York, Buffalo, Boston, Cleveland, Pittsburgh and Chicago in 1896. The founding of the International Union of Bricklayers and Allied Craftsmen in 1865 was the culmination of developments that began more than four decades earlier. Organization in the masonry trades in the United States began as early as 1823. The Laborers' International Union of North America was brought into being in 1903 through the efforts of AFL President Samuel Gompers, when 25 delegates from 17 different cities met in Washington, D.C., representing 8,000 workers. (For a history of the different building trades unions, see *The Builders*, 1983, published by the Building and Construction Trades Department of the AFL-CIO.)

Union officials are often criticized for giving special favors to friends or kin and spending the union's money too freely. Members resent high salaries and cars for business agents. Many see their union officers as politicians whose main concern is to stay in office. If a union official does something for the members it can be viewed as trying to build a following. In general, there is loyalty to the union rather than for any union official. Even those with relatives who are union officials speak of them as office holders rather than leaders. The shop stewards in the field who work alongside members are seen as the real leaders of the men since they are solving job construction problems as well as looking out for the interests of the men on the job.

Most unionized construction workers will not violate union practices regarding strikes and picket lines. In 1982, on the Exxon job in Clinton, New Jersey, several of the trades had their contracts coming up for renewal. All settled except the electricians who set up a picket line. It came at the height of the construction season and many of the trades were angry because of the loss of work when it was available. Picket lines were set up and the men respected it. One laborer commented, "When guys are on a picket line they're trying to better their conditions, and it's not up to me to spoil it. I don't ask questions. They're construction guys like me and the union says I gotta respect their line, so I do it."

An operating engineer also commented, "We're not allowed to go through a picket line even if we wanted to. They'd be after us and our cards would be lifted. We'd have to go before the executive board of the union and then . . . bam, I don't know what, but they don't let you off easy for something like that."

The rule is that a man must accept strike and picket line practices of his own union and he must support the actions of fellow construction workers by not crossing their picket line no matter what the consequences. A man named Frank was a superintendent for a major sheetmetal contractor that we currently use on many of our projects. The sheetmetal workers contract was up for renewal in 1997 and the union struck. Frank was making a very good salary with good benefits, but not only did he carry a book, he believed in what the men struck for. His boss was trying to work some of his jobs with supervisory personnel and Frank was considered a key guy. When Frank refused to cross the picket line, his boss did not fire him (that would have been too blatant), but he demoted him to journeyman and took away all of his perks. Frank was extremely resentful when I ran into him on one of our renovation projects. He said he was no longer a super nor was he given responsibility for the large sheetmetal jobs. In fact, he was given assignments as far from his home as possible. He was pissed off at the boss, who he had known since he first went into business. Frank was the kind of guy who personally busted his hump to knock out a job and he would take responsibilities on his own to satisfy a customer. He was a big factor in my choosing his company to do work for us and when Frank was no longer available for my jobs I began to look around for other companies. This was all because Frank would not cross a picket line, which his boss should have understood would have caused big trouble for him with the local union.

UNEMPLOYMENT

In 1996, construction, along with agriculture, had the highest unemployment rate of any major industry, twice as high as the average unemployment rate (U.S. Bureau of the Census, 1996, p. 419). With 6 percent of the labor force, the construction industry had 10.1 percent of the unemployment. In fact, this same reference shows that construction workers going back to 1975 consistently had twice the rate of unemployment as the rest of the country.

A basic element of the way of life of construction workers is the instability of employment. On any construction job, a tradesman or tradeswoman is needed only at certain times. Unless it is a large project where a worker's craft is sequenced from one floor to another, or from one part of the project to another, there is the inevitable interruption of a worker's employment. In addition, there is the problem of weather. In cold, rainy areas of the country, a man or woman can lose a substantial percentage of their income during winter months. When it rains, site work cannot proceed. When winds are high, high steel workers have to knock off. Unemployment in construction is higher in February than in August. The loss of days of work in construction does not come in regular blocks of time. Often this means that a worker cannot fall back on unemployment insurance since most states require a waiting period before benefits begin.

The pervasiveness of concern with the threat of unemployment manifests itself when a job is in its completion phase. I had a large $100 million project in Newark, New Jersey, in 1991. When the job was nearing completion the men asked almost daily if we were planning other work, if there were projects coming up they could find out about, or whether I was going to another job and if I needed workers. The completion phase of a project is a sad time because groups who have worked together are now breaking up. Workers also feel the tension of not knowing when their next project will begin.

Mike Cherry captures the mood of the wind-down phase of a project in this quote from his book on high steel workers (1974, pp. 204–205):

On June 24th, Crockett came over to me while I was making up a bundle of old cables and told me that it was my last day. He had to lay somebody off, he said, and the other stay-behinds were all local books. . . . Then he handed me my check. This slowdown was temporary, he said, and perhaps we'd all get together again when things picked up.

Construction workers have a sense of the insecurities they face in their industry, but those who are self-confident about their skills know that eventually they will be in demand and will be able to find work again. They may have to go to the hiring hall, or begin contacting friends, relations, and supers to make the necessary connections that will lead to another job. But they maintain the spirit of confidence embodied in the following remark by Mike Cherry: "Hey, you know I was lookin' for a job when I found this one."

CONSTRUCTION ERRORS AND MISTAKES

One of the negative impressions about construction workers is that they commit mistakes and they are indifferent about errors. There is a growing feeling among Americans that quality of work in general has deteriorated and that there is little pride in workmanship in modern America. Perhaps construction workers are particularly vulnerable to this charge because the public, as homeowners, has had direct contact with them, using construction workers for building new homes, making alterations, or for repair work. In construction one is dealing with a bulky, complex product that takes a long time to produce, is the subject of the work of many hands, and is affected by weather, all of which contribute to the inevitability of errors. Construction work is not subjected to the same kind of control that is attained in a factory, and thus the acceptable tolerances are greater. Furthermore, the fact that so many parties are involved with the planning, design, layout, and building of structures increases the chances of errors. For an extended discussion of mistakes in construction and how they are dealt with, see Riemer (1979, pp. 121–138).

Mistakes are the inevitable result of any kind of work or activity; at the very least, they are the unintended result of human effort. The treatment of errors by construction workers is no different from the manner in which errors are treated in society as a whole. Trade-offs are made whereby the seriousness of a mistake is weighed against its physical or human consequences. If an error could endanger persons or cause damage to property, there is no choice to be made—it must be corrected. Any other course would be legally criminal if the defect were known and willfully ignored. In most other cases in which less serious errors occur, contractors, architects, and construction workers weigh the seriousness of a mistake against the cost of correcting it. If the fall of a pipe was less than specified but would still permit water within it to drain properly by gravity, it would make no sense to rip it out and reinstall it.

The following incident illustrates the point.

On a downtown Buffalo road project we had to build four bridges spanning over a number of streets so we could connect Route 33 with the New York Thruway. We bought the steel for these bridges from a Pennsylvania company. The New York State Department of Transportation specifications stated that if steel sat outside for more than 120 days before erection we had to apply a new shop coat of protective red lead paint to prevent the steel from rusting. Through our own errors of timing and coordination (we had the steel shipped too early), the steel sat outside all winter. When the time came to build the bridges, the factory shop coat was examined by me and by my super, and we found it to be perfect, except for a few scratches. The state inspector, going strictly by the book, demanded that we repaint the steel in spite of the fact that (he admitted) the shop coat paint looked fine. This would have cost time and thousands of dollars. We appealed to the state transportation department and they sent an inspector from Albany to examine the steel. In this case reason prevailed because after he examined the paint he said it was fine and we only had to touch up the scratches.

Another instance of a series of mistakes happened on one of those projects where you can't win for losing. Sometimes it seems as though the construction gods have it in for you and everything you do from day one is fated for failure. I was working as a project manager for a contractor in the northern United States. They bid on a hospital job in Florida and they decided to do the job themselves and send key men to Florida to take charge of the project. This was their first mistake because if you are a "Yankee" contractor in the 1970s going into the Dixie heartland, you'd better have allies or, better yet, hire a local contractor. The next mistake, an even bigger one, was that our bid was $1 million (yes, I said *$1 million*) lower than the next bidder. The bonding company was willing to let us out of the bid, but my bosses refused and figured they could make up the $1 million by shopping for low prices among bidding subcontractors and by trying to expedite the project and finish it before the projected completion date. Well, when you try to buy a project out cheap you are bound to get unqualified contractors, which is exactly what happened. The company used three roofing contractors to get the roof built right, and finally had to rip the entire roof off and start again. We could not find a qualified electrical contractor in the area and wound up going to Daytona for a qualified (and union) contractor, who did a good job but was costly. We used a disastrous contractor to lay the floors for the operating rooms and had to rip up all the floors and get someone else to finish it. Our HVAC (Heating, Ventilating, and Air Conditioning) contractor installed an underground steam line that blew up and destroyed the emergency entrance we were building. We had to rebuild the entrance and the HVAC contractor had to reinstall the steam line. I am not making all this up, it really happened.

One of our major difficulties was our failure to find competent local contractors, and I believe this was because there were no union contractors to be found. It has been my experience with regard to commercial and industrial construction, that union contractors tend to be more qualified than nonunion contractors with regard to this type of work. It was certainly true in the 1970s. It has changed somewhat today and I would not want to assert categorically that nonunion contractors are unqualified for commercial work. The industry has been steadily going nonunion so there are a lots of good nonunion firms in the market.

Construction workers are aware that their careers and the longevity of their employment depend on their performance. This may be more true for construction workers than for other occupations because performance in construction can be easily traced back to the crew or the journeyman doing the work. Construction work depends on the individual worker for quantity and quality of work due to the hand technology involved in the work process, thus there is a strong motive for construction workers to perform reasonably well as it will result in respect from fellow craftsmen as well as a reputation for good work that will further a man's future employment prospects. Workers who simply put in their time on a job or do sloppy work are not the first hired when workers are assembled for a project. Given the localized, community-like nature of the construction industry, workers get known and ranked by the type of work they do by foremen and supers in the local region.

To those who question the attitudes and responsibility ethic of construction workers I offer the following example.

I was project manager for a Niagara Falls general contractor that cleaned up the Love Canal, one of the biggest environmental disasters caused by chemical contamination. We built a treatment plant to remove the leachate (chemically saturated water leaching from the canal into adjoining private home property). Our work included the installation of a drainage system, underground holding tanks, and the new treatment plant. We also capped the contaminated area of the Love Canal with three and a half feet of clean clay.

We had 50 men working on the project. They had to take showers every day after work, wear special suits that were discarded each day to be washed and decontaminated, and use respirators whenever they worked in a manhole or a deep excavation. They worked in soil saturated with a deadly chemical—dioxin. This chemical ate steel pipe and shoe leather. Men had to wear heavy, treated rubber boots over their work shoes. They worked in an environment putrid with the odor of chemicals, received no extra or premium pay, and had no idea what they would encounter when they dug into the earth. Yet not a single man quit or refused to perform all the work required, nor did anyone refuse to use the uncomfortable and clumsy safety devices while performing his work. The only incident occurred when a telephone installer came to put phones in our trailers, took one sniff of the air, and left, saying, "This is not for me." Our own men stayed on the job from start to finish, and completed the project on time without any serious incidents.

Construction workers, as well as other blue-collar workers should be given recognition for all the dirty, heavy, smelly, uncomfortable jobs that many people would not dare to do themselves. Blue-collar workers do not get good press because the people who write about them are not blue-collar workers themselves, except in very rare cases. By and large, what working people do is largely ignored. When a movie actress who was also a public personality came to the Love Canal, she covered herself with publicity as a fighter for saving our environment. She addressed a crowd of 400 people outside the gate, in front of the press and television cameras. However, when she entered the contaminated construction site, she sped through the area in her car with the windows closed, and she never took the time or trouble to stop and talk to the workers.

4

THE JOB SITE

CRAFT ROLES

One of the important roles on a construction job site is the craft role. The significant difference between manufacturing and construction is the absence of the interchangeable worker in construction. The most striking thing about a sizeable building under construction is the myriad specialty trades working with hand tools to execute specialty hand-tool procedures based on the individual worker's knowledge and experience. Each day on the construction project, a variety of workers regularly apply unique sets of skills to different sets of circumstances (Finkel, 1997, p. 83). To perform a craft role, a man or woman must possess certain skills and knowledge. Knowledge and skill is displayed in what a craftsworker produces and in the services performed on the job site. A carpenter's knowledge will result in wooden products, a mason in stone, brick, and block walls, an ironworker in steel framing, and so on. Each craft contributes to the total structure. There are 20 main trades in construction, plus teamsters. Table 4.1 covers the major ones. Some trades not covered include elevator constructors, acoustic ceiling carpenters, insulators, and others. Craftsworkers like plasterers and marble polishers are becoming fewer in number.

In the table, the term *function* is used to denote a service rendered by craftsworkers as part of special training. the term *responsibility* refers to an obligation to perform craft skills as well as behaving according to the customs of the trade.

PRESTIGE

Generally, the greater the skill the larger the wage scale, and the greater the danger the greater the admiration. Both high wage scales and performing work

Table 4.1
Craft Roles

Craft	Knowledge	Skills	Function	Responsibility
Carpenter	•Geometry •Measurement •Blueprints •Knows properties of wood and metal substitutes for wood (metal studs and door frames)	•Hammering •Sawing •Fitting •Fastening •Gluing •Measuring •Leveling •Shimming	•Frames •Forms •Drywall •Millwork •Cabinetry •Wood floors •Trim	•Provides own tools •Builds from blueprints or verbal instructions •Lays out own work •Directs helper •Directs apprentice
Mason	•Geometry •Measurement •Blueprints •Knows nature of brick block stone, and mortar •Knows bonds •Scaffolding	•Setting masonry •Applying mortar •Leveling •Bedding mortar •Striking joints •Parging •Breaking •Sawing •Measuring •Coursing •Making walls plumb	•Builds walls •Sets veneers •Builds foundations •Builds fireplaces •Builds shafts •Finishes concrete	•Provides own tools •Builds from blueprints •Lays out work •Directs helper •Directs apprentice
Operating Engineer	•Controls devices on construction machines •Knows load capacities of machines and cranes •Safety procedures •Reads grade stakes •Engines	Mechanical: •Lifting •Lowering •Blading •Grading •Tracking •Digging •Placing •Leveling •Hauling •Loading •Tamping •Excavating •Backfilling •Raising steel •Raising materials •Standby on equipment	•Moves earth •Moves rock •Excavates •Fills in earth •Shapes earth •Grades earth	•Operates machines •Hand signals •Protects equipment •Safety
Ironworker	•Measurement •Blueprints •Size and weights of structural and reinforcing steel •Safety devices	•Balancing on beams •Bolting steel •Riveting •Shimming •Climbing •Shimmying •Cooning •Torch cutting •Welding •Leveling •Hammering	•Erects steel •Connects steel •Places rebars •Ties rebars •Fabricates miscellaneous iron •Erects steel stairs	•Provides own tools •Makes structural steel plumb

Table 4.1 *continued*

Craft	Knowledge	Skills	Function	Responsibility
Laborer	•Measurement •Blueprints •Torch burning •Uses laser •Mixes cement •Use of concrete •Jackhammer •Bush hammer •Tamper	•Shoveling •Carry loads •Mixing •Place loads •Screed concrete •Level concrete •Unloading •Torch burning •Tamping, grading	•Heavy labor •Assists journeyman •Moves materials and tools •Operates some equipment	•Takes foreman's orders •Protects tools and materials •Cleanup •Trash removal
Electrician	•Circuitry (electric) •Power systems •Electric devices •Electric motors •Lighting fixtures •Blueprints •Measurement •Controllers	•Piping •Wire pulling •Wire connecting •Panel connecting •Circuit tracing •Testing •Connects motors •Grounding •Energizing •Interlocking •Temperature control •Power manholes •Overhead power •Underground power	•Installs lighting and power systems •Installs communication and data systems	•Tools •Safety •Energizes systems •Repairs
Plumbers and Steamfitters	•Pipe, fittings, and valves •Water systems •Waste systems •Drainage systems •Heating systems •Air conditioning systems •Boilers •Humidifiers •Filters •Plumbing fixtures •Radiation •Blueprints •Measurement	•Pipe fitting •Threading pipe •Cutting pipe •Soldering •Welding •Brazing •Rigging equipment •Hanging •Fastening •Testing •Repairing leaks •Pressurizing •Bleeding air •Charging refrigerants •Caulk joints	•Waste, water drainage systems •Heating and air conditioning systems •Gas systems •Air systems •Chemical systems	•Install systems free of leaks •Repairs •Testing
Painter and Paperhanger	•Properties of paint, thinners, removers, varnish, shellac, wallpaper, and all coatings and wall coverings	•Spraying •Brushing •Pasting •Gluing •Matching •Fitting •Removing •Sanding •Mixing •Blending	•Apply finish paint and wall coverings	•Mix paint •Check colors •Match patterns •Prepare surfaces •Protect unfinished surfaces

Table 4.1 *continued*

Craft	Knowledge	Skills	Function	Responsibility
Concrete Worker	•Properties of concrete •Troweling machine •Concrete pumps •Concrete forms •Concrete dressings •Slabs, walls, columns	•Float concrete •Troweling •Screeding •Pouring •Vibrating •Loading and unloading concrete buckets •Pumping •Bullfloating •Raking	•Pours and finishes concrete	•Tools •Finished surfaces
Sheetmetal Worker	•Properties of sheetmetal •Blueprints •Sheetmetal locks •Types of hangers •Geometry •Measurement •Air flow theory •Fan mechanics	•Cutting •Fitting •Locking •Connecting •Hanging •Measuring •Setting equipment •Setting diffusers •Setting filters	•Connects sheetmetal •Installs fans and blowers •Installs ventilation and exhaust systems •Installs air-conditioning systems	•Tools •No leaks •Correct sizes •Balances air quantities
Teamster	•Mechanics of trucks, lowboys, and concrete mixers	•Driving •Braking •Turning •Backing up •Dumping •Operate controls •Washing •Cleaning •Turn concrete drum	•Operate truck to deliver materials and supplies •Move earth off site or from one part of site to another	•Truck at right place and time •Safety •Protect equipment

under dangerous conditions enhance prestige in the construction industry. A prime example is the erection of structural steel for large commercial structures. I was recently involved with building a hotel in Jersey City, New Jersey. While we were erecting the structural steel frame of the building, a delegation from the insurance company that oversees our safety program came to the building to inspect the floors and look for safety violations. The executive from the insurance company remarked, "I've been involved with many buildings, especially in New York City, and I always hold my breathe during the structural steel phase of any project. I don't know how those guys can do what they do, walking on that steel." The two of us looked up at an ironworker 120 feet in the air, standing on a beam and waiting to catch another one. I also remember in 1992, when we were completing the structural steel for the Blue Cross/Blue Shield Building in Newark, New Jersey, and I was standing on the roof of a companion building that we built for New Jersey Transit. I watched an ironworker 250 feet in the air, at the very edge of the building, standing on a beam and waiting to catch and connect the last beam at the corner of the building. After he received the beam and positioned it perpendicular to the beam he was standing on, he had to bend over to line up the holes by using the pointed end of his wrench, and then insert the eight bolts into the holes. He was not tied off and all I could think was, "Don't lose your balance and don't get dizzy and topple over." The other amazing thing about watching ironworkers at work is when you see this mass of steel laying on the ground waiting to be lifted into place. Each piece has some kind of marking on it and the ironworker has this blueprint that he's looking at. I've stood next to these workers and I must say the blueprint looked to me like a bewildering mass of unintelligible symbols, and here is this guy, probably only a high school graduate, figuring out what piece crosses what piece, what column is positioned at what point in the building, and at what elevation columns and beams are supposed to be set. We are not talking about an erector set. This is a hundred times, nay, a thousand times more complicated. Of course, learning how to lay out steel and direct its erection only comes with long years of training and practice and not every man in the crew can do it. Only general foremen and superintendents who have earned their place and prestige are entrusted with the job. Usually they are older men who have been in the trade a long time, and who have earned the respect of the men and enjoy well-deserved prestige for their competency. This is the other aspect of erecting structural steel that is often overlooked when people look up to see the guy walking the steel, but it's also the super down below who is feeding up the right piece for the right place.

Discretionary use of one's time is highly valued and those who have it enjoy high prestige. Crafts requiring more skills than others, like carpentry, masonry, electrical, plumbing, sheetmetal, pipe fitting, and millwork, usually result in permitting craftsworkers to layout their own work and organize their own time (Finkel, 1997, pp. 108–110). Certain crafts enjoy exclusive practice of the trade because of the special knowledge required. For example, most construction men make it a point not to mess with electricity because it can be dangerous and most don't know how to handle it, especially high voltage, high power feeders.

The association of dirty work with less prestigious work is sometimes expressed by a foreman who threatens to punish a man by sending him into a hole, the mud, or a sewer. On one of my sewage treatment plant projects, we had a laborer known as "Dirty Johnny" because of his perpetually dirty appearance. He actually took pride in his nickname, and enjoyed describing the size and shapes of feces he encountered floating in a new pipe. One day we had to tie in a live sewer line and needed a man to work inside the pipe. Johnny was the man chosen. He jumped into the trench and crawled into the pipe with laughter and alacrity. When he came out, smelling awful, he cried out, "There'll be no flies in Buffalo tonight 'cause they're all goin' home with me."

VALUES AND SANCTIONS

A successful construction project benefits all who are associated with it. Two important elements of a successful project are completing it on time and performing the work at a level of quality that meets the requirements of the plans and specifications for the structure. For the contractor a successful project is also one in which he realizes the profit that he has projected in his bid. Men on the job are constantly reminded by the general contractor, and by their own boss or supervisors that target dates must be met. On large projects, the general contractor or the construction manger will conduct weekly meetings to review the schedule, discuss any job problems, and project goals for the next phase of construction. At these meetings subcontractors will be reminded about upcoming tasks, about materials and equipment that will be needed, and about any deficiencies that the general contractor or the architect's inspectors have observed. At these meetings, the subcontractors have a chance to voice their own criticisms or concerns regarding other contractors or the construction manager. Minutes are produced and reviewed from week to week to add or correct any omitted items or misstatements. The general contractor or construction manager hopes that through these meetings and their general leadership to create a positive atmosphere on a project, one that is self-propelling. This leads to good relationships between the employing contractors, the owner, the architect, and the men performing the work. Men associated with successful projects are often rewarded with other work. When we finished the Amherst Sewage Treatment Plant in Amherst, New York, on time, within budget, and at a profit to my boss, I was rewarded by being selected as project manager for another treatment plant. And so were all the contractors associated with the project because we used the same team of subcontractors and rather than have them bid against competition, we negotiated all the subcontracts. I completed two office buildings in Newark, N.J., for the state of New Jersey under a time constraint because the occupants had to get out of their current building since it was found to be full of asbestos. I was able to get the state moved into the buildings according to their timetable. I was rewarded with a bonus and another important assignment, and again we used the same teams of contractors for my new project, the twin New Jersey Transit Building and the Blue Cross/Blue Shield Building. The other side of the coin is a bad project that promotes negative behavior, construction mistakes, losses to the contractors, and a bad reputation for the contractor, the men, and the supervisor.

Table 4.2 lists the values and sanctions that can result in positive benefits for adhering to construction values, and the negative results for not conforming. Table 4.1 on crafts deals with knowledge and skills used on the job site; Table 4.2 deals with social behavior on the job site. Construction workers learn the norms and values of their trade as part of their socialization process, norms, and values that are as important as knowledge and skills.

I have presented above values and sanctions for construction craftsworkers. For a comparison with industrial craft workers, there is the following list presented by Norman Best (1990, p. 120) regarding the code of ethics among craftspersons in industry:

1. They must be qualified—meaning that a person could produce the necessary product in a capable way.

2. The item or work must be produced in a graceful way with a minimum of effort. Running at a job, huffing or puffing, or being an eager beaver were considered second class.

3. Consideration for one's fellow workers was essential.

4. Patience—a cool head—when everything goes sour was necessary.

5. Toadying to the boss and ranking fellow workers was looked down on.

6. Ranking fellow workers to a boss was simply taboo.

7. Lending a hand, demonstrating by doing—not by talking.

8. Sticking one's neck out, to a boss, in support of a fellow worker in trouble was the epitome of a good guy.

9. Criticism of a fellow worker was something to be handled with consummate skill, usually to be associated with a quiet demonstration of a better procedure.

10. Expressed concern for fellow workers and their problems should be limited to areas of shared concern.

11. A willingness to accept the tough jobs with confidence was essential.

In addition to those that I have discussed, these attributes listed by Best could certainly be applied to construction workers.

TIME DIMENSIONS ON CONSTRUCTION PROJECTS

Every construction project has a limited time frame. This is one of the reasons why economies of scale have not worked in the construction industry. In manufacturing, the work process can be projected over a long period of time and machinery can be applied that will efficiently reproduce the same operations over and over. On a construction project with a limited time frame, it would not make sense, nor would it be economically rational, to introduce a special piece of machinery that might costs hundreds of thousands of dollars or even millions to be used exclusively on that project. This might make sense with a nuclear power plant, but how many nuclear power plants are built each year? This limited time dimension on construction projects has inhibited the use of factory methods in the construction industry.

A project that did use factory-like methods was the building of Levittown, Long Island. In Levittown the "factory" was set up in the field and the large number of units built, 17,000 homes, plus schools and firehouses, permitted economies of scale. The project lasted five years, a time dimension that permitted Levitt to introduce repeatable operations. The units only had four or five models, which were turned differently to give them a different look, which again permitted production similar to the mass production in factories. Long time periods and repeatable operations, extremely rare in construction, were present in the building of Levittown, a successful project that permitted the developer to offer homes at reasonable prices, $6,600 for the first homes built in the early 1950s.

The following is a cogent example of the difference between factory methods and construction methods as it relates to the time dimensions of construction projects. In 1972 I went to work for Stirling-Homex, a company that at that time was the largest manufacturer, developer, and installer of manufactured housing in the United States. During that period it was believed that manufactured, factory-made

Table 4.2
Values and Sanctions

Values	How Expressed in Behavior	Positive Results for Conforming	Negative Results for Not Conforming
Getting to work on time	•Arriving early and socializing before starting work	•Companionship •Fellowship •Compatibility	•Docked pay •Ridicule •Disrespect
Performing work correctly and efficiently	•Performing work correctly the first time	•Assignment to responsible or interesting tasks •Promotion to foreman status	•Complaints from supervisor or foreman •Layoff •No rehiring for other projects
Cooperating with other crafts	•Performing a work task at request of another craftsman or foreman •Permitting other trades to complete their work to allow proper sequencing of one's own trade •Performing work task to make work tasks of other trades easier	•Harmonious relationships •Pooling of resources •Mutual assistance	•Quarrels and disputes •Isolation •Bad relations with other trades
Following instructions and orders	•Doing exactly as instructed in a timely fashion	•Fulfillment of needs of project •Fulfillment of role assigned •Performance of one's function •Sense of achievement	•Criticism for breach of trust •Dismissal from job •Sense of failure
Honesty about one's work	•Admitting mistakes •Taking responsibility for one's errors •Performing corrective work if necessary	•Other's trust •Good reputation •Improves hiring prospects in future	•Other's suspicion •Humiliation if caught in a lie •Dismissal from job •Poor hiring prospects in future
Willingness to perform difficult or dangerous work	•Exposing oneself to risk on a scaffold, in a trench, or at the edge of a building •Working in conditions such as extreme cold or heat •Working in dirty conditions—mud, sewer, tunnels •Doing heavy, back-breaking, grueling work like pushing concrete or lifting heavy loads	•Respect and admiration from other workers •Praise for effort •Selection for special tasks •Selection for difficult tasks •Possible premium pay	•Contempt or ridicule unless old or hurt
Taking care of tools and equipment	•Using tools with care and safety •Picking up tools	•Trust •Good reputation •Respect	•Dismissal •Anger from other workers

housing was the wave of the future. It was thought that with factory methods, housing costs could be brought so low that the industry could meet the demands of all home buyers, particularly the middle- and low-income buyer, which could solve the problem of providing affordable housing in the United States. The federal government sponsored and funded a research program to find methods to make houses in factories, and some major corporations like U.S. Steel participated in the program.

I was hired as Chief Estimator for Stirling-Homex and worked in their corporate center at Avon, New York, just south of Rochester. The company had built a state-of-the-art factory for producing houses. Their houses could be produced in modules of two, three, and four packages which could then be assembled whole on the construction site. They had three lines (double rails), along which the houses moved, like an assembly line. The production process started with flooring and floor joists built on a mechanism that could then be flipped so that a platform made of plywood with joists underneath started down the assembly line. As the house moved down the line, different trades moved on to the platform to frame walls and ceilings, after which drywall was clad with wallpaper, with cutouts for switches and receptacles. Components were prefabricated and applied to the frame. Kitchens were already built with sinks and plumbing, cabinets and counters, flooring, walls, and ceilings in separate modules, which were then dropped into prepared locations on the platform. Stirling-Homex used nonunion labor and many women in their factory. Women were involved in electrical work, drywall installation, wallpaper installation, carpentry trim and cabinetry, and plumbing work. The three lines each turned out 3 homes an hour, 25 in a day, and 75 total homes for the three lines, or 450 homes in a six-day week. There was a tornado that destroyed 450 homes in Mississippi and this factory was able to produce that amount of homes in one week and ship them by rail so that three weeks after the tornado struck, people were living in their new houses. The factory was very efficient, but the field work required to set the houses and make them work could not keep up with the factory. In order to install these houses, foundations had to be built and utilities had to be brought into the basement—water, sanitary sewer, gas, electric, and a storm-sewer system, along with roads and curbs. The modules in combinations of two, three, or four, had to be put on trailers and brought to the construction site. The homes were then lifted off and placed in a marshalling yard. When the foundations were ready they were lifted again and trucked to the construction site, where they were lifted a third time and placed on the foundation that was built either of concrete or concrete block. At this point, the interfaces between the two, three, or four modules (depending on the model) would have to be completed and the utilities would have to be hooked up to the plumbing, fuel, and electrical feeds in the modules. After that the plots would have to be graded, the site landscaped, and the driveways blacktopped. Finally the roof joints between the modules would have to made waterproof, a task that proved to be very troublesome.

There were many more details that had to be worked out, too many to detail here. Stirling-Homex hired a large force of salesmen who went all over the country, selling housing to housing authorities who gave them contracts within the jurisdiction of various housing programs in existence at that time, FHA 235 and FHA 236 programs, as well as public housing programs. These salesmen also sold various colleges on the idea of using this type of housing to build houses for faculty members. Stirling-Homex had lots of contracts on the books, and they had a super-efficient factory. In order to justify the capital investment put into the factory, they turned out houses by the fistfulls and the factory showed a handsome profit. But the stumbling block was that the field work could not keep up with the factory. It took a long time to prepare a site, and put in the sewer, water, electric, roadway, and sidewalk systems. It also took a long time to build the foundations, get the modules to the marshalling site, set the units on the foundations, and then to finish the various models of houses. The research department was very imaginative in designing different looks for these houses and in engineering how they were to be built by the factory, but they could not solve the inability of the construction worker in the field to keep up. The factory kept pounding out the houses and the organization of the field work fell further and further behind. The whole house of cards came tumbling down when Stirling-Homex, having something like 10,000 homes stored in marshalling yards throughout the country, listed these not-yet-set modules and therefore not yet existing houses as accounts receivable from the various authorities for whom they were built. Stirling-Homex was a public company—its stock rose from $5.00 to $30.00 during its heyday. The Securities and Exchange Commission (SEC) that overseas the stock market, picked up on their listing modules as accounts receivable and directed their accounting firm to adjust their balance sheet accordingly. When they did this, Stirling-Homex ceased to show any profits and within a matter of weeks, the stock plummeted and shortly after they went bankrupt.

After Stirling-Homex went down, manufactured housing ceased to be a viable alternative to traditional ways of producing housing in the United States. There still are companies that make modular housing, but on a much smaller scale and their percentage of the housing market is very small. In fact, I did a public housing project in Erie, Pennsylvania, where I built 200 units of housing on separate, single-family plots, using units manufactured by the ALCO company in Michigan. The units came in two halves and were easy to place on the foundations and build the interfaces. We used poured concrete foundations. I used separate subcontractors in the traditional manner to take care of whatever tasks had to completed in the field. We still had to store the units in a marshalling yard and bring them in by truck with a crane. But it was a successful project, and poor people in Erie, Pennsylvania, were able to rent these houses for $65.00 per month, and live in single-family homes on separate plots. That was a good program but it has never been applied on a large scale in this country. Factory-made homes are not cheap or shoddy. In fact, they are stronger than conventionally-built homes since they have to withstand being lifted up and lowered four times—once when they leave the factory and have to be put on a trailer; a second time when they have to be lifted off the trailer and set on the ground at the marshalling yard; a third time when they are lifted at the marshalling yard and put on a truck to be taken to the housing site; and a fourth time when they are lifted at the housing site and set on the foundation. No conventional house is subjected to those kinds of stresses.

After I lost my job with Stirling-Homex I went to work for Mort Brodsky in Rochester. I was employed as a project manager to build Eastbrooke, a condominium project of 650 residential units. It took us two years to complete the project, including all the roads, sidewalks, and utilities. That number of units was about 2-weeks factory time for Stirling-Homex, without, of course, the field work. I still believe that a great opportunity was lost in 1972 when the factory-made home ceased to be a viable option in the residential market. The government program, "Operation Breakthrough," led by George Romney, the head of Housing and Urban Development (HUD), was an attempt to sell the country on the factory-made home, but the collapse of Stirling-Homex and the inherent problem of matching the factory to the field, caused that program to collapse.

To repeat, it is important to recognize that the time dimension on construction projects is unique and different from the way other products are made in this country. Every construction project has a limited time frame once it comes into existence, but it takes a long time for a project to become a reality. Land has to be acquired, financing has to be arranged, and approvals have to be secured from the local authorities, or sometimes from the Corps of Army Engineers if it is near a waterway or impacts an environmentally protected area. In Secaucus, New Jersey, where I am presently employed, all projects are reviewed by the Hackensack Meadowlands Development Corporation, a nonprofit, quasi-public authority that is charged with protecting the Meadowlands. Some owners will not build unless they secure a client or tenant for the building, which adds time to the project. The building then has to be designed and the plans submitted for review and approval. For all of these reasons it can take years from the time a project is conceived before it goes ahead. It took 20 years for our road project in Buffalo to be approved that connected the New York Thruway with Route 33. A construction project begins after the bidding process leads to the selection of a low-bid contractor and the signing of a contract. The contractor is then given a letter to proceed or a verbal instruction to proceed by a certain date. Verbals are not accepted on any public work, which has to be officially awarded by some governmental body and then official notice comes in the form of a registered or certified letter, with a copy to the bonding company. All public work must be bonded. Bonding a job means that if the contractor should go broke or fail to complete the project for one reason or another, the bonding company, which is like an insurance company, must step in and hire a contractor to complete the job at the bonding company's expense. When all work is performed on a project to the satisfaction of the architect or engineer representing the owner, or the owner himself, the contract is considered complete and the owner makes final payment. There is always a one-year guarantee period during which the contractor has to correct any defects that may appear in the construction or the equipment furnished or the systems installed.

During the construction process, there are several crucial beginnings and endings affecting interlocking phases of the work. Various methods have been devised to assist the contractor in developing a systems approach to scheduling the different phases of construction work. One of these, called the Critical Path Method (CPM), is based on listing all major events that will take place on the construction job and assigning time in hours or days for completing each event or task. These events are then plotted in a network diagram with arrows outlining those events which logically precede others. The critical path is the stream of events that take the longest time and it is that path the general contractor has to pay particular attention to in order to make sure it does not extend the time of construction. This plotting of CPM events can be a huge and complicated task. On the Amherst sewage treatment plant we were required to provide such a CPM network. We had to build a special room to hold the sheet of paper on which the network was plotted—the paper went completely around the entire room and covered all four walls. Every day, my engineer would go into the field and see what work was done and then return to that room to record it on the CPM. At the end of each month, the resident engineer would pay our company for the work completed based on the markings on that CPM network. See Diagram 4.1, which outlines the key phases of most construction projects. Each box could have hundreds of tasks. The CPM for the Amherst treatment plant had 5,000 activities.

On another job, the Exxon project in Clinton, New Jersey, we also used CPM, and we had 20,000 events in our network diagram. Again, we built a large room and all four walls of the room were covered with the CPM print-out used to follow the progress of the job. CPM does not produce the job, and I'm not sure that it really helps in getting a job completed. On the Exxon job, the CPM helped the bureaucracy complete its paperwork in processing requisitions and monitoring change orders. The change orders were enormous. The project started at $169 million and there were $40 million in change orders, so the entire project wound up at $209 million. The Exxon project took three years to build and was comprised of a 10-story office building, a pilot plants building where they tested gasoline products in mini-refinieries, and a building containing 550 laboratories. We built two sewage treatment plants on the job site, along with a heliport and complete electrical substation. The construction manager's team to run the job comprised 73 people. Exxon had 15 of its people on site, and the architect also had 15 people on the site. These 103 people were housed in 18 trailers attached with hallways. We had computers, typewriters, printing machines for the drawings, and all kinds of copiers. We had a separate plan room to house the drawings that totaled 1,300 sheets. With all the copies that had to be made and all the different drawings, plus individual shop drawings, it took a staff of six people just to file and keep up with the drawings and books of specifications. We also had a team of 10 estimators, with computers, computational office machines and copiers, turning out estimates for change orders. A $1 million change order was nothing for Exxon (that year, 1981, Exxon's sales were $130 billion dollars). Exxon had excellent engineers on the job who were interested in the quality of the work, knew exactly what they wanted, and had the money to pay for the best.

The main point that I want to make about the Exxon project is that with all the bureaucracy, the planning, and CPM networks, the actual construction in the field was executed and completed in the traditional way—with supers, foremen, and

Diagram 4.1
Key Construction Phases on Building Projects

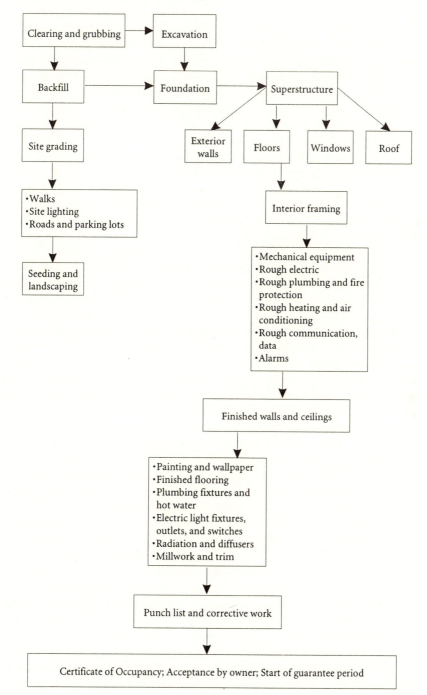

subcontractors. The leadership in the field was led by John (one superman of a superintendent). In my 42 years in the industry he was the best I've even seen or worked with. John could discuss electrical work with the electrical contractor, heating, ventilating, and air conditioning with the HVAC contractor, concrete with the concrete contractor, and plumbing with the plumbing contractor—in other words, the details of every trade with the experts and specialists in the trade. He mastered the 1,300 sheets of drawings and I believe he knew every detail on them. He was up and on the job at 5:00 A.M., pouring over the drawings, looking over the schedule, and making plans for what had to be accomplished that day. He ran the job meetings like an orchestra leader, asking pointed questions, answering questions from the floor, making sure contractors who needed to talk to each other were communicating, and making sure that every contractor that walked out of the meeting knew what was expected of them. John was a man in his fifties with unlimited energy. I know about his energy because he used to walk me over the job, which covered 100 acres with him marching on the double in front of me, pointing out what he needed here and what he needed there. I was chief engineer on the project and John was the general superintendent and the two of us made a pact to work with each other. He could scare you with his scowl or charm you with his smile. Any problem, any trouble, any tough situation demanding attention, and John was there. He always had his roll of drawings with him, which he had edged with a strong tape so they would last through the project. John had a certain air of confidence about him that gave everyone the feeling that whatever problems might come up were solvable. He touched others with his can-do attitude so that none of us who worked with him were afraid to tackle any assignment. John also treated contractors and tradesmen as individuals. He had a personal relationship with the men on the job and though our work force was comprised of about 1,000, it almost seemed that John knew everyone of them by face and name. I, myself, knew a large number, but John was so involved every day in every aspect of the building process that I'm sure he was acquainted with most of the workers, from the lowliest laborer doing clean-up work to the most skilled carpenter doing trim work. The project was brought in on time, and I can say without the least thought of contradiction, that its success was due to the leadership of this remarkable superintendent.

The point I'm trying to make in using the Exxon project as an example is that bureaucracies and extensive paperwork techniques like CPM do not build projects—people do. Projects need leaders like John and they need good contractors with their own core of superintendents, foremen, and skilled craftsworkers. It's the personal relationships between these various actors that gets things done on time and properly. Sure, we had problems and troubles on the Exxon job. Every job has them. One problem was the face brick on the various buildings. The project took 13 million pieces of brick that had to be laid up. The brick that was selected was too porous and permitted water to saturate it and leak through into the interior of the buildings. The architect had designed weep holes, that is, openings in the mortar to permit water to pass through and then drop into the cavity between the brick and block. Every brick design allows for a cavity between the brick and the back-up block so water can pass through, drop to the base of the outside wall, and then pass out through the weeps. You cannot keep water out, especially from a driving rain, but you can design a wall so the water that does get in can find a way out. A big fight took place with the architect pointing the finger of blame at the brick contractor, the brick contractor blaming the brick supplier, and the owner blaming them all. The issue was resolved by employing a contractor to apply a coating over the brick to waterproof it, with the three parties—the contractor, the supplier and the architect—each paying for one-third of the cost.

In addition to the beginnings and endings of construction phases and the total start and finish of projects, there are daily beginnings and endings. The workday starts with foremen and superintendents arriving early—around 6:00 to 7:00 A.M., to plan the day's activities. Workers start arriving 5 to 30 minutes before the 8:00 A.M. starting time. I must state that the overwhelming majority of construction workers show up for work on time. During the day, men might be shifted several times from task to task. The day's work is interrupted by a half-hour lunch break and two 15-minute coffee breaks, one in the morning and one in the afternoon. Work ends at 4:30 P.M. for most trades, but some trades, like the electricians in New York City, have negotiated a 3:30 P.M. quitting time for their workers. Some men report before the regular starting time if a special task is required. On a road project, a street might have to be kept free of cars and thus a flagman will come in early and wave all cars away. In winter, mason's helpers report early to heat the sand so it will be usable by 8:00 A.M. Some men work after 4:30 P.M. to clean up or to complete a work task. If rain is expected men have to stay late to protect freshly-poured concrete with polyethylene. If a concrete pour is held up, men will have to stay late to finish troweling it before it hardens.

REGULARLY RECURRING ACTIVITY

The essence of organization consists of patterned recurrence of behavior that persists for varying lengths of time. The regularities and uniformities are structured into behavior by rules and standards that we call norms. In construction, some of the rules come from the unions. For example, most unions require that the first man hired must be the steward and that the last man hired is the first man fired within a particular trade. In actual practice this is not always followed and contractors do have the right to fire a man regardless of when he was hired if the man is incompetent or did something to jeopardize the work or other men. Other rules come from external sources. Every state and every large city has a building code that prescribe that the construction of walls, pipes, ducts, ceilings, roofs, windows, doors, floor slabs, and so on, must conform to certain standards that protect against fire, leaks, collapse, and other hazards. There are also rules pertaining to safety on the job, rules that have been formulated by state agencies as well as the federal Office of Safety and Health Administration (OSHA).

While rules and standards function to regularize work behavior, regularization is somewhat mitigated by frequent changes. It is unusual for a man to be at a single work station for any length of time. He may perform the same activity, but he would do it in different locations and under varying conditions.

I will explain with an example from the Elm-Oak Arterial project in Buffalo, on which I was project manager. The following is the way manholes were built:

1. Each morning two laborers in a four-man crew came to work a half hour early. If it was cold they heated the sand, then they loaded sand and mortar on the truck assigned to their crew. They checked the mortar mixer to make sure it started and attached it to the back of the truck. They placed the mason's tools on the truck and were ready to produce by 8:00 A.M. The previous day they had placed concrete blocks at the manhole location where work was to be started or continued.

2. At 8:00 A. M., with the two masons riding in the cab and the laborers in back of the truck, they proceeded to the work area.

3. When they arrived at the excavated area for the manhole, the masons went down into the hole. Beforehand, the laborers checked the shoring and bracing and adjusted and tightened them to make sure they were secure. If any mud had slid into the hole, all four men worked to shovel it out. Masons are not supposed to shovel according to union rules, but the informal norm on this job was that they shoveled, if necessary.

4. When the hole was ready, one laborer stayed in the hole and the other went on top. The man on top mixed the mortar and sand in the mixer and send it down in pails. He also slid blocks down on a wooden chute. The laborer in the hole caught the blocks and handed them to the masons. The 12-inch solid blocks used to build the manhole weighed 100 pounds each and had no openings at the top, making them extremely difficult to handle. The mason had to cradle them in his arms before he set them. The laborer in the hole placed mortar boards where they were within reach of the mason. The laborer piled fresh mortar on the mortar board as the mason used up the mortar with which they bedded and bonded the blocks set in place.

5. The masons set the blocks handed to them in a bed of mortar and then filled in the sides with mortar. The plumbed (made straight) and leveled each block laid, using their hand levels. With their levels they checked the top of the block for level and the sides for plumb. When the manhole was completed to the top, it was "parged" on the outside with a two-inch layer of mortar spread with a trowel that sealed it and prevented water infiltration.

This description is what was supposed to take place each day. However, something always happens to vary the pattern. If it rains, time is spent pumping water out of the excavation. If the surveyor has a bust (makes a mistake), the manhole might be in the wrong place and might have to be torn down and rebuilt. Some days the mortar mixer breaks down. Many times the banks of the excavation cave in so severely they cannot be dug out by hand and a machine must be used to redig it. Sometimes, a gas, water, electric, or telephone line is in the way of the manhole below the pavement, and the crew must move to another location until the utility company moves their line. On some occasions, a manhole crew catches up to the sewer line crew and gets laid off for a week or two. Other times, they fall behind and a second manhole crew must be hired. From time to time, someone gets hurt or there is an accident. A block might jump off the chute and injure a laborer or mason. The mason might get some mortar in his eye. And this is only one operation among many others that are going on at the same time.

With the many possibilities in construction for interruptions in regularized work, recurring activity is maintained through solving the frequent, sometimes daily, breaks in the planned work process and changing or modifying the projected work for the day or week.

RECURRING SOCIAL SITUATIONS

The Physical Framework

The construction site is a physical frame within which social events take place. The site is subdivided according to function and the designed placement of structures. Trailers and work shanties are located near work areas. They are places where men and women (if there are any on the job) dress, keep their tools, eat lunch, and socialize. Other areas are set aside for material compounds and storage trailers and are usually fenced in with a locked gate. Heavy machinery is kept in a locked compound area that contains a fuel pump and a gasoline tank. There are locations for the water supply and toilet facilities. There are always public telephones on the job as well as phones in the various trailers occupied by contractors, resident architects and engineers, and owner's representatives if they maintain a presence on the job.

An entire construction site may be fenced in and guarded by watchmen. The site and its various facilities become familiar to the men who learn to use them to satisfy their needs. They also know where to find the persons they need to communicate with to perform their work or have questions answered and problems solved. Today bosses, supers, and foremen carry cell phones so they can reach each other or their men quickly when they need to talk or give instructions. The project architect or project engineer have their own trailers with their professional personnel and they keep the various drawings and documents up to date and available for contractors' supers and foremen to use if they need to look at a drawing or check a design detail.

Events

Events are work tasks. These events have social consequences because they involve various individuals acting in work roles with each other. Work events require communications between foremen and journeymen, between journeymen within the same trade, or between journeymen of different trades. There is also a network that involves inspectors, employers, owner's representatives, architects, engineers, and union representatives, all of whom touch on the work process that is going on within the construction site. Construction people and the ancillary personnel need to talk with each other to get things done. Failure to consider the social aspects of events and to get along with those who have information can have adverse effects on a construction project. Trades might have to be notified not to work until another portion of the project is completed. Trades might be asked to do extra work desired by the client. Problems, mistakes, and questions requiring answers might have to be communicated to the project architect for analysis and decision. If a craftsworker is not sure of the intent of the plans and specifications, and proceeds with the work event without engaging other responsible parties, he has ignored possible adverse consequences. I have found in the past, and still follow the practice today, that it is better not to proceed with work if there is a question. It is prudent to contact the project architect, or the owner, and find out what they want in the way of a finished material or a particular design, get them to initial a drawing or send a letter, and only then is it safe to let the contractors proceed. But, when there is pressure to get a job done and I need to meet a deadline, I will take a chance and go off on my own, hoping I'm not going to pay too dearly for my actions.

Work events can have social consequences involving nonconstruction people. On a road project when streets have to be closed or restricted, public agencies like the fire and police departments must be notified, as well as ambulance companies, hospitals, and bus companies. If traffic has to be detoured, the driving public is inconvenienced. Newspapers and radio and television stations must be made aware of detours and closings so as to warn the public. On road projects, construction workers often become directly involved with the public who may be physically in the way and preventing men from performing their work. Sometimes the public acts irrationally, such as when drivers verbally attack flagmen or flagwomen trying to direct traffic around a congested construction site. Sometimes automobiles parked near a construction site have to be kept out of the area next to the structure going up. Structural steel has to be fireproofed with a sprayed-on fireproofing material, and even though tarps are draped on the side of the building, the fireproofing material can be blown by the wind and fall on a parked car. Steelworkers erecting steel on the edge of a building might drop a bolt and hit a passerby, which is why sidewalk bridges are built for pedestrians to walk under. I was involved on a project where we had a horrible accident occur. We were building the Bectin-Dickinson Headquarters in Franklin Lakes, New Jersey. We had buildings on both sides of a main road, connected by an overhead bridge. We had to construct curbs along the roadway. Our curbing contractor was a small entrepreneur who had his relatives working for him. One day, while he was building curbs alongside a main road, a driver plowed into the boss and several of his workers. The boss was decapitated and his son-in-law was killed. The man also struck another driver in the rear, drove her across the road and into a tree, killing her. It turned out the man was drunk and a bottle of whiskey was found under his front seat. Getting involved with the public can be deadly, for the public and for the construction worker.

The social consequences of work events are as important as the physical consequences of applying work skills; they must be considered in planning work. Failure to do so can lead to drastic actions such as shutting down an entire project.

Objects

Objects on construction projects are tools, equipment, and materials. All three, along with the labor of craftsworkers, must be present for production to take place. Tools and equipment are objects that must be available to craftspersons when they require them. Materials come to the construction site in a continuous stream during the life of the project. Movement of materials to the project and to the work station is a social event involving teamsters, operating engineers, laborers, field clerks, and suppliers, as well as foremen and superintendents who must plan for and order materials so they are present when needed. Moving and handling materials requires social communication between craftsworkers and foremen, and to suppliers, manufacturers, and truckers. Bringing materials to the job site is part of a system that must be continuous as long as work is being performed. Sometimes cranes are required to unload and raise heavy equipment to floors or to the roof of a building, equipment like cooling towers, pumps, central air conditioners, boilers, heavy electrical switchgear, and elevator equipment.

Concrete is an important material, composed of a mixture of sand, stone, and cement. Usually, a contractor will issue a purchase order to one supplier for all the concrete to be furnished on the project. The project architect or engineer will specify the mix to be used for the different types of concrete to be poured for different parts of the building. When a concrete pour is planned, the foreman tells the construction clerk how much and what type he needs and the clerk calls the concrete plant, giving it time of delivery, the type of mix, and the location. There is a time limit within which concrete must be mixed and delivered, usually 90 minutes from the time it leaves the plant. If it goes beyond that time it can be rejected by the project inspector. Concrete ordering must be planned, orderly, and systematic if waste and losses are to be avoided. As in all construction, things can go astray—a concrete truck breaks down, a heavy rain interrupts a pour, mechanical trades leave out sleeves, or ironworkers do not get the rebars installed on time.

Individuals

It takes time on a construction project for men to get used to working with each other. On the Elm-Oak arterial road project in Buffalo, it took about five months for the period of adjustment. Men in the various crews had to learn to work with their foremen. An operating engineer did not get along with the labor foreman on his crew and had to be reassigned. The labor foreman on the mason crew was sent to another job when he argued with his crew. I fired the bridge superintendent who was too abrasive and not particularly competent. Some operating engineers seemed better suited to one machine rather than another and reassignments were made. After five months the men came to know each other's personalities and work habits and the crews stayed together until the following year's winter layoff.

Conflicts

Conflicts are inevitable on construction projects. If they interrupt work they are serious. If there is an absence of conflict because of absence of communication between trades, that too is serious. Conflicts can arise when one craft pushes another to get its work done so the complaining craft can proceed with its work. This is healthy conflict because it moves the job.

Conflicts arise between owners and contractors. Both want a speedy project because a job that comes in on time is mutually beneficial. But the owner views quality as primary, while the contractor wants to meet his costs and considers productivity primary. Low cost and high quality are often in conflict. There are also personal conflicts and craft rivalry. Men working under hazardous and arduous weather conditions are irritable and short-tempered. Some days work goes badly and everyone is grouchy. Men must accommodate each other as tradesmen and as individuals. However, horseplay and verbal joking serves as a means of blunting and controlling hostility. Joking behavior was described by anthropologist A. R. Radcliffe-Brown (1952), who saw it as a means of preventing open aggression and ensuring a stable system of social behavior. It also serves group solidarity. Insiders are permitted to insult and argue with each other, call one another names, and physically joust with each other, but let an outsider try the same thing and they will be punished.

On the Amherst sewage treatment plant project, we had a labor foreman known as a "duker" (a man good with his fists). He was also mild-mannered with a wonderful wit. One day he was fooling around with our prize clown, Chi Chi, when a concrete truck pulled up. The driver became impatient and wanted to get his truck unloaded. He saw Chi Chi and Frankie, the labor foreman, fooling around and ignoring him. He insulted Frankie and ordered him to get the truck unloaded. When he was still ignored, words were exchanged. He jumped down from his cab shouting, "You wanna make somethin' outta it?" and put up his hands in a fighting pose, a bad mistake. Within seconds he was lying on the ground in the same pose, his nose broken and his face covered with blood.

ADMINISTRATIVE ROLES ON THE CONSTRUCTION PROJECT

Project Manager

The role of project manager is that of a leader and an interpreter. He is the primary administrative officer whose function is to convey the policies of contractor management to the men executing the work. He does not interfere with the work, but does his job by working through the superintendent. Given the informal nature of construction work, however, project managers like myself often have direct contact with subcontractors as well as with the construction workers. I have never felt comfortable sitting in the field trailer and ignoring what goes on with the work itself. The project manager plans the overall direction of work through progress schedules that he transmits to the work forces and the specialty subcontractors through the superintendent. There is usually an overall progress schedule, in the form of a bar chart or a CPM network chart, which is reduced to paper and is the formal completion schedule. Next, there are daily, weekly, and monthly schedules that are conveyed to the contractors verbally or through the weekly meetings. Construction work is so flexible and changing that no schedule can be hard and fixed.

Job conditions can dictate changes in the sequencing of work or in priority locations for work on the job site. Late delivery of equipment and materials can hold up certain work and force a change in plans while waiting for the equipment and materials to arrive. Elevators, heating, ventilating and air-conditioning equipment, and electrical power and switchgear equipment are among the critical items that have to be ordered long in advance to have them arrive on the job on time. Windows and door frames (especially if they are welded rather than knocked-down frames) are also long-lead items. The project manager must include in his schedule time and provision for material deliveries and equipment needed to progress the work. Many of these items are ordered by specialty subcontractors who must be given the schedule and put on notice when certain items will be needed on the job. The project manager also monitors costs and productivity to see if they are staying within the budget and time frame projected for the various items of work. The project manager also carries out various administrative duties with relation to the owner, architect, and engineer. He must prepare the monthly requisitions for payment, conduct correspondence with the owner, architect, and engineer; process change orders and makes sure they are documented; convey the wishes of the owner, architect, or engineer to the various trades; prepare, with the architect and engineer, the final punch list of unfinished work and defective work and follow through with getting the punch list completed; arrange for the Certificate of Occupancy with the local building inspectors; and help the accountant prepare the request for final payment from the owner.

The project manager plays an interface role between contractor and owner. He overlays the work function with the administrative function. Project managers depend on craftsworkers for the execution of work and on the contractor's top management for policy decisions. Often they are compelled to act against their better judgment in carrying out their employer's policies. In this respect, they are less independent than the journeymen who are usually the sole judges on how to carry out the work involved in their craft.

Highway and Heavy Construction, a construction journal, stated in an editorial that "it is the men who make construction companies go" (March 1996). Any project manager who ignores this truth will be ineffective. In industrial production, where technology controls the movements of men, workers perform a limited set of operations each day and attitude is less important than in construction where the craftsman controls the carrying out of his tasks. Thus, a project manager is only as good as his ability to create and maintain a positive attitude among workers and supervisors that will induce them to be cooperative and productive. Today managers in industrial settings are also learning that attitude can be very important and they have tried to create new forms of managing workers that will permit more decision making and more control over the work process by workers on the line.

Resident Engineer or Project Architect

The resident engineer or project architect represents the owner on a construction project. His main function is to ensure that the contractor will perform work in accordance with contract plans and specifications. To carry out this function, the engineer or architect employs inspectors who oversee the work and pass judgment on whether it meets plans and specifications. The engineer or architect evaluates the contractor's requests for payment and approves, rejects, or modifies requests as they relate to the amount of work accomplished by the contractor at the end of each month. The architect or engineer initiates changes and changes orders requested by the owner through modifications and additions to the drawings. They evaluate and approve or disapprove the contractor's proposals in response to any requests for owner-initiated changes. No project of any size is ever completed without the advent of changes to the drawings and price changes to the contractor. As mentioned, during the Exxon project, we had $40 million in change orders. Usually the requests for changes go to the architect, who would make changes to the drawings or create new drawings to reflect the changes requested by the owner. The architect would then transmit changes through a formal paper transmittal to the construction manager, who would have estimators figure the cost of the changes and give the changes to the various subcontractors involved for pricing. When all the figures were in, the change proposal would be sent to the architect, who would evaluate the proposal and then send it to the Exxon administrator on the job site. He would look it over, and based on the architect's evaluation and his own evaluation, he would either sign it or request answers to questions or revisions of certain figures. When all figures were revised to the satisfaction of the architect and owner, the Exxon representative would sign it and the construction manager would make sure that the changes were made in the field.

In the 1980s, I did two projects, one for a township and the other for AT&T. On both projects, we had a resident engineer who represented the township in one case and the owner in the other. Each one had a different working style in carrying out their duties. The following example presents a description of these differences.

Engineer No. 1 was a take-charge guy who often claimed he, not the contractor, was "running the job." He wanted to play all roles, contracting as well as resident engineer watching the job for the owner. He ran his office without allowing any interference from his employers, the township. He made decisions, right or wrong, and stood by them. He ruled his staff of inspectors with an iron hand and instilled enough fear in them that none of them would dare to make an independent decision. If there was any question regarding whether to accept or reject our work, they would have to check with the resident engineer. He loved to be out in the field, talking to the foremen, the men, the super, discussing the work, and giving his opinion about everything we were trying to accomplish. We all tried to be respectful and we all listened to him, in spite of the fact that he was not supposed to talk to the men directly or to interfere with the work. According to the formal rules of the project, he was supposed to communicate with me if he wanted to communicate anything out to the field. My super and I never did get along well with him, though we respected his knowledge. We finally had our confrontation. He held up one of my requisitions for payment over a difference of interpretation regarding completion of a section of work reflected on our CPM network. I kept trying to reason with him, but to no avail. Finally, I asked for a meeting and I had to go through my "throwing over the table" act. It was something I planned to do in advance to show my frustration and anger and prove that I was not going to put up with his arbitrary and dictatorial behavior. It worked, and I did get my payment requisition signed. I also sent him a letter demanding that he not talk to the men in the field, that it was breaking up the chain of command. He gave in to my demand and we completed the job without further incident. In spite of his arrogance, my super and I respected him for his strength of character even if we had to show that we weren't going to be pushed around.

Engineer No. 2, who represented AT&T, contrasted sharply from Engineer No. 1. Rather than take a vigorous role in the work process, he preferred to stay in his office, and not be bothered by field problems, leaving the job of solving engineering problems to his assistant. We were lucky because this engineer developed a tremendous respect for my superintendent and trusted him, a trust, I might add, that was warranted. With my super leading the forces in the field, we were able to build a 120,000 square foot building, in the middle of the winter, in just nine weeks. It took 250 men working at least two shifts a day, but when the day arrived for AT&T to bring in their computers, we were ready for them. This building had a printing plant; it was also the building from which 30 million phone bills a month were sent to AT&T customers throughout the northeastern United States. I learned early in this project that my best bet with regard to Engineer No. 2, was to do all my business through my super since he had such a good relationship with the guy. He was retiring and soft-spoken, sometimes remarking that he wished he had gone into another profession. He was envious of those with less education who made more money than he did. He hated writing or receiving letters because they would become a record that a superior might read. He wanted to take no chances with being criticized. I liked the man but I can't say that I respected his knowledge the way I did with Engineer No. 1. At the same time, the job went smoothly, in spite of the pressure of the short time period. The job was going so fast that my boss, who visited the job every two weeks, couldn't believe his eyes when he saw the changes each time he arrived. My boss said he felt like Rip Van Winckle who woke up to find the whole world had changed.

Both engineers wanted their projects built well and in accordance with plans and specifications. Engineer No. 1 viewed successful projects as a personal triumph that would further his career. Engineer No. 2 wanted to have a quiet project with no fuss or problems and very little paperwork.

Superintendent

The superintendent is probably the key person on any construction project. I have said many times that you can overcome a bad project manager or a bad foreman, but you can't overcome a bad super. The super is the link between the plans and specifications and the execution of the work. He masters the intent of the plans and specs and discusses the way the work is to be carried out with the workers. The superintendent is also the liaison between the crafts; he decides which crafts work in which particular location on the project. A poor super inevitably leads to a bad project.

The following may be considered a model of behavior for a superintendent:

1. His overall style is democratic and consultative. Most of the time he tells the foreman what task must be accomplished and permits the foreman and journeyman to organize the work and carry it out as men knowledgeable about their own craft.

2. If something goes wrong he tries to find out why and correct the mistake. He does not humiliate the man who made the mistake but gets angry if the man lies or tries to cover up an error.

3. He responds to a foreman's or a worker's request as a "now" problem.

4. If he has to say no to any request from any man on the job, whether worker or management, he says so clearly without anyone getting the wrong impression. I had a super who used to convey a definite no by responding to a request that he was rejecting in the following sentence: "You have as much chance as seeing God as getting what you're asking for."

5. He never leaves the job site until every man who is working completes his tasks for the day. The only exception is when a trade decided to work another shift or decides to work overtime for an extended period. Even in these instances the super may decide to stay on the job to oversee the work.

6. He involves himself with paperwork in a minimal way, permitting the construction clerk to handle most of it. But he knows how to find what he needs even if the trailer or his desk looks like chaos. I've always been amazed at how some supers can reach into a pile of papers and pull out the right one that he needs.

7. He tries to conduct all business face-to-face, preferring to talk to a person on the job rather than over the phone. In this respect most construction supers hate e-mail and all the other modern-day electronic devices designed to eliminate person-to-person communication.

8. He socializes with the men who work for him, on the job and off the job.

9. He makes it a practice to have regular social events with the men from all crafts on the project.

10. He is never intimidated by threats from any quarter—the men, the boss, the owner, the architect, or the union.

11. He does not hesitate to tell friends who work for him they are wrong if he believes it to be true.

Foreman

Foremen in construction are working foremen. The foreman gets extra pay, but it is not much above the regular union scale. Sometimes a contractor will make a special arrangement with his key men, like foremen and supers, and offer them extra pay, bonuses at the end of the year, overtime, and so forth. One contractor I worked for paid double-time to foremen and key men for five hours each week, the five hours between 35 and 40. Construction foremen are close to the men they lead. Every crew needs someone to plan the work, assemble the materials, and assign the tasks—the function of the foreman. The foreman is in touch with the superintendent and finds out how the work of his own crew fits in with the rest of the project. Foremen carry out the overall strategy of the superintendent, assigning tasks to members of his crew in accordance with the superintendent's goals.

One of the norms in construction is that a foreman takes responsibility for all successes, as well as mistakes, made by members of his crew. An incident occurred on one of my projects in which the foreman violated this rule and was caught. The foreman was a friend of the superintendent. Nevertheless, he was called a liar and embarrassed himself when he tried to blame his men for work that was done sloppily and unacceptably. Even if his men had screwed up the work, the foreman was still responsible since he was supposed to oversee the work.

Foremen sometimes have a broker function. They make arrangements with various supers to perform work and then serve as employment brokers getting jobs for the men in their crew. Sometimes crews under a certain foreman move as a group from job to job as the need arises for their specialty.

Journeymen

The journeyman's and journeywoman's role is his or her craft role. Management's norms and craftsworker's norms may or may not coincide. The craftsworker's style is to maintain his independence and keep control over the evaluation of his work within his craft. He will accept the right of the superintendent or foreman to tell him what tasks to perform, or if he has made a mistake, but no outsiders.

Tom is a journeyman operating engineer. He calls himself a "hardhead" because he insists on doing things his own way. If an employer tries to tell Tom how to do his work he gets indignant (and almost hysterical) in his rejection of such interference. When Tom talks about his work he sounds more like a contractor than an employee. He says he's been with the company 15 years and that he quits every month and gets fired every other month. Tom enjoys getting his employer's goat. Once he broke a gas main while digging in the street. His boss asked him, "Why the hell did you do that, Tom? You cost me money and you got our name in the paper besides." Tom answered with a straight face, "Oh, it was a dull day and I figured we needed some excitement."

5

INDEPENDENCE AND AUTONOMY

INTRODUCTION

The content and significance of construction projects relates to two processes. One is the technological and organizational requirements of the firm. The other is the social and personal requirements of the employees. Industrial organizations have focused on the first aspect. An extensive literature exists on the technological content of occupations (U.S. Bureau of Labor Statistics, 1996–1997). Technology is supposed to provide for rapid and error-free output of goods. The goal of industrial engineering is the adjustment of work to the demands of technology. The capabilities of the worker are evaluated in relation to machines, equipment, and the physical aspects of production. The worker's role is seen as only one element, although a human one, within the system of technology. The most influential ideas that accompanied the rise of industrialism were the division of labor and man as an economic animal. The economic-man concept provided the rationale for our present economic reward system. The division of labor concept was the basis for the specialization of work tasks.

During the late nineteenth and early twentieth centuries, business and industry employed a technology and social organization derived from the mechanistic model of human behavior. Taylorism was its practical expression (Taylor, 1911). In Taylor's model, the human role is that of a cog in a complex production system dominated by costly equipment. In mechanical systems, all elements are completely controlled through mechanical design. Initiative and self-organization are not acceptable since they increase variability, reduce control, and run the risk of failure. Mechanical systems rigidly specify task assignments that specify certain desired work behaviors. The drive for reduced variability encouraged the idea of creating minimum skill requirements for task performance. Jobs were designed to be specialized and fractionated so they could be rapidly acquired with minimal training. To ensure successful outcomes, economic reward systems were based on precisely specified behaviors in the workplace.

Based on the mechanistic model, modern business and industry has tried to retain for itself maximum control in how it uses its work force. Business and industrial organizations strive for maximum interchangeability of workers. The organization's goal is to reduce its dependence on the availability, skills, or motivations of individuals.

In mass production factory work, the product is not turned out by any one worker or group of workers, but by the plant as a collectivity. Usually, the individual worker finds it hard to pinpoint his or her own contribution to the overall productive process. The mass production principle is not confined to factory work, it also affects office work, and even professionals who are members of large organizations dedicated to the bottom line, that is, the making of profits. The inefficiencies that have developed in mass production industries due to its inflexibility and bureaucratic command structure, have affected the thinking of managers in large organizations in the 1990s. Managers have recognized the necessity for batch production based on quick-reacting changes in goods production that adjusts to changes in demand driven by mass advertising and strong competitors. Some firms are now paying more attention to worker motivation and decision making on the shop floor and are becoming more flexible in their rules for workplace behavior. At one time it didn't matter what workers thought as long as they built a better mousetrap and built it faster. Now it has become clear that commodity production of any kind must take into account worker motivation. But we mustn't go too far in believing that worker motivation, feelings, or ideas take precedence over the machine and technology in the eyes of managers of industry and commerce. Workers are still expected to follow the rules, and the rules of behavior are dictated by the uses of technology, especially computer technology.

The trends and practices in industrial and factory production have not taken hold in construction because the technology of the construction industry makes these practices inappropriate.

The special features of construction include the following:

1. Work takes places on a site and on a building that is unique in location, and as regards most commercial and industrial structures, unique in configuration and design.

2. Employment on a construction project is of limited duration, averaging one to three years. Journeymen working for specialty subtrades are on the project over a lesser time period and on an intermittent basis.

3. Weather conditions in the form of rain, wind, freezes, floods, mud slides, heavy snows, and catastrophic events cause interruptions of construction work.

4. Construction products are large, sometimes monumental, and take a long time to produce. This makes them subject to changes of all kinds—in the overall economic environment, within the industry, among material suppliers, in the supply of labor, and within the firms chosen for work on a project.

Given the variability and unpredictability of events that may impact construction projects, it is not possible to subject them to the kind of regimen and consistency that is present in the production of goods such as automobiles, food products, textiles, chemicals, computers, computer chips, furniture, and the vast array of products offered in the nation's shopping centers. Other features of the construction industry, such as the predominance of skilled labor, small size of most construction firms, and worker control of the work process, all lead to a large measure of autonomy for the construction worker that limits the ability of contractors to subject the work process to the kind of regimentation present in factory production. (For a discussion of management techniques in construction, see Applebaum, 1982, pp. 224–234).

OWNERSHIP OF TOOLS

People living in nonindustrial cultures in the past, including preindustrial America, made their own tools and produced the goods needed for their survival. This was true of farmers, hunters, herdsmen, fishermen, and craftspersons. In industrial cultures there are almost no occupations where people produce the goods they consume. Most individuals must work for wages that are then used to purchase goods for consumption. Even self-employed entrepreneurs produce goods that they do not consume themselves, but must sell in the marketplace for income that is then used to buy what they need. In preindustrial cultures it is the farming household or artisan shop based on the family that is both the producing and consuming unit. In industrial society, it is the business corporation or individual enterprise, not the individual family, that is the producing unit.

The divorce of the worker from control of the producing unit and from his tools, has had enormous impact on the structure and culture of industrial societies. Many thinkers and philosophers have cited this social aspect of modern cultures as an obstacle to satisfying work, giving rise to worker alienation and failure to realize their full life's potential (Durkheim, 1949, pp. 233–255; Hayes, 1946, pp. 306–307; Fromm, 1961, pp. 44–58).

Construction is one of the few industries where significant numbers of workers own their own tools—carpenters, masons, electricians, cement finishers, ironworkers, sheetmetal workers, plumbers, drywall installers, and others. While they still work for others, construction workers have a sense of independence and autonomy because of their ownership of tools. Ownership of tools also gives them the possibility of working for themselves by becoming small, specialty-trade contractors. It is a possibility that many construction workers realize, sometimes combining working for others along with working for themselves after working hours or on weekends. Having this possibility gives them a powerful bargaining position in their relationship to employers as they have a choice to quit and go into business for themselves if working conditions or pay scales do not satisfy them. There are 1.48 million construction workers who are self-employed (U.S. Department of Commerce, 1997, p. ii).

Sometimes ownership of tools and equipment by a journeyman makes an employer dependent on him. On the Elm-Oak arterial project in Buffalo, one of the bricklayers owned his own truck, tools, and some equipment. Though working for the general contractor, he acted like an independent entrepreneur. The fact that he had his own truck and equipment meant that the boss did not have to supply those items to put him to work. After he was given his assignment every morning, he made his own arrangements for materials and equipment that he loaded on his truck, after which he picked up his laborers and drove them to their work station. This bricklayer also owned his own scaffolding, heaters, and accessories that he loaned to his boss, and for which he was compensated when he used them on the job. A large number of men on the Elm-Oak project had their own trucks and used them to move tools and materials. Thomas Brooks, labor historian, commented (1979, p. 8): "The construction worker's pride in his craft and his autonomy is rooted in ownership of his tools, through which he symbolically owns his job and controls his destiny."

It requires little capital for a construction worker to go into business, often no more than some hand tools, a skill, and a contract. A mason on the Blue Cross job remarked that all a craftsman needs to go into business is a pen (to sign a contract for construction work). The aspiration to have one's own business is strong in the United States. Blauner quotes an auto worker as follows (1966, pp. xvi–xvii): "The main thing is to be independent and give your own orders and not have to take them from anybody else. That's the reason the fellows in the shop all want to start their own business."

AUTONOMY IN THE WORK PROCESS

Construction workers, particularly skilled craftsmen, exercise autonomy over their work, and management relies on the craftsworker to create the product. Sometimes management has goals that conflict with those of the craftsworker. Management is interested in speed; craftsworkers know that speed is the enemy of quality. If management is conscientious they will stress performance rather than speed.

Quite often, if a construction worker considers working conditions onerous or unsatisfactory, he will not hesitate to quit, having enough self-confidence that he can find another job. At a company dinner that I attended in Niagara Falls, one of the men quipped that he should organize a "second-timers" club since so many men at the dinner had quit the company and were later hired back. Mike Cherry comments as follows (1974, p. 183):

A casual dislike of the boss is probably not a central factor in a white-collar's decision to leave his job, but it is often the sole issue in whether or not a construction worker stays on. If the boss wants a thing done one way which the worker thinks should be done another, or if the worker thinks the boss has spoken to him in an unacceptable tone of voice, or if the man simply disapproves of the way the captain runs the ship, he is likely to make a "shove it up your ass" speech and leave.

CONSTRUCTION UNIONS AND WORKER AUTONOMY

A significant portion of union agreements in the construction industry deal with the prevention of encroachment by management on worker autonomy.

Building trades unions, wherever possible, utilize the closed shop to restrict management control over workers, which means that all workers on the job are union members and hiring will be done through the union. Of course, men who have worked previously for the contractor can be hired back through negotiations with the boss or super and then the business agent is notified accordingly. The carpenter's union agreement states that a "commercial qualifying card" shall be a condition for employment. The card can only be issued by the carpenters district council in a particular area.

In most industries, business firms control supervisory personnel. This major tool of management does not exist for unionized construction workers since foremen are always union men and most supers carry a union card. Foremen feel more loyalty toward the men and their union than toward management; this is less so with superintendents. Supers must not identify too closely with management as this will lessen their effectiveness that is based on their closeness to the men they lead. If a foreman violates a union regulation or becomes autocratic, he can be fined or brought up on charges before the union executive board. This position of foremen as union men lessens management's power to control construction workers or dictate to them.

Construction unions have other means to protect worker autonomy. In union shops, unions, not management, control entry on to the projects. In urban areas where the construction unions are strongest, one must become a union member to get a job. The unions control the apprenticeship programs in the construction industry; they administer the schools and provide the candidates for apprenticeship. Employers sit on apprenticeship boards, but it is the union that has the final say on whether or not a candidate will be accepted into the union.

Union agreements in construction include provisions to prevent union encroachments on management's autonomy. Unions are not supposed to place any restriction against the use of machinery, tools, or labor-saving devices. In practice, there are restrictions on how machinery is to be used. For many years, pipe-threading machines for steamfitters and plumbers were restricted to three-inch pipe and above. This is no longer true. Unions tried to prevent the use of copper and plastic pipe because it was faster to install, but they lost that battle. In general, unions have limited power to restrict the use of a new technology in the industry or to prevent the use of prefabricated products that are becoming more prominent in construction. Power tools for screws, nails, and fasteners are now a fixture in the industry. On many projects, doors and windows come premounted on frames. In residential construction, which is mainly nonunion, roof trusses come prefabricated, walls may be cut and assembled in the factory, windows are mounted on frames that merely need to be set into walls, and even stairs may be assembled and dropped into place.

Unions are not supposed to place any restrictions on labor output, however, it is in this area that unions exert great power. Almost every trade has informal norms as to how much a journeyman is supposed to produce each day. It may go up or down over time, but for each time period in which production takes place, a bricklayer lays so many bricks or blocks a day, a carpenter produces so many lineal feet of partition wall, a drywall installer places so many boards a day, an acoustical ceiling journeyman installs so many square feet of grid or so many square feet of ceiling tile a day, and so forth. Complicated installations like an air conditioning and pump room that involves heavy equipment like a Trane Centravac, a series of pumps, filter systems, gauges, and large pipe diameters like eight, ten, and twelve-inch pipe cannot be subjected to any fixed time frame. A contractor puts a bunch of men into the equipment room, which could be as large as 5,000 square feet, and the steamfitters could be in there for months laying out and installing the equipment. On the Blue Cross/Blue Shield building, the air-conditioning system involved 2,500 tons of air conditioning, and with all the pumps and equipment and the three cooling towers, it took a crew of steamfitters three months to build out the equipment room, which did not include the heating systems, which had a bank of four boilers and their own pumps that took a different crew two months to lay out and build. Contractors have a good idea of what the norms are for their trade and when they figure a job they use labor figures that reflect what the men are producing in the current period. Mostly they use historical records to give them an idea of what the men are doing. For a large equipment room like the Blue Cross/Blue Shield job, the contractor will look for production output for a similar installation of that size and see how long it took the men to install it. Different job conditions or difficulties of installation may slow up a job within certain limits, and a good super or foreman can help to find short cuts or to speed up output, but there is little that management can do to get the men to produce a significant difference from what is the informal norm. In resisting attempts to speed them up, construction workers maintain their own control over the work process. Many supers have tried to set deadlines for various trades and many have been disappointed. They learned to ask the foreman when *he* thought he could finish a piece of work, and then ask them to give the job a kick in the ass, and in most cases the super would be accommodated.

I interviewed a mason who was a refugee from the Soviet Union and learned his trade building factory chimneys. He was able to get into the union when he came to New York. He ran into the problem that on the jobs where he worked, he was criticized for working too fast. He was even warned and threatened with physical harm if he didn't slow down, so he left the union and decided to go out on his own. He depended on the contractor to supply him with laborers because he didn't want the problem of making payrolls. He was fast and very proud of his skill, and when he was in the union he resented being told to slow down. Still, establishing norms of output by workers exists in all industries, and it is one of the weapons workers have to try to control the pace of their work.

CONTROL OVER THE NORMS OF PRODUCTION

O'Brien and Zilly (1971, p. 10) state with regard to output in construction that "on the local level there are still unwritten laws that govern the output." The approach to estimating costs illustrates construction worker control over output norms. The chief estimator for a northern construction firm told me that he estimated labor costs "after the fact." When the company was bidding for a project, cost figures were examined to ascertain what the men were currently producing—this was used as a production norm. The chief estimator said that while he might try to calculate improved methods for expediting materials or consider using a less expensive material or a new tool, labor output was beyond anyone's control other than the journeyman.

Worker control over production norms is not so much a question of restricting output as deciding it. As discussed in Chapter 1, the men on the Amherst sewage treatment plant project decided to pour a thousand yards of concrete in a single day. No one in management told them to do it. The superintendent, foremen, and key journeymen decided and planned it on their own initiative. After the thousand-yard pour, the concrete foreman, said, "If they'd leave us alone we can take care of the work and make money for the company. We did a thousand yards in a day, but I've done better."

Another feature in construction that strengthens worker control over production is the personal relationships between bosses and workers. Management personnel often come from the ranks. These men have worked with, or been friends with, the men they supervise or employ. This familiarity permits men to assert their control over how and how much they can work. A pipe foreman once remarked about his boss, "He and I used to lay pipe together, just like this, in the trenches. Now, whenever he sees me working he tries to tell me how to do it, and how many feet I should lay. I just tell him to get lost. And he knows that he's gonna get a good day's work outta me."

One example of factory-like methods employed in construction is the use of "flatplate" construction in high-rise apartment buildings. Flatplate construction means that the floors are supported on interior, reinforced concrete columns rather than steel on the exterior frame. Every floor is the same and every column location is the same, except for additional columns for shear walls in the core of the building. Depending on the size of the floor, the concrete contractor can set up his operations on a three-day pour cycle—first the columns, then the floors, then the movement of forms, rebars, and other materials, plus the laying of sleeves and electrical boxes for the next floor. The three-day cycle forces the men to do the forming, laying the rebars, and setting the sleeves and boxes in a prescribed time period without deviation, and if they have to speed up so be it. It works well and the floors and columns go up fast. But when they reach the top of the building, the well-run, machine-like sequencing is over. It might last three months, that's the way it is in construction. There are no long production durations that compare with mass production in factories. Gerald Finkel makes the same point in his following remarks (1997, p. 87):

Unlike other industrial development, the construction industry has never been able to attain the efficiencies of large-scale production. This comes in spite of the present-day fact that there are more firms with a national and international focus now than at any other time in market-based construction history.

Part of this failure is simply the fact that there are millions of dollars of small-scale alteration and jobbing type projects. These jobs lack the essential features of volume production. There is little repetitive activity, no central site, small and erratic inventories, antiquated business controls.

The most interesting concern is why, then, have economies of scale not developed to any large extent on the biggest projects or within the biggest firms. Cassimatis provides an insight, albeit from the 1960s, that is relevant to the present construction industry. He notes that the traditional relationship between general contractors and specialty subcontractors must be continually renewed from project to project (Cassimatis, 1969, p. 68). Whereas manufacturers can enter into long-term agreements with suppliers and their labor force, construction employers find themselves continually reestablishing procedures and flows as they enter into relationships with new sets of subcontractors and their workers.

RELATIVE DEMOCRACY

On construction projects, within each trade and between trades, there is a sense of democratic equality. No particular trade is considered superior to any other. Every trade makes its contribution without which no building would be complete. The painter of a wall is no less important than the carpenter who built it. The window caulker is just as vital as the glazier. No mason could lay block if his laborer did not mix the mortar and erect the scaffold. Within each craft each journeyman gets the same wage. The wage differential between the major trades is not significant. One trade may command slightly higher wages, while fringe benefits and conditions are better for another trade. Construction workers are respected because they perform work that meets the standards of the trade, not because any one trade ranks higher.

Construction workers consider themselves the equals of others, regardless of salary or rank. Employers are treated with respect, not deference. Engineers and architects are recognized for their knowledge, not their titles. Every man and woman on the job, and associated with a project, is expected to carry his or her load. At a sewage treatment plant project in western New York an older laborer was given the cleanup job. He also ran errands, picked up small tools, and performed odd jobs. No one looked on his work as menial nor looked down on him. He was so respected that he was made labor steward.

REFUSAL TO WORK

In most industries refusal to work can be cause for dismissal. In construction, however, workers can determine that conditions are unsafe or unsuitable for work. The carpenters' agreement, for example, states that "employees will not be required to work in inclement weather." The carpenters' shop steward and the men themselves jointly decide if the weather is inclement. This type of decision making prevails among high-risk trades. Construction men are paid "show-up" time if they report for work and the weather becomes unsuitable for them to go to work.

While most superintendents are union men and wish to maintain their good standing with the men, there is a possibility that a superintendent may not agree with the men that the weather is too bad for work to commence. On a sewage treatment plant project in western New York, the superintendent once opposed the men on whether to work or not. The super also refused to pay show-up time and claimed the men could have worked. The company had to back him up, but privately they criticized him. This man continued his arrogant ways and alienated the men further. He was finally taken off the job and sent to another project. He had trouble at the new project and was eventually laid off by the company.

Construction workers usually assert their autonomy and refuse to work in a deep trench excavation that does not have its sides protected by metal or wood shoring. A super I knew told me about a project where one of the workers working for him died in a cave-in. It was a sewage treatment plant project. The soil was very unstable and the engineer and the township authorities knew it. The contractor had taken soil samples and recommended that all trenching, which in some cases was as deep as 20 feet, be shored with metal shoring. He also gave them an estimate to provide the shoring, which would have been extra since it was not called for on the drawings. The township refused to approve the shoring and the contractor was not going to provide for it out of his own pocket. The project went ahead and there were several near misses, with the sides of the trench giving way, but the men had enough time to scramble out when they felt the earth tremble and they saw little pebbles of earth rolling down the sides. There wasn't enough room on the site to lay the trenches back, so the best the contractor would do was to provide "shields" for the men to work in. Shields are steel boxes made of I-beams with heavy plates on two sides. The men work inside the box while laying pipe, but the ends are open to permit the pipe to be dropped to the bottom of the trench. The super said that on the day of the fatal accident, he was standing on the side of the trench when suddenly he felt like he was on an elevator going down. The sides of the trench collapsed and the soil covered up the shield in which two men were working. One guy was near the top and they were able to locate his arms sticking up through the dirt and they dug him out in time. The other guy was at the bottom and there was no way to locate him. They kept digging until they found him, but by then he had suffocated and his lungs had been crushed from the weight of the dirt.

A crane operator will not lift a load if he believes it is too heavy for his machine or if the angle of the crane can tip it over. High steel erectors will not work on a windy day or when the weather is icy and the footing is slippery. Federal and state governments protect the right of workers to refuse work under unsafe conditions. A man fired for refusing to work in an unsafe work environment can appeal to the federal Office of Safety and Health Administration (OSHA). A project manager who orders men to work in dangerous conditions can be fined and jailed if it results in injury or death ("Safety Net Result: Money Spent, Lives Saved," 1976, p. 16).

Jack Haas (1977, p. 166) describes a situation where high steel ironworkers determined for themselves that it was unsafe to work and refused to do so:

The decision to work or not may be a group one; when a decision is made to thwart the foreman or contractor's usurpation of their autonomy the group will invariably act together. In one example, the foreman directs the workers to shovel snow off an iron beam; the group chooses not to work, and the men leave the job. Other workers remain free to decide for themselves whether or not to work. The perspective of worker autonomy is enacted and reinforced.

AUTONOMY IN HIRING AND FIRING

Hiring, firing, and layoffs usually take place on the construction job site and not in the company office. Men seeking work contact the superintendent, foreman, or shop steward on the project, or register themselves at the union hiring hall. The home office is then notified that workers have been hired and the office secretary is given the relevant information regarding the individual who fills out a W-2 form. In many cases the superintendent or foreman contacts the union business agent and asks him to have men sent to the job. A superintendent or foreman needing workers contacts those he knows at their homes and tells them to report for work. Officers of the contracting firm may express concern about the numbers of men on the project, but rarely do they participate directly in the hiring and firing process. This is not true of small firms with only a few employees or where the boss works alongside his men. In such cases the owner does his own hiring and firing and serves as his own super or foreman. Commenting on the autonomy of construction workers as a result of the hiring process, Richard R. Myers wrote (1946, p. 1), "Perhaps more than workers in any other industry building workers function as independent units, each worker pursuing employment and making arrangements to apply his skills according to personal contacts, personal preference and a personal schedule."

This comment was written over 50 years ago, but is just as true today as it was in 1946. Most general contractors still do all their hiring through personal contacts and the local business agent.

Bennie Graves studied construction workers in the pipeline industry and found that the autonomy of the workers was related to their autonomy in hiring and firing. Men were hired through contacts with relatives or friends or made their own deals with superintendents and foremen. The superintendent became dependent on the men in the summer when work loads were high and manpower scarce. The men were dependent on the superintendent in the winter when work loads were low and manpower high. This reciprocal dependency placed the workers on a relatively equal footing with the super who hired them. Graves describes the relationship (1974, p. 422), "Autonomy requires that networks [workers, foremen, superintendents] rather than outsiders [unions, employers, public officials, pipeline owners] must control most day-to-day aspects of hiring, firing and conditions of work."

A man who secures his job through his own efforts is independent even of the union. A labor foreman talked about this at the annual Christmas party of a northern United States contracting firm. He said that since he secured his job through his own contacts, he could hire his own men and form his own crews without going to the union. He contrasted his situation with that of another foreman who secured his job through the union and was obligated to take any man the union sent him. The first foreman said, "I got my job myself so I owe nothing to the union. I get my own crews and so the men I hire owe me. The man who hires you or helps you get your job is special and respect is due him."

Generalizing, it can be said that the nature of hiring and firing in an industry is an important clue to the level of autonomy of workers in that industry.

AUTONOMY AND TAKING DIRECTIONS

Construction workers assert their autonomy and independence by the way they take or refuse to take directions. I was project manager on a 15-story building in a northeastern city. The superintendent who ran the job described himself as a "hardheaded Dutchman." He was extremely competent, had been a journeyman carpenter, and had run a lot of large projects as a superintendent. He was also qualified as a building inspector, had taken and passed many tests for a number of townships, and had the necessary credentials to inspect a number of trades—building, plumbing, electrical, and structural. The superintendent was a man versed in all aspects of construction. He was a forthright person, scrupulously honest, who prided himself on acting on his belief that he was right most of the time. He was not the kind of person to be pushed around by anyone—his boss, the workers, the unions, or building industry politicians. The local laborers' union had a reputation of playing rough with contractors who did not cooperate; here were all the ingredients of a major struggle. At one point the laborers tried to teach him a lesson by moving his car from in front of his trailer to several blocks away. He had to report his vehicle stolen and have the police find it for him.

The situation finally reached a crisis when the super needed to get the floors cleaned up after the drywall crews. With all the debris on the floor it was impossible to schedule other trades until the floors had all the rubbish and debris removed. Every time the super told the labor foreman that he wanted the laborers to clean up a certain floor they would clean up a different floor. The super told them to stack the trash by the trash chute and throw the material down. They piled up the trash by the chute from the floor to the deck above so thick that it was impossible for anyone to move around the trash to throw it down the chute. Finally, it got to the point where the super conceded that he couldn't do anything with the laborers, so laid them all off. Then he hired a contractor who had muscle with the laborers. The new contractor put the laborers on his payroll and was able to get them to take orders from him while he took orders from the super. This is a lesson in how much autonomy and power a construction union and construction workers can assert in a struggle with contractor management.

6

ACCIDENTS, DANGER, AND DEATH

The construction industry has the highest incidence of accidents and deaths than any other single industry in the United States. According to the U.S. Bureau of Labor Statistics, the construction industry accounts for 20 percent of deaths in private industry, but employs only about 5 percent of nonfarm employees in the private sector. Of the fatalities in the construction industry, 32 percent are due to falls; 25 percent to transportation accidents; 20 percent to exposure; and 18 percent to contact with objects, including equipment. Five percent are due to assaults and violent acts. (U.S. Bureau of the Census, 1997, p. 439).

FALLS

A Slippery Fall

One of the causes of accidents in construction is bad weather. When a job site becomes wet and muddy from rain or snow, it is dangerous. Men lose their footing, heavy equipment slides out of control, visibility is poor, and workers are absorbed with their own states of discomfort rather than watching out for danger in the external environment. Here are some examples.

Larry was working as a surveyor on the Amherst sewage treatment plant project. One day he was on a 20-foot wall with a concrete pouring crew. His job was to give the men top-of-wall elevations so they would know where to stop the concrete at the top of the forms. It had been raining for nearly a week prior to the pour. The ladders, planks, walls, and ground were muddy and slippery. Larry was on the wall when the lunch-time horn sounded. He covered his surveyor's instrument and started toward the ladder. Reaching over with one foot to catch the top rung, his other foot slipped and down he went. He later recalled his thoughts during the fall, "As I was falling and going down I thought, 'this can't be happening to me.' I knew

I'd be hitting concrete. I hoped I wouldn't break my spine or my neck. Then I hit. Something cracked the back of my head. It was like a window shade shot down and everything went black."

Larry landed on his buttocks. In this regard he was lucky, but he could not keep his head from snapping back and striking the concrete. He remembered coming to, "First thing I saw when I opened my eyes was my dad bending over me. I had no sensation. Not anywhere. I figured I hit my spine. I couldn't even move my fingers. I was panicky. 'My God,' I thought, 'I'm paralyzed.' I was scared shit."

So was everyone else. No one knew then what the damage was. Someone called an ambulance, which soon arrived and roared off with Larry to the hospital. At the hospital, the doctors said that the fall had numbed his body sensations but that nothing was broken. The temporary paralysis was relieved with a shot and the warmth of the hospital bed and blankets. The next day he was back on the job.

The superintendent, in mock seriousness, told Larry, "I'm docking you for the time you were gone. What's this shit, taking off when we got a pour going." Larry laughed, "Up yours, I'm reporting you for unsafe ladders." The super had the last word, "No more jobs for you over two feet."

The above incident reveals that construction men anticipate accidents and try to react accordingly, but they do not coddle themselves or each other and they try not to show fear. As things turned out, Larry had another accident and was permanently injured, or so everyone thought, including Larry. At the age of 27 he gave up construction work and went on permanent disability. He later moved to another city to seek another type of employment. Although the doctors told Larry he would always walk with a limp, he told himself they were "full of shit," and embarked on a program of exercising his leg and lifting weights. It gradually improved, and within two years he was strong enough to return to work and took his place once again in the construction industry. Returning to work he had renewed strength and vigor, quickly worked himself into a superintendent's position, and was soon running his own jobs.

At the Amherst treatment plant project, the pile-driving crew was sheet piling a sewer trench 25 feet deep. Steel I-beams placed at the top of the sheets across the trench were used to brace the pilings. The men had to go back and forth across the I-beams to get from one side of the trench to the other side. One day the hammer that drove the sheets into the ground and eventually to rock 25 feet below, got hung up on the crane boom and the operator could not release it. It was dangerous, for if the weight dropped out of control, it could pull the crane over onto the men below. When the foreman saw the situation he started running across one of the I-beams, slipped and went down. Directly below him was a foundation for a manhole with reinforcing rods sticking up in the air. Luckily the foreman missed the steel rods that could have impaled him. Instead, he landed hard on a steel mat of crisscrossing reinforcing rods, broke six ribs, and punctured his lung. The problem was how to get him out of the trench. When the fire department ambulance arrived, he was wrapped in blankets and strapped into a stretcher. Then the men in his crew rigged a cable and hook to the stretcher and lifted him out with the crane. He never returned to the job.

CAVE-INS AND EARTH SLIDES

The federal Office of Safety and Health Administration considers trench excavation one of the most dangerous jobs in construction work ("Call Off the Underground Menace," 1977, p. 27). Due to the frequency of cave-ins and death I never met a sewer line worker who did not have experience and near death from a trench cave-in. Earth slides are also dangerous and fearsome. The following is a description of an incident that occurred on our Amherst sewage treatment plant project.

Preparing to start work on our project we stripped the topsoil and stockpiled it on the job site. Each pile contained about 15,000 cubic yards of dirt. Later in the project, another contractor, working on the second phase of the project, started a large excavation about 200 feet from our topsoil piles. In order to make room for other structures that had to be built we were asked by the project engineer to place one of our topsoil piles on top of the other. This created a mound that was 30 feet high and contained 30,000 cubic yards of dirt weighing about 60 million pounds. I recall walking alongside the pile and straining my neck backwards to see the top. Our superintendent had warned the township engineer that we were overloading the soil with such a concentrated load, especially with another excavation going on only 200 feet away. The combination of an excessive load in one place close to an open excavation near it led to a massive earth slide.

On the day of the slide I was inspecting the job while walking alongside the topsoil pile. I saw several bulldozers and trucks on top piling up more and more dirt. Later, sitting in the field shanty, I heard someone shout over the two-way radio that there had been an earth slide. I grabbed a camera and ran with others out of the shanty, heading in the direction of the topsoil pile. When we arrived at the scene, where just a short time before I had to strain to see the top of the pile, I could hardly believe my eyes. The topsoil pile was gone. It had sunk out of sight.

Where had it all gone? The weight of the dirt had pushed the clay below it down and toward the open excavation 200 feet away. The new excavation was now filled with the dirt that had been pushed up from below as the topsoil pile pushed its weight toward the excavation that provided a large area of no resistance. The dirt had slid below and emerged in waves of solid, frozen-looking clay, jaggedly haphazard in all sorts of weird shapes.

At the now-gone topsoil pile, two bulldozers were overturned and buried. Their tracks were off and their cabs were jammed with dirt. One dump truck was pitched forward with its nose stuck into the ground. Another dump truck was on its side with only one half of it visible. In some places the earth was cracked open more than ten feet. Cracks ran in all directions.

I questioned the men and no one could describe what happened—it took place too fast. They all exclaimed disbelief at the sight. No one had ever seen such a massive dislodging of earth.

The fact that no one was hurt, killed, or buried was because the event happened during lunchtime and no one was working on top of the pile. If it had occurred before or after lunchtime, two bulldozer operators and two truck drivers would have been buried and suffocated. The men who saw what happened were awestruck, humbled by the power of natural forces over which they had no control. Our superintendent took no satisfaction in having warned the town engineer. We all learned to respect the power and unpredictability of the earth when it is deeply disturbed.

HIGH STEEL

Men who work on the skeleton of a building—carpenters, masons, and others—often must work on scaffolds at great heights, but they do not risk their lives each day the way high steel men do. Concrete workers, carpenters, and masons stand on platforms and scaffolds. A high steel worker must walk on beams that are only inches wide—from a perilous eight inches to a risky 24 inches. They work exposed: the skin of the building is not up to protect them from the wind. Men who are able to work hundreds of feet in the air, walking on narrow beams of steel, are rare. Other construction workers respect their nerve and courage. Some construction men step in and out of danger from day to day, or week to week, but the high steel worker faces danger every minute, hour, and day while in the air connecting steel. He dare not make one false move, as he wrestles heavy steel sections swinging at the end of a crane that can move unexpectedly and knock him from his perch. A sudden gust of wind could swing the steel into him and send him down to death or injury, or he could slip or simply lose his balance, and his life, in a split second.

High steel men are dependent on others for their safety. A crane operator explains (Terkel, 1972, p. 23):

This is a boom crane. It goes anywhere from 80 to 240 feet. You're setting iron. Maybe you're picking 50- , 60-ton and maybe you have ironworkers up there 100, 110 feet. You have to be real careful that you don't bump one of these persons, where they would be apt to fall off. At the same time they're putting bolts in holes. If they wanted a half-inch, you have to be able to give them a half-inch. I mean, not an inch, not two inches. Those holes must line up exactly or they won't make their iron. And when you swing, you have to swing real smooth. You can't have your iron swinging back and forth, oscillating. If you do this, they'll refuse to work with you because their life is at stake. They're working on beams, anywhere from maybe a foot wide to maybe five or six inches. These fellas walk across there. They have to trust you.

MISCELLANEOUS ACCIDENTS

Faulty Equipment

Many accidents occur because of the failure of mechanical devices. One worker commented as follows (Terkel, 1972, p. 24):

A lot of stuff that comes out of the factory isn't exactly right. It's faulty. They don't know until it's used on the job. It's not just one person that's hurt. It's usually four or five.... There was 11 of them in an elevator downtown. The company that built that elevator, it was supposed to be foolproof. . . . It fell 12 floors and they were all hurt bad. Two of them had heart attacks when this was falling. There was one fella there that was completely paralyzed. He had 11 children. The only thing he could move was his eyes, that's all.

In 1978, 51 men were killed in a single accident in Willow Island, West Virginia, when an entire scaffolding system collapsed. The scaffolding ripped away from the sides of a cooling tower in a circular fashion, sending all 51 men working on it about 170 feet off the ground to their deaths in a heap of concrete, metal, and twisted debris. Federal officials of the Occupational Safety and Health Administration said it was the worst disaster they had seen, except for those related to mining. An investigation disclosed that the scaffolding system was faulty (*Buffalo News*, April 29, 1978).

A Sharp Trowel

What could happen with concrete finishing that is dangerous? The trowel they use is razor sharp. One day Jim's hand slipped into the side of his trowel and was slashed open from his small finger to his wrist. The foreman put a handkerchief over it. I asked to see it and then was sorry that I did; it was such a sickening sight. I told Jim not to look. We took him to the hospital and had to wait an hour before a doctor came to look at it. When Jim took the handkerchief away, the blood squirted out in a looping arc, landing on the doctor's coat, leaving a stain from shoulder to sleeve. The doctor pushed the handkerchief back over the cut. It took more than an hour to fix Jim's hand with two rows of stitches and a splint to keep the skin together. Jim was back on the job the next day, ignoring the doctor's admonition to take a week off and not use the hand.

Two Nails

Mike was helping to strip concrete forms when two nails at the end of a plank went into his hand. Because the nails were crossed on the board, they went into his hand the same way and were locked and crossed when they came out the other side. They entered the back of his hand between his thumb and index finger and came out in his palm. There was no way to get the nails out without tearing away the flesh. The nails were at the end of a 12-foot board with the weight of the board exerting pressure on the nails in his flesh, putting him in terrible pain. The board was cut off as close to his hand as possible, but the real problem was how to get the nails out. In spite of his pain, Mike figured out a way. He told one of the men to get a nail cutter and cut the nail heads off. Then they lifted the board off the nails and slid the nails out of his hand. He was taken to the hospital for a tetanus shot and bandaging. Mike was back on the job the next day.

This rapid spring-back is characteristic of construction workers. They are contemptuous of those who baby themselves after an accident. They are equally contemptuous of men who stupidly endanger themselves.

Orange and the Propane Tanks

One lunch hour at the Amherst treatment plant project, a laborer named Red was smoking a cigar near three propane tanks. He was standing inside the large intake chamber built to receive the town's sewage before it was sucked into four huge sewage treatment pumps. The men were using it as a storage area and a place for them to warm up, using propane tanks. The inevitable happened. There was a leak in one of the tanks and Red, smoking too close to the tanks, set it on fire. Witnesses said that Red seemed to freeze, unaware of the danger, until someone yelled, "Get the fuck out of there, you dumb bastard!" Red and everyone else in the intake chamber managed to get out in time. The three tanks blew and shot out of the chamber like naval shells, with the steel jackets folding up like cardboard. The heat inside the chamber was so intense that large chunks of concrete peeled off, making the walls and ceiling look as if they were hit by artillery fire. The piping inside the chamber melted. For a long time after that incident the men needled Red for smoking next to a propane tank. They kept asking him when he was "going to stop smoking his dumb-ass cigars." He did stop for a while, but it was not long before he was smoking again, oblivious of dangerous gasses on a construction job. He showed up at a farewell party for one of the men a few months later, and someone remarked, "What, are you still around, Red? I figured you must have blown yourself up by this time."

Danger on construction projects can come from the most unexpected sources. There was the time Chi Chi was working a concrete bucket behind a 12-yard concrete truck. The driver had backed the truck into position, jumped down from the cab, and started toward the rear to set the drum in motion. Suddenly, the truck began to roll backward, as the gear had somehow jumped into reverse. Chi Chi managed to scramble out of the way without being crushed, but the truck continued to head for an open excavation where men were working 50 feet below. By some miracle, the concrete bucket got jammed underneath the truck and slowed it down long enough for the driver to jump back in the cab and release the reverse gear. If the truck had gone over the edge, a grievous tragedy would have occurred.

Dick recalled how a concrete truck rolled over him; in fact, it rolled over his head. It was a miracle that he was still alive. Fortunately, it was a very wet, rainy day, and the ground was extremely muddy. Dick's head was pushed into the pliable ground so that he was not completely crushed. He suffered a concussion and many broken bones in his face, but he lived. After many months in the hospital he recovered and was able to get back into construction and become a superintendent. The men kidded him about his accident, attributing his "dumbness" to the truck rolling over his head. However, he is far from dumb—wild, yes, but not stupid.

The federal Occupational Safety and Health Administration, in response to the dangerous nature of the construction industry, monitors safety practices on various construction projects throughout the country. OSHA inspectors visit construction sites and look for safety violations like open stairwells, gases and chemicals that might explode, unsafe ladders or scaffolds, debris that could catch on fire or block stairwells, trenches that are unprotected, unsafe electrical extension cords, and many others. OSHA publishes a manual that sets forth safety regulations. Hard hats are a must. Any worker who chooses not to wear one is flirting with danger since objects are always falling in a building under construction. Fire extinguishers are important as small fires are constantly breaking out from any number of causes. OSHA standards are particularly stringent with regard to elevator shafts and types of scaffolding on tall buildings. Yet, in spite of all precautions, there are a thousand ways in which an accident can take place each day. If a person is in construction chances are high that he or she can be injured. In addition, construction is physically demanding and therefore results in bodily injury to many workers.

THE NECESSITY OF APPEARING FEARLESS

Mike Cherry, discussing high steel workers and danger, commented that it was important for a man in that kind of work not to show fear, especially to himself (1974, p. 149). This attitude sums up the general outlook of most construction workers. Lenny recalled when he first started working as a surveyor. One of his first jobs was the Queenston–Lewiston Bridge over the Niagara River gorge, 368 feet above the river. He talked about the first time he had to walk out on the steel and hold a rod for the man on the "gun" (the transit, a surveying instrument that measures angles and elevations). The other men in the crew watched to see how he would react. They knew he was scared, but they wanted to see how he would behave before they decided whether to work with him. Lenny said that the foreman of the bridge crew would watch men who were sent by the union to erect steel. He would take one look at how a man walked out on the steel, and if he was dissatisfied he would remark, "You're not a bridge man. Go back to the hall." Jack Haas, in his study of high steel workers, noted:

Workers who perceive physical danger develop mechanisms to control their reactions and the reactions of others. Individually and collectively they struggle to enhance the security of their situation. Symbolic or real threats bind workers together in an effort to protect themselves. Part of the defense, however, lies in controlling one's personal trepidations and insecurities and maintaining an appearance of fearlessness. (Haas, 1977, p. 168)

The need to mask fear does not mean that men are foolhardy or will work under any conditions without complaining. One day in January, we were making a deep connection into an existing city sewer line and built a manhole at the location. The sewer line was 30 feet deep and in order to make the connection we had to create an enormous excavation at an intersection. We had several slides and cave-ins on that excavation, as well as broken electrical cables and telephone lines. We finally managed to get the hole shored with large timbers, boards, and steel braces. The assistant superintendent on the project was responsible for setting up all excavations for the block layers building manholes. The bricklayer foreman said he was not going to permit the removal of any of the braces holding the timbers and boards, even if they were in the way of building the manhole. He said that the braces would have to be built into the manhole and burned out after the manhole was complete. The braces were hydraulic shoring braces that were rented and cost a good deal of money. The assistant superintendent taunted the bricklayer foreman for showing fear over working in the hole without the braces. All of the other men in the crew jumped on the assistant super for being willing to jeopardize the lives of men over a matter of money. No one questioned the courage of the bricklayer foreman. Rather, he was seen as exercising good judgment in protecting the welfare of the men working in his crew.

CONTROL OF THE WORK ENVIRONMENT FOR SAFETY

Jack Haas talks about perception of danger among ironworkers who erect steel (1977, p. 168):

The single characteristic they all share is their perception of danger; this perception produces a set of perspectives around the problem of danger that is rigorously and continuously enforced. The workers attempt to increase their control over their work environment and lessen the dangers. . . . This perspective emphasizes the ironworkers' commitment to increasing worker autonomy and thus a control over their environment. They strive to maintain control by collectively supporting individual and group decisions to judge for themselves safe and unsafe working conditions. They support the actions of fellow workers who decide whether or not to work in inclement weather. Fellow workers accept or reject the judgments of work superiors who may not give precedence to ironworkers' considerations and who could consequently pose a threat to their personal and collective security.

The manhole incident is a good example of this type of mechanism. When the assistant superintendent seemed to be primarily concerned with the cost of the braces rather than the safety of bricklayers, the other men came to the support of the bricklayer foreman. The foreman was asserting control over the environment in which his men would work.

Another example occurred at the SUNY library project in Buffalo. Structural steel was being erected in the winter. There was a big push to get all the steel erected so the concrete floors could be started earlier in the spring in order for brickwork to start early enough to enclose the building before the following winter. The architect's representative insisted on steel erection to continue every day except when there were high winds. One weekend there was heavy rain followed by very low temperatures. On Monday, the ironworkers' steward sent one of the men up to check the steel for ice. The report came back that it was too slippery to work. The architect's representative told the foreman to chip off the ice. The foreman refused. The following conversation took place:

Architect's rep: "You mean to tell me these men came in to work and they're not going to because you refuse to chip off the ice?"

Ironworkers' foreman: "That's right."

Architect's rep: "Get the general contractor. Let's hear what he has to say."

Architect's rep to general contractor: "I'm ordering you to work. You're aware of the schedule. We need the steel so we can get the floors started so we can close the building in by the fall."

General contractor's project manager: "I have no control over this matter."

Architect's rep: "Who decides whether they work or not today."

General contractor's project manager: "They do."

What the architect's representative did not understand, and what was clear to everyone else, was that when it comes to safety, no one dares challenge the right of the men to determine for themselves what is safe or unsafe. In a publication, *Workers's Bill of Health Rights* (Wallick, 1972, pp. 109–114), there was not one provision that gave workers the right to refuse to work if it was unsafe, although informally this is a right that construction workers enjoy because they have a large measure of control over their own work environment as well as their own work process. OSHA today does permit workers in construction to register complaints with them if they believe working conditions are unsafe. If they receive such a complaint, OSHA will investigate and issue a violations order requiring the contractor to correct the unsafe condition.

IDENTIFICATION WITH THE INJURED

Observing the prevalence of accidents in their industry, construction workers often say, "there but for the grace of God go I." They feel it is only a matter of luck who will be the next victim. The percentage of injured workers can be very high on some projects. On the subway project in Washington, D.C., one of three men was injured (Scott, 1974, p. 254).

Paul, a foreman, was talking about Sam one day. Sam was killed when a concrete truck went over him. Paul was Sam's foreman, and he felt that when he went to the funeral everyone was looking at him as though asking why he was alive and Sam was dead. Paul said he could not forget the wide, innocent eyes of Sam's daughter looking up at him and not understanding what was going on. Paul said it made him think about how his own daughter might have looked if he had been killed instead of Sam.

All construction men find ways to identify with those who get hurt. One of our men was struck by a section of 84-inch pipe that weighed 12 tons. It swung around while the men were trying to place it in a trench and hit the worker in the chest. He was described as "a good worker, a family man, a man who spoke with an Irish brogue and was liked by everyone, a guy who smiled a lot and who had the gift of gab." When they got him to the hospital his workmates were told that he had some crushed ribs but would be all right. What no one realized at the time was that he had lost consciousness while on the way to the hospital and had a stroke, therefore, for a short time, the oxygen supply to his brain was cut off. As a result of the stroke the man suffered the loss of his right arm along with a considerable loss of speech.

The worker hired a lawyer and sued for damages. During the trial, the lawyer for the insurance company kept badgering the construction men who were witnesses, called them "dummies" and "stupid," implying that they were not intelligent enough to recall anything accurately. He tried to catch them in contradictions to discredit their veracity. Some of the men did become confused and contradicted themselves.

The company lawyer focused on the man who was injured. He demanded that the man raise his arm, implying that he was faking it and could move his arm. The man tried painfully to comply, while the lawyer shouted that he was a fake. One of the workers who was a witness jumped the rail and charged the lawyer. The other men, while restraining the man started shouting obscenities at the lawyer, threatening him with bodily harm when they got him out of the courtroom.

Paul commented on the court scene:

We all felt that we were being insulted and attacked as a body. You could see that the guy was paralyzed. Also when he was questioned he had difficulty getting the words out. It was as if the lawyer was mocking his disability. And this guy was going to have to live with his disability for the rest of his life. I tell you the truth, I took it personally even though he was not a member of my family. I could have killed that lawyer. We all could. What happened to the guy could have happened to any one of us.

PHILOSOPHIZING

One Friday, a bunch of us were sitting around at lunch, swapping stories about accidents and deaths on construction jobs. Out of the eight men in the room, seven could recall, from personal experience, a serious accident or death they had witnessed or been involved in. George told how he was toppled into an excavation where his arm struck a rock and was shattered. The arm was hanging limp when they pulled him out and it started to swell from the bleeding. It was repaired with two cobalt plates and eight screws through the bones in his arm. Phil told about his brother Stan who was buried in a trench cave-in and had suffered internal injuries. Phil said as they were digging him out they could see blood coming out of his nose and ears. Another man in the group was working on a sewer line job when five men were drowned one night when heavy rains caused a flash flood that filled the trench in which the men were laying pipe. None of the men questioned the fact that they had to work under dangerous conditions. They all commented about how safety practices were ignored by everyone, including themselves, but they seemed to take a fatalistic attitude about accidents and death. Dwelling on the five men drowned in the flash flood, it seemed that the men might have refused to work if they figured that heavy rains would cause a flood that could threaten their lives, but it seemed farfetched that anyone would have foreseen the possibility and acted on it.

We were searching for an answer why various construction accidents happen. Why are some fatal and others not? Why are certain men killed and others spared without a scrape? Some men agreed that accidents are often mistakes, but when we returned to the drowning incident, it was agreed that the flash flood was not the result of a mistake. Finally, after a long silence someone said, "What's the use of looking for a why? An accident is something that happens and there is no why. It just is. That's all there is. An accident is just that, it has no why." Blunt realism such as this epitomizes construction worker culture.

7

JOB SATISFACTION AMONG CONSTRUCTION WORKERS

INTRODUCTION

Contemporary models of job satisfaction generally take into account two sources of variations: (1) the needs and values and individual characteristics of workers, and (2) the nature and organizational structure of jobs, firms, organizations, and industries. When the characteristics of individuals interact in a positive way with the characteristics of jobs, there is a high degree of job satisfaction. Workers needs and job requirements also vary with age, race, sex, and levels of education. While individual characteristics are related to job satisfaction and should not be neglected, the literature on work satisfaction suggests that it is the structural or job-related characteristics that are the most critical in producing satisfied workers (Hanson, Martin, and Tuch, 1987, p. 288). Some of the aspects of job characteristics that have been studied in connection with work satisfaction include organizational attributes, job control by management, worker autonomy, skill levels, specialization, socialization on the job, promotional opportunities, hours of work, wage levels, worker decision making, and others. A distinction is sometimes made between extrinsic and intrinsic factors—external and internal job characteristics. Internal or intrinsic factors include work benefits such as autonomy, control over the work process, interesting and challenging work, chances for socializing at the workplace—factors that have to do with the nature of the work itself and the work environment. Extrinsic or external factors include rewards such as high wages, good fringe benefits, job security, and medical insurance.

While the literature on work satisfaction often places most stress on job characteristics, we need to question whether this is the whole story or just the major element in job satisfaction. Workers' needs and characteristics should also be considered. For example, older workers tend to have more work satisfaction than younger workers. The reason may be that older workers have the better jobs, they have had enough time to accommodate to their work environments, and they are no longer restless or anxious about the need to rise in the job hierarchy (Mottaz, 1987, pp. 387–409). Another example of worker characteristics is that white males tend to have more job satisfaction than racial minorities and women because, on average, they have the better jobs (Waldinger, 1996, chapter 6). Another case involving worker characteristics relates to female workers, who may have more satisfaction in their work regardless of wages or status, if their hours are flexible enough for them to combine responsibilities at work with those at home. Many women may not value high wages and promotions as much as flexible time to care for their families. Thus, individual needs and values can have an impact or even offset the objective job characteristics.

The discussion on work satisfaction among construction workers focuses on factors isolated by researchers as significant sources of job satisfaction. I then relate these factors to construction workers.

SUPERVISION

Herzberg and his associates (1967) compiled data in which workers were asked what made them satisfied or dissatisfied with their jobs. Supervision was mentioned more frequently than security, job content, company and management, working conditions, and opportunity for advancement and wages. The only aspect of the job mentioned more frequently was relationships with coworkers. Silver singled out supervision as an important element in a construction worker's view of himself and his work environment (1986, pp. 128, 148–149). In addition, Silver questioned his research population of construction workers, asking them "How often is your performance evaluated during the job (1986, p. 43). Silver found that only 25.6 percent of the workers stated that they were supervised constantly or frequently during the day. The overwhelming majority, 74.4 percent, said they were supervised 1 to 3 times per day, 2 or 3 times per week, once per week or less, and never. Sixty-three percent were supervised 2 or 3 times per week, once per week or less, or never. Silver's questionnaire also showed conclusively that construction workers were largely left alone with regard to how to perform their work. Only 7.6 percent of the workers questioned stated that they were told how to do their work (Silver, 1986, p. 42). Of those questioned, 62 percent said that they alone, the construction workers, decided how to do their work. Another 30.4 percent said that job conditions determined how they did their work, but it was they, the construction workers, who decided how to perform their work. Although Silver questions the strength of autonomy among construction workers (1986, p. 41), his own figures from his research demonstrate that construction workers have a high degree of autonomy and a very low level of strict supervision.

Much research on supervision is concerned with the degree to which supervisors consider the desires of their subordinates. One study by the Survey Research Center at the University of Michigan (Katz, Gurin, and Floor, 1951), contrasted employee-oriented and production-oriented supervision. Employee-oriented supervisors establish supportive relationships with subordinates, take a personal interest in them, and are understanding when mistakes are made. Production-oriented supervisors view their subordinates as people to get the work done and are concerned with achieving high levels of production. Research evidence points to work satisfaction being related to employee orientation of supervisors. Supervisor behavior that is employee-oriented includes the following (Likert, 1961, pp. 16–17):

Recommends promotions, transfer and pay increases.

Informs workers on what is happening in the company.

Keeps workers posted on how well they are doing.

Hears complaints and grievances.

Thinks of employees as human beings rather than people to get work done.

Will go to bat or stand up for workers.

Usually pulls for employees or both employees and company, rather than for himself and for the company only.

Takes an interest in the employee and understands his problems.

Is part of the work group and is interested in people who are in the group.

Likes to get ideas from people in the work group.

A number of studies have been conducted on the relationship between supervision and job absences, turnovers, and grievances (Fleishman and Burtt, 1965; Fleishman and Harris, 1962). Findings show that supervisor consideration correlates with low rates of absences and grievances and high job satisfaction. The relationship could be opposite, that is, supervisors display a greater degree of consideration for subordinates they perceive to be satisfied. Subordinates who are critical and dissatisfied are less likely to be recipients of warmth and personal support.

Using the ideas on the relationship between supervision and job satisfaction, let us examine the construction worker. Absenteeism, turnover, and grievances exist among construction workers, as they do among any group of employees, but they are much less prevalent compared with factory and office workers. Workers are absent because of sickness or injury, or the need to attend to personal affairs or family problems, but chronic absenteeism, lateness for work, and turnover of workers is rare to nonexistent. The men are accounted for as plans are made for the next day's work. If a man does not show up and does not call, a call goes to his house. If someone is absent from a crew, the shifting of men must take place. Every absence must be explained. If a man must take care of personal business and informs his foreman, he will usually not be docked. Construction workers may express dissatisfaction when they go on strike, which normally happens when their contract with the employers' association expires. They might be asking for more money, greater benefits, or better conditions. This represents an attempt to improve their situation rather than dissatisfaction with their lot as construction workers. A lot of blue-collar workers would gladly trade places with them, and they know it.

Consideration for subordinates by superintendents and foremen is generally high. Many of these men know each other and their families through kinship, friendship, and socializing. After work, many participate in activities together—drinking, bowling, going out to eat, going to sporting events, or playing in team sports. Foremen and superintendents are considered part of the work group. If a man is seriously hurt he is visited by some of the men and his condition is reported back to the others. Foremen will often give money to a gofer (an apprentice who runs errands) and ask him to buy coffee and doughnuts for his crew. Some foremen, when talking to crew members, often put a hand on their shoulders, or hold them by the arm or back of the neck, exhibiting a feeling of warmth and human consideration for his workers.

In construction, supervision is the key to the success of a project; yet, supervision is rather loose. Supervision is based on knowing and planning more than on cracking the whip. Supervision in construction is responsible for organizing the necessary materials, equipment, and labor, and interpreting the drawings so the men execute the work properly with regard to workmanship, dimensions, and shape. Construction is unlike manufacturing where materials, workers, and machines are assembled at specific work stations. A construction project is a large site where workers, machines, tools, and materials must constantly be moved from one work area to another. It is the job of the super to plan these moves in the proper sequence, knowing when and which trades must be alerted to start their operations, while being aware of the others' schedules. The project manager's job is to prepare a detailed construction schedule showing the time frames and sequences of the various trades, but it is the superintendent who carries out the plan, modifying it when some trade is late or another is too fast, adjusting it when materials do not arrive on the job on time, or adding to the schedule when changes are made or additional work is requested from the architect or owner.

Supervision is loose in that the superintendent does not direct the work. This is not always true. In the case where a contractor is small and the boss himself works alongside his men, he also supervises them. In some smaller projects fathers and sons do the work. On larger projects, superintendents tell the foreman of a crew what he needs done and when he needs it. The foreman who directs the work and works alongside the men, plays both an authority role and a cooperative one.

Supervision in construction is democratic in style, depending on the workers. It is not possible to subject the workers to a strict routine. Supervision cannot be too authoritarian since it must ultimately depend on the journeyman to produce the work. Authoritarianism in construction (and perhaps elsewhere) inevitably leads to resistance. Supervision cannot be laissez-faire either because, after all, the work must be coordinated between trades. The democratic style of supervision is inevitable in a work situation where craftsmen are the main producers and, therefore, control the work process. Project managers are ultimately responsible for bringing projects in on time and within budget. If the contractors and their workers do not cooperate they can be dismissed. But contractors have contracts which cannot be canceled without cause. If management has unreasonable expectations about what they expect from the contractors and workers then they are at fault and the job will be a failure. Many contractors have men who have been working for them for a long time and they have a positive relationship that has resulted in jobs coming in on time in most cases. Still, they rely on the subcontractors and their workers and have a loose, informal relationship with them based on personal knowledge and goodwill. Nothing else will work in construction and other industries are learning the same thing.

Field supervision—foreman or superintendent—is the highest rank a journeyman can aspire to in construction, thus, there is never a wide gulf between the workers and their supervisors. The foreman of today was the worker of yesterday. For example, on the Elm-Oak arterial project in Buffalo, as the work progressed the general contractor expanded the number of operations on his waterline installation. He had to split up the old crews, making new ones, and appointing new foremen. He needed crews to pressure-test and chlorinate the lines; make new house connections from the new mains; install new fire hydrants and street valves; and so forth. Workers who had never been foremen found themselves in charge of an operation and a crew. It took about a month for them to become confident in their new positions. Soon they began to demand things—tools, equipment, and materials. They became angry if their crew members were delayed by logistics. They were kidded by the other workers in their crews, and their responses were mock threats to give their hecklers "dirty jobs in the hole." The kidding helped relax the new foremen because it meant their workers were backing them up. These new foremen were effective because they shared problems (and the search for solutions) connected with the work process with their subordinates. The situation called for democratic leadership that paid off in the workers' acceptance of the new leadership. This was a case where the objective nature of the job rather than the individual characteristics of the workers, resulted in a behavior pattern that was favorable to work satisfaction. Riemer (1979, p. 68), however, points out that there is a mutual interdependence between dynamic and structural components of construction projects so that the behavioral patterns are the result of external and internal factors, subjective and objective elements, and a continual interplay between individual and job characteristics.

A supervisor has the right to command and his subordinates are obliged to obey, however, a superior's authority over subordinates extends only as far as workers voluntarily permit themselves to be governed by a superior's directives. In construction, the formal organizational chart does not guarantee that high authority directives will be effective. Effectiveness of authority must be established in the course of social interaction in the field that is appropriate to the situation. Supervision that is loose and informal, and shows consideration for subordinates, is the most effective in construction. This has been found to be true not only in construction but in many other fields. Today, in the 1990s, the auto and steel industry have quality circles, decentralized worker decision making, and flexible organizational structures that are similar to leadership patterns in existence in construction for many decades.

PARTICIPATION IN DECISION MAKING

One of the basic findings by those who research job satisfaction is that workers obtain satisfaction from influencing decisions and controlling their work process. Baumgartel (1956) studied scientists in 18 laboratories and found significantly more positive attitudes where they were permitted greater participation in work decisions. Jacobson (1951) found the same thing in an automobile plant, as did Wickert (1951) who studied telephone operators and service personnel. Ross and Zander (1957) studied 2,680 female workers in a large company and, like Wickert, found that those who remained satisfied enough to remain with the company were able to influence their job conditions.

Morse and Reimer (1956) carried out research on job satisfaction among four clerical operations of a large insurance company. Two programs were set up—an autonomy program and a hierarchically-controlled program. Job satisfaction was measured before and after the experimental year. There was an increase in satisfaction under the autonomy program and a decrease in the hierarchically-controlled one. Two other studies found that workers display higher job satisfaction when they are able to make decisions about products, goal-planning, division of labor, and work assignments to group members (French, Israel, and As, 1960; Kay, French, and Meyer, 1962). Silver (1986, p. 109) states that constraints on construction workers preventing them from fully exercising their skills and knowledge in the production process are sources of low morale. Finally, General Motors auto workers in Lordstown, Ohio, in March 1998, voted to retain a provision in their local union contract that continues to give them a voice in their job conditions, even though it resulted in their accepting a lower hourly rate compared with auto workers in other plants. They are entitled to bonuses if their efficiency and output exceeds a certain standard but recently their bonuses had fallen to the point where they were making less than the average auto worker in other plants. In spite of this situation they still voted for continuing the autonomy provision in their local contract.

There is evidence that workers who are satisfied with their jobs tend to have greater opportunity to influence decisions that affect their work and their job environment. Relating this generalization to construction workers, we can examine the activities of a typical work crew installing waterline pipe on a downtown road project. This crew installed 5,000 feet of water main pipe under the street in the downtown area of Buffalo, New York.

Each morning, the crew would decide what fittings they needed, based on where they had left off the previous day. The foreman would ascertain if he needed a pavement breaker and if so, he would request the machine and an operator. The foreman would have to make sure the public did not park cars in the work area and so one of the men was assigned to come in early and keep the cars away.

There were four men in the work crew: an operating engineer, who ran a back hoe machine that dug the pipe trench; a foreman, who directed the operation from the top of the trench, signaling and talking to the machine operator on top and to the men below; and two laborers in the trench, who set pipe, bolted up fittings, and did whatever hand digging was necessary. One of the laborers also served as flagman, directing traffic when the machine had to move back and forth into traffic while backfilling the trench. The crew put up movable construction signs each time they moved to a different work area. These signs warned the traveling public that construction was going on in that area.

The men worked collectively solving daily problems. Their greatest difficulty was at each street intersection where they encountered existing underground utilities—gas, electric, telephone, sewer, water, telegraph, cable television lines, fire alarm, city steam, and other underground services. Sometimes the waterline would have to be installed in a snakelike configuration over and under these various utility lines. At times, utility companies would have to be called to remove and relocate their lines so the waterline could get through. The foreman and the crew would decide among themselves whether they could get through an area. If additional waterline fittings were needed they would call the field office and tell the clerk to order them. The crew would examine the plans to see what provisions were to be made for house services, fire hydrants, and street valves. There were times when the crew called on the project manager or the superintendent to make a decision. The state engineer would be consulted if a design change or a monetary change order had to be authorized. It was up to the waterline crew to bring these problems and questions to the attention of the project manager, the superintendent, or the state inspectors.

It was rare for crew or foreman decisions on the waterline main to be overruled. It only happened once, and that involved a matter of safety. The men were not using the steel box that served as a safety shield because it inhibited their production. Nevertheless, they were ordered to use it. If any worker got hurt the superintendent or the project manager would be held responsible. This crew developed a solidarity and camaraderie so strong it was noticed by the other men. They drank together and went out together.

George Strauss sums up the construction workers as follows (1963, p. 16): "If we take the building tradesman as the classic example of the craftsman, we find that he behaves in many ways like a professional. . . . Craftsmen like to decide how they will do their work."

MEMBERSHIP IN AN INTEGRATED WORK GROUP

A considerable body of research exists that asserts that there is a strong relationship between greater job satisfaction and work based on integrated work groups. Herzberg and his associates, basing their findings on 44 articles on job satisfaction, concluded that "these findings indicate that the cohesiveness of the work group is an important factor in determining the morale of workers (1957, p. 132). There is additional research that demonstrates that coworkers' social groups and kin-based networks increase job satisfaction (Hurlbert, 1991, pp. 415–430).

There are two aspects to integrated work groups. The first relates to techniques and the technology employed in particular work settings. Since the techniques used in construction usually involves teams, crews, and gangs, construction work inherently fosters cohesive work groups. The other aspect of integrated work groups is social. On most construction projects, a community social structure is created along with the physical structure. Friendships are formed and grow between men who know each other from previous jobs or meet in the same crew for the first time. A social system of leadership and groups based on the trades and social roles of men within the trades is established on the project and is recognized by workers who must navigate within that system. Informal leaders, in addition to the formal relationships between supers, foremen, shop stewards, and journeymen, emerge through reputations based on skills, knowledge, and personality. Channels of communication are established. Social interaction takes place at work, during lunch and break times, and after work at the local bar, restaurant, bowling alley, social club, or other meeting places in the neighborhood. All this activity builds group feeling, a sense of "us" and "the others." Networks and contacts are all-important in the construction industry, for new recruits trying to break into the industry and for veterans looking for work from job to job as projects are completed. Social cohesion is a matter of survival as well as a source of job satisfaction.

Within the community of men on the construction project, small groups and cliques develop, usually based on trade affiliations, but also on previous friendships. Hub Dillard explains (Terkel, 1972, p. 24):

You're tense and most everybody'd stop and have a beer or a shot. They'd have a few drinks and then they'd go home. They have a clique, like everybody has. Your ironworkers, they go to one tavern. Maybe the operators go to another one. The carpenters go to another place. They build buildings and tear 'em down in the tavern.

On a western New York sewage treatment plant project, the pile drivers had a clique and a special reputation as a wild bunch. They did crazy things, engaged in horseplay, and were always fighting with each other, both verbally and physically. One time they toppled a crane into a small steel building on the job site. They thought it was hilarious seeing men scatter in all directions as the crane slowly started to tip and then came crashing down on the empty building. Another time they lost their foreman, who fell into a trench, cracked his ribs, and never returned to the job.

The pile drivers drank in the same tavern where several other trades drank. They had their own place at the bar and made plenty of noise. Sometimes they gathered at one corner of the room and shoved several tables together. They welcomed no outsiders and no one showed any inclination to join them. They were viewed as rough, sloppy, and uncaring. They usually finished their work, but were held in low regard by the other trades because they took their time and delayed other crews.

On another western New York sewage treatment plant project, the pile driving crew had a different foreman. This group had an entirely different personality. They worked efficiently, had no mishaps, and were either ahead of the other trades or on schedule. They gained the respect of all the other trades. One of the members who had been in both crews was asked why he thought they were so different, "I guess every crew has its own ways. To tell the truth, I enjoy both. Don't ask me why."

In addition to integrated groups that form on the job, there are crews that go from job to job. On the two sewer plant projects mentioned, the work overlapped and required 30,000 cubic yards of concrete to be poured on the two jobs. The work was not continuous and concrete workers were hired as needed. It worked out that the concrete crew could move as a body from one project to the other, meeting the needs of both in this intermittent manner. The crew had been in existence a long time. They worked like a machine. Each man knew his job as well as the moves of the others in the crew. George Strauss talks about this arrangement in construction (1958, p. 65): "In some cases (particularly among ironworkers) crews went from job to job together—even from one city to another. Often they took their own foremen with them. If the boss fired one of the crew, the rest quit too."

The effect of integrated work groups on output and productivity has been much studied. An investigation of construction workers in Chicago demonstrated that both productivity and job satisfaction went up when a system of letting men choose their own work partners was introduced (Van Zelst, "Sociometrically Selected Work Teams," 1952, pp. 175–185). Applying the sociometric principles of Moreno (1937) to 38 carpenters and 26 bricklayers, work teams were regrouped into mutual choice crews and researched over an 11-month period. Controlling for other factors that might have affected output, Van Zelst found that it was clear that group output was traceable to the system of letting the men choose their own work teams. There was also evidence that job satisfaction increased. There was a drop in the number of workers who left the job during the period of the experiment (1952, p.183). Van Zelst concluded ("Sociometrically Selected Work Teams," 1952, pp. 184–185), "It must be noted, however, that the building trades with their buddy-work-teams are especially suited for a sociometric regrouping. . . . The end result in this study has been a happier, more productive worker, who has given management a 5% savings in total production cost."

One worker in the study summed up his feelings (Van Zelst, "Sociometrically Selected Work Teams," 1952, p. 183):

Seems as though everything flows a lot smoother. It makes you feel more comfortable working—and I don't waste any time bickering about who's going to do what and how. We just seem to go ahead and do it. The work's a lot more interesting too when you've got your buddy working with you. You certainly like it a lot better anyway.

The picture of the construction worker's situation contrasts with that of the factory worker. Work on the assembly line leaves no time to socialize because "the line-tender must do all the work that the endless belt brings before him" (Chinoy, 1955, pp. 71–72). Job dissatisfaction is reflected in the high rates of absenteeism and turnover among factory workers, especially among those who are low-paid and unskilled, such as the many workers in textile, light manufacturing, and electronics factories. Many factory workers perform their tasks alone (Levison, 1974, p. 61):

Another aspect of blue-collar work is loneliness. Many working-class jobs are very consciously designed to keep people apart. In many factories the noise level alone prevents any conversation beyond a shouted remark or two. In others the work stations are far apart or the job too difficult to permit any real communication. Rules against talking are also common, either written down on paper or delivered by the supervisor. The attitude is that if you're talking you're probably not doing the job. Only where the work is necessarily done in teams, *like construction work,* (emphasis added) is there any opportunity for real contact.

The situation described above has changed somewhat since the 1970s. There has been a conscious effort by some of the larger corporations, like auto companies, to introduce quality circle teams and more lower level decision making by workers on the line. But this trend has been extremely limited, and the bulk of manufacturing work, especially in the low-wage, nonunion sectors, is still ruled by bureaucratic and authoritarian approaches to the workers who are pressed by supervisors to work silently and speedily.

Miners provide an example of an occupation where work in teams is a source of job satisfaction (Friedmann and Havighurst, 1954, p. 176):

Coal miners had a very personal sense of being pitted against their environment and expressed feelings of accomplishment and pride at having conquered it. . . . The whole gang is pitted against the mine. Victory is dependent upon each man's holding up his end. Victory is not only the sense of having cheated death . . . it is also the sense of having achieved life through one's own efforts and those of one's fellow workers.

In British mines, coal was extracted by pairs of miners who shared all necessary tasks (Trist and Bamforth, 1951, pp. 3–38). These pairs usually chose each other as work partners. They were a close, integrated team, sharing a dangerous and difficult job. There was some division of labor, but each man carried out all tasks. The system was inefficient, costly, and not easily mechanized. When machinery and mechanical conveyors were introduced, there was a separation of tasks and specialized labor. The former short wall work areas were replaced by long walls. Instead of two-man groups, large gangs of men worked in rotation, each group carrying out only one task.

This change should have resulted in a large increase in output, but it did not. Coal production hardly rose, and absenteeism increased. Reported illness among the workers rose and tension levels became high. The Tavistock Institute of Human Relations investigated the reasons for the rise in worker dissatisfaction.

The Tavistock Institute found the breakup of the two-man teams had two results. First, the men lost their sense of identification with the job. They no longer were close to the whole set of tasks, including caring about how much coal they produced. Second, rivalries between gangs interfered with coordination of the various stages of the job, a coordination easily achieved by the former two-man teams. One task was exceptionally dirty and considered "bad work." The group assigned to that task had low social status and responded by slowing down the whole mine operation. Miners with previously high morale in the face of hazardous mine conditions now found themselves without the support of a closely knit team. Trist and

Bamforth reported a consequent real drop in job satisfaction (1951, p. 38). Since the 1950s, the British coal mines have been thoroughly mechanized and downsized. Many pits were closed down and tens of thousands, if not hundreds of thousands of miners were laid off forever. The British mine industry, once one of the proudest parts of English industrialization, is now a shadow of what it once was. Whole mining towns and villages have disappeared, along with mine families. This situation became particularly severe during the Thatcher years when the cry was for laissez-faire capitalist approaches to the British economy, with an emphasis on profitable investment and depriving the British worker of union protection and government benefits.

In summary, most people are more satisfied with their work when they work as members of a group rather than in isolation. Most workers prefer jobs that permit interaction and are more likely to quit jobs that prevent contact with others. Congenial peer relationships are cited by workers as one of the major characteristics of good jobs. On the other hand, "low job satisfaction is related to ... lack of opportunity to interact with coworkers" (Kasl, 1974, p. 176; Hurlbert, 1991, pp. 426–427). Construction workers are fortunate that the technology of their work demands that tasks be performed with teams, gangs, and crews. Human sociability is an intrinsic part of the construction work environment. Construction work requires cooperation within crews and between trades. Thus, the cultural pattern of work behavior as well as thought patterns in construction fosters feelings among the workers that they are part of an integrated group.

BELONGING TO AN OCCUPATIONAL COMMUNITY

There is satisfaction from the feeling of belonging to a group in which one shares ideas and beliefs, and where members engage in similar behavior. The notion of occupational community is based on the idea that men who work in the same trade, craft, or occupation share experiences and a way of life so that as a group they have a culture. (For a full discussion of occupational cultures, including construction, see Trice, 1993.) Entry into an occupational community is through membership in a trade or craft based on acquisition of the requisite skill. Belonging to a craft implies that one is a certified member of the group, sharing a standing within the craft with other members. This provides the individual with self-esteem and prestige shared with other members of the community.

Trice describes an occupational community in the following way (1993, p. 26):

[F]orces are present that facilitate group identity among members. ... The specific forces vary in strength from occupation to occupation. The major ones are: (1) esoteric knowledge and expertise, (2) extreme or unusual demands, (3) consciousness of kind, (4) pervasiveness—the occupational culture permeates non-working life, (5) ideologies that confer favorable self-images and social values to the tasks, (6) the extent to which members of the occupation are members' primary reference group, and (7) the abundance of consistent cultural forms. When all these closely related forces for cohesion are active, the occupational culture tends to be known as a community.

An occupational community represents a particular relationship between work and non-work lives that, in its ideal form, is rare in modern societies. It implies that members of an occupational community are affected by their work in such a way that their nonwork lives are permeated by their work relationships, along with their attendant value systems. However, as Gerstl comments (1961, p. 37), "work offers few positive satisfactions and is not a central life interest for the majority of industrial workers." In our society, our work lives are often isolated from our other familial, political, and religious roles. Many people believe they do not start to live for themselves until they leave work—like the packinghouse worker who says that he is anxious to get home from work so he can "try to accomplish something for that day" (Blum, 1953, p. 96).

Differing from this condition are attitudes and lifestyles of many craftsmen, described as follows by C. Wright Mills (1953, p. 223):

The craftsman's work is the mainspring of the only life he knows, he does not flee from work into a separate sphere of leisure; he brings to his non-working hours the values and qualities developed and employed in his working time. His idle conversation is shop talk; his friends follow the same lines of work as he, and share a kinship of feeling and thought.

A good example of Mills' craftsman is the stone mason who even daydreams about his work (Terkel, 1972, p. xlvii): "I daydream all the time, most times it's on stone. All my dreams, it seems like it's got to have a piece of rock mixed in it."

Occupational communities typically can be broken down into four components: (1) self image; (2) accepting evaluations only from peers; (3) integration of work and nonwork lives; and (4) sharing problems and experiences.

Self-Image

Self-image is the way a person views himself. This self-perception is not accidental. It is based on the social role of the individual that receives support and confirmation from others. When a man's self-image is centered on his occupational role, those who give him support and confirmation are his workmates. Robert Park states (1968, p. 94): "The conceptions which men form of themselves seem to depend upon their vocations, and in general upon the role which they seek to play in the communities and social groups in which they live, as well as upon the recognition and status which society accords them in these roles."

People who value their work and get satisfaction from it are likely to take their self-image from their occupation. Construction workers have a positive self-image based on occupation. There are indicators in construction that support high prestige. Construction workers are among the highest paid of all blue-collar workers. They enjoy autonomy in control of their work based on their knowledge and skills. Some researchers have likened construction craftsmen to professionals (Stinchcombe, 1959, pp. 168–187). They are given the freedom in their work to independently organize and perform their skills just like professionals. Construction workers have been referred to as the "aristocrats of labor" (LeMasters, 1975). This reflects the prestige and self-image enjoyed by construction workers. George Strauss likens construction workers to professionals (1958, p. 65): "The construction workers studied were intensely proud of their craft, showed strong social unity, and were independent and self-assertive. Their identification with their craft approximated that of a doctor or lawyer."

Construction workers have titles that identify their membership in a craft or trade. It is a title that certifies membership and identity, and gives those who bear this title prestige and a sense of belonging. If a man is on a construction project, he is known not only by name but also by trade. Even if someone does not know his name a worker will be known as "electrician," "bricklayer," "carpenter" or whatever his tools and work identify him as belonging to a certain trade. The importance of occupational title to self-image is explained by Becker and Carper (1956, p. 344):

Kinds of work tend to be named, to become well-defined occupations and an important part of a person's work-based identity grows out of his relationship to his occupational title. . . . Occupational titles imply a great deal about the characteristics of their bearers and these meanings are often systematized into elaborate ideologies which itemize the qualities, interests and capabilities of those so identified.

The positive self-image of construction workers is revealed in two other ways. One is the frequency with which they take their families to past projects they have worked on and point with pride to their participation in the job. The other is their encouragement to their children to enter the industry. In contrast to industrial workers, building tradesmen in many instances are willing to have their children follow in their footsteps. Many construction projects have fathers and sons working on the job. Relatives, especially brothers also often work on the same project or in the same construction company. In the Hartz Mountain construction division there is a superintendent who has both a brother and a son who work for the company. Hartz had a subcontractor with a son (who is a carpenter foreman) and a brother on his payroll. A Hartz mechanical subcontractor has two principals who are both sons of men who started the business. Hartz has a drywall subcontractor whose two principals are brothers. These family relationships are ubiquitous and universal in the construction industry.

Accepting Evaluation Only from Group Members

Just as doctors and lawyers believe that only their colleagues are competent to judge them, construction workers also accept judgment of their work performance only from fellow tradesmen. A remark made frequently by construction men to inspecting authorities and owners is, "You can inspect the work when it's done, but don't tell me how to perform my job." At a New York State sewage treatment plant project, the resident engineer, who performed his administrative duties well, created much hostility when he tried to tell the men how to perform their work. After many showdowns, the resident was forced to confine his review of the work to the final results and allow the craftsmen to judge their performance through their own craft foremen and skilled journeymen. The insistence on judgment of performance by one's peers is explained by Gouldner regarding professionals (1960, p. 468): "Continued standing as a competent professional often cannot be validated by members of his employing organization since they are not knowledgeable enough about it. For this reason, the expert is more likely than others to esteem the good opinion of . . . peers."

Occupational communities not only use peer review to evaluate work skills of colleagues, but their habits and personality traits as well. Caplow remarked (1954, p. 127): "Those which are disapproved are the ones which interfere with the smooth functioning of the working group: pugnacity, carelessness, taciturnity, nervousness, dishonesty, self-pity, and the like. In a sense, the rules of comportment which are applied are extensions of the tacit rules encountered in the 'normal' family."

Convergence of Work and Nonwork Life

Members of an occupational community tend to prefer friendships with people who do the same type of work. This means not only being friendly with people at work, but spending time outside working hours with workmates. Workmates predominate as best friends. In their study of printers, a craft that in the past had all the characteristics of an occupational community, Lipset, Trow, and Coleman found (1956, p. 70):

Large numbers of printers spend a considerable amount of their leisure time with other printers. In interviews many printers reported that their best friends are other printers, that they regularly visit the homes of other printers, that they often meet in bars, go fishing together, or see each other in various places before and after work.

I tested the question of friendship by taking a sampling from the Amherst sewage treatment plant project. I asked 11 men to tell me how many "close" friends they had who were construction workers. "Close friends" were defined as men they knew more than five years, exchanged home visits, and shared after-work activities like bowling, hunting, fishing, or drinking. I told them to consider close friends those who had all three characteristics, not just one. I also asked them to list nonconstruction friends.

The following table shows the results:

Subject	Construction Worker Friends	Nonconstruction Friends
E.K.	4	1
D.C.	3	0
B.M.	1	1
I.P.	3	2
K.O.	0	0
P.R.	2	1
S.F.	1	0
B.L.	0	2
P.C.	3	1
C.C.	2	0
B.H.	2	1

This table indicates the tendency of construction workers to choose friends and social contacts from among their occupational group.

Among workers other than construction-related occupations it is by no means common for men to have friends from their occupational group. Occupational communities rarely exist among urban factory workers (Blauner, 1966, p. 483). Many workers attempt to insulate their nonwork lives from any work influence. Goldthorpe and his associates found that the majority of men in their study sample neither had relationships of any depth with their workmates, nor were they interested in finding friends from their workplace (1968, p. 56): "Taking the sample as a whole, only around one in four of our affluent workers could be said to have a "close friend" among his mates in the sense of someone with whom he would actually plan to meet for out-of-work social activities."

Sharing of Problems and Experiences

Physical danger and discomfort in construction is shared by construction workers during their workday. Construction men and women like to swap stories about these kinds of experiences. They often relate such incidents in a humorous manner as several others join in with their own variation on the theme.

One favorite source of tales concerns difficulties with construction equipment. Many construction firms operate on the principle of trying to keep company-owned equipment as long as possible, even if it is obsolete and falling apart. Arguments about less down time and more efficiency with more modern equipment have not dissuaded construction contractors from their policy. On a road project in the northeastern United States men were given construction machines that were notorious for being faulty (and were given nicknames accordingly). One of these machines was a small bulldozer, the subject of many stories, one of which was told one day at lunchtime by Lenny, as follows:

We're on Elm Street on the state job and I've got the mini-beast, you know the one, the Case 190, and we're doing some clearing and grubbing. It's January and we got to jump it every morning to start it. One morning we're pumping gas into her and it's leaking all over the carburetor. Frankie's putting on jumper cables and don't you know he gets 'em missed up, causes a spark and sets the beast on fire. I'm across the field in a car with the inspector and I see Frankie running towards us. I spot the fire so I grab a fire extinguisher and start running. When I get there I push the spray nozzle and my prick could have pissed more of a spray. Then we run and get the water truck and drive it hard across that field. It was so bumpy our hard hats were hitting the top of the cab. We get there and open the hoses and the fuckin' water truck is empty. So we get a second water truck over and finally get the fire out. We all feel like heroes. This one got a singe here, that one got a burn there, but no one's burnt bad.

That Friday I'm in the office to turn in my time sheets and who do I run into but one of the bosses. He says to me, "Hey, there's Smokey the Bear. I heard you put out a fire on the Case 190. You dumb bastard, why didn't you let that piece of junk burn? We could have put in a claim and collected for a new one."

I told him that if I ever see his house on fire I'm goin' to remember what he told me and I'm goin' to let it burn. Was I pissed. Here I thought I'm a hero and instead I get my ass chewed out.

During the same lunch hour, another man told a story about a crane that would not turn to the right. Every time the men used it they would tie a rope to the boom and three men would pull the rope to turn the crane. One day, the boss came out to the job and saw what the men were doing. He commented in all seriousness, "Boy that crane sure works fine."

The men also liked to tell stories about goof-ups, embarrassing moments, fooling inspectors, and funny situations. Another man told about an incident on the same job. They had a old-timer on the job who they used as a flagman. They stationed him a half mile from the construction work to wave off the traffic to the other side of the road. The flagman was too far way to see what was going on with the construction. He would bring a chair, his lunch bucket, and something to read when there was no traffic. At the end of the day's work or at night if they worked overtime, one of the men from the construction gang would drive to his station and pick him up. One night the men went back to their hotel and forgot to pick up the old-timer. They found him the next morning, in his same spot, still flagging traffic. He was so used to working overtime he figured they must be working a 24-hour shift.

These stories help to cement the feelings of togetherness among the men. Although many stories are humorous, they relate to problems and difficulties that they all share. Stories foster a sense of group membership, often articulate values and ideas they unconsciously share, and give everyone who participates feelings of comradeship. Following is a conversation that took place in a round-robin fashion one day after work:

A Sewer Rat. Fred said that Harry, his foreman, was a natural sewer rat. Every so often Harry would tell Fred, "Come on, let's take a walk," which meant a walk through a seven or eight foot sewer main to inspect it.

Stealing. This was a favorite subject of Lenny's. He said some days he gets up in the morning and sneaks an extra pair of socks to put in his coat pocket, "just to start the day off right." Lenny mentioned another guy famous for his stealing. On Lenny's birthday the guy stole a box of cigars for him. Then he found out it was the wrong brand, so he took it back, got a refund, and on the way out, stole the right brand.

Charlie. Lenny talked about Charlie, a "hard luck" guy. Charlie was attacked on the Union Road job by a truck driver with a wrench and wound up in a hospital for severe head injuries. On one road job, Charlie got caught in the cab of a back hoe that caught on fire, and just barely got out without being burned alive. On another job Charlie was sent a cherry picker (small crane) that had a busted transmission before it came out on the job. Charlie was blamed for it and was laid off for a week. Lenny recalled that Charlie was sent to Chicago during the blizzard of 1978 to help with the snow removal. Lenny said that he remembered thinking that they'd better not send Charlie because if there was another Chicago fire like the famous one, Joe would sure to be blamed for it, or there might be another St. Valentine's Massacre and Charlie would be one of those massacred. About two months after the conversation, Charlie had a heart attack and died.

The Good Old Days. Timmy and Fred were talking about the "good old days," when men would have to shape up for jobs. The contractors would come around and pick out the men they wanted. They talked about the old union meetings when an apprentice would have to ask for permission to speak. Many of the apprentices were the sons of members, and if they got up to speak at a union meeting their fathers would give them a cuff (smack with a cupped hand). Fred said in the good old days, laborers in the union would vote by lifting their shovels if they wanted to vote aye. Now, Timmy chortled, the union has the meeting stuffed with hard guys who give their neighbors a jab in the ribs and the man responds by saying "A-i-e-e-e!" in pain, up jumps his hand, and the chairman says it's an aye vote.

Everything That Can Be Broken, Has Been. Lenny talked about a guy who was hit by a pile driver and had almost every bone in his body broken. Lenny said the guy had so many plates in him that when it rained he "rusted." This guy was flagging on a road job when a woman ran two barricades and hit him. He was still waving his flag as he went down. When Lenny bent over him, he said, "Don't worry, Lenny, everything that could be broken, has been."

I've Always Wanted To Do That. Harold told about the time he was working on a concrete sidewalk gang. They had just finished a good stretch of work—about 50 feet—and the concrete had just been broom finished and all the joints were struck. Along comes this very old man. He stops at the edge of the newly finished sidewalk, and looks from side to side. Then he looks at the men and with lips pursed and face determined he walks right through the entire length of the concrete sidewalk, leaving his footprints in the fresh concrete. Then, he turns to the men and says, "All my life I've wanted to do that and I never thought I'd get the chance. Now, I've done it and it feels good," and off he goes with a broad grin on his face.

Carmine. Carmine said that once some inspector tried to talk to him. Carmine told him, "See my foreman." The inspector asked, "Who's your foreman?" Carmine answered, "I don't know."

Dirty Sal. The men were talking about "Dirty Sal" who was even dirtier than "Dirty Johnny." Lenny said this man, who was a laborer, always smoked a cigarette that he never took out of his mouth. In the winter, the mucus would run out of his nose and merge with the cigarette. One time Lenny was down in a manhole on a sewer line with Sal. The water in the sewer line was full of fecal matter. When lunchtime came, Sal threw away his cigarette, rinsed his hands in the filthy water, climbed out of the manhole, and sat down to eat lunch. He offered Lenny half his sandwich but Lenny declined.

Frankie. Frankie says, "The other day I knew it was quitting time because my sock slipped down to my toes and it was hurting."

Frenchie. I dropped a piece of pipe and some bum picked it up for scrap. Fred replied, "That was no bum, that was Dirty Sal."

What's a Shovel Worth. Sid: "Al confiscated my shovel." Al: "You're being charged for it." Sid: "Okay, I found a pick. Can I get credit for a pick?" Al: "All right, a pick's worth half a shovel." Sid: "Do you see pointed ears on me?"

Killed By a Flying Shit House. The men were talking about the Niagara Falls power project on which many men were killed. Lenny mentioned one man who was killed by a portable toilet, called a "Johnny-on-the-spot." It was being lowered on to the job site when it slipped and landed on the man. Lenny commented, "What do you tell his wife? Something serious, like 'Your husband was killed by a flying shit house.'"

Dom. Sal told about a laborer, Dom, who was always in the toilet. Sal said Dom sat on the toilet so much he had a ring around his ass. Sal said Dom could somehow sense when the big boss, was coming on the job. All the men would be working when suddenly Dom would start screaming at the other laborers to work faster or he would bawl out the concrete truck driver. Sure enough, at that moment the boss would appear, be impressed with Dom's performance, pat him on the back, and say, "Keep up the good work, Dom," and leave. Sal quipped that the boss must have had a special odor that Dom could pick up.

Poison Ivy. Lenny mentioned that he always picked up poison ivy. All he had to do was "get near the stuff and it would jump up and grab me." Lenny said he was working on a job, surveying in a field full of poison ivy. He had covered himself with gloves and long pants and felt protected. It was a hot day so he took off his shirt. He was still protecting his hands which were down in the bushes. Suddenly, a large black insect landed on his chest. Lenny slammed his opened gloved hand flat against his chest, and yelled, "Gottcha!" His gloves, filled with poison ivy, left their imprint on his chest when the infection broke out. After that he took a ribbing from the rest of the men, who kept slamming their palms against their chest, shouting "Gottcha."

We Always Look Backward. Alan asked, "How come we do so many things looking backward?" Fred shot back, "That way we can see where we came from. We never look ahead, we might get confused."

Labor Trainee. Tim commented about a labor trainee who was laid off. He said the man stood around like a statue so much that he was covered with pigeon shit when he left. Tim said he had to ask the man to lift his feet so he could grade under him. Tim said, "When I asked him to hold a grade string for me, the man said, What, again?"

I Have to Start Stealing. Lenny said he checked his finances and came to the conclusion that the only way he could make ends meet was to start stealing. He said at the rate his wife was spending, it would have to be a grand larceny.

A Big Kiss. During the conversation, one of the gradall operators came in to say goodbye since he had been laid off. Lenny jumped up and gave him a big, smacking kiss on the cheek, and said, "I told you when you left I'd give you a kiss good-bye." Fred yelled to the man, "You'd better get a tetanus shot!"

Keep Your Shovel. After the guy left, Lenny told the rest of the men in the room, "We'll be laying off the next two weeks. Any man who still has his shovel can stay."

I'm Going to Finish the Job. Sid told a story about Bob. Bob was shot in Vietnam and had a bad leg. He was also a fearless person, one of the few men willing to crawl inside a 24-inch pipe for hundreds of feet to check for leaks without the fear of getting stuck or being in a cramped, pitch-black place. Bob was on the Military Road job, in a 24-inch pipe checking for leaks, when he suddenly got a cramp in his leg. He got panicky, thinking he might not be able to crawl out, so he scrambled back out of the pipe. When the boss found out he told Bob he was not to go into the pipe anymore. Bob got angry, started stamping his feet on the ground like an angry bear, and shouted at the boss, "I don't give a fuck if you fire me, I'm going back in that pipe to finish the job."

OCCUPATIONAL PRESTIGE

Job satisfaction comes, in part, from one's belief that his job carries prestige and is important to the community. Construction workers can point to the physical evidence of their work, talking with pride about significant projects they worked on—power plants, thruways, bridges, convention centers, large office buildings, and so on. The larger the project the greater the pride. One of the projects we worked on, the Katherine Cornell Theatre at SUNY, Buffalo, was featured in the trade magazine, *Architectural Forum.* I showed a copy to the men, and as they were looking at it, they described with great pride how they executed some of the work associated with the job.

Construction men like to talk about work feats. Men talk about how many bricks they've laid in a day, or how many thousands of feet of road blacktop or cubic yards of concrete poured. Some tradesmen become famous for their work production. One day I listened to the workers talk about a man who was phenomenal at building manholes. They said that even when this mason became old he could still wear out three laborers trying to keep up with him. One of the supers said he was stuck one day and had to get a manhole built, so he went to see the old mason. The mason told the super to get all the materials at the excavation, get him a laborer, and wait at the hole at 5:00 P.M., after work. The super said he was waiting at the hole at 5:00 P.M. when, to his amazement, a bus pulled up in front of the hole. The bus door flew open and out stepped the old mason, dragging his tools in a bag. He had talked the bus driver into stopping at the manhole. He finished the manhole in two hours, with the super and the laborer feeding him block and mortar.

Construction workers also talk about the arduous and dangerous nature of their work with pride. Work that is dangerous carries prestige because the men who perform it are viewed as special. High steel workers are treated this way. Part of the culture of construction is the satisfaction from doing what is conceived as difficult work, winning out over the elements, and showing persistence in the face of adversity. Construction work is often hard and dirty, requiring one to work in foul weather, breathing in dust, and being soaked to the skin by rain or snow. A construction man's hands are usually swollen and scarred, with a high incidence of broken or missing fingers. Construction workers enjoy the challenge of difficult tasks and the satisfaction that comes from overcoming challenging obstacles.

JOB INSECURITY AS A SOURCE OF DISSATISFACTION

Unemployment is a major source of concern and dissatisfaction among construction workers. During the winter of 1977–1978, on the Elm-Oak Buffalo road project, we had one severe blizzard every two weeks. This caused frequent layoffs and many complaints from the men. Usually, management tries to keep its key people working, even in the winter on days when the weather is too bad for work to continue. Thus, it was a great surprise to us when we were directed to layoff some of our key workers, men who had been with the company 15 or 20 years. One of these men remarked with bitterness when he was laid off,

I came over here to work with the road crew from the building division where I never lost a day; now I get laid off. I've worked through my lunch hours; I'm always on the job an hour early. I'm always pushing to make costs and this is the thanks I get. Fuck the roads division. I'm going to talk to the boss and get back into buildings.

Unemployment compensation is based on the four-day week. For this reason, many of the men ask to get laid off after working a Monday or a Friday. Most construction unions now have supplements to unemployment compensation. Men with 20 to 26 weeks of work for the year are eligible for benefits. One of the carpenters returned to a downtown road project after being laid off for one month. He was kidded about enjoying the time off and became very angry. When asked why he was so high strung, the man replied, "Because I've been off for a month. Christ, I was ready to go to work in a supermarket. Everybody tells me I'm a damn good carpenter but that don't mean shit. This shit's been going on for years. If things don't change I'm going to open a little bar. I don't care how little I make. At least it'll be steady."

The construction industry, along with agriculture, has the highest rate of unemployment. In 1995 the unemployment rate was 11.5 percent; in 1996, it was 10.1 percent. During those years unemployment in agriculture was 11.1 percent and 10.2 percent respectively. Unemployment for all other industries averaged 5.6 percent in 1995 and 5.4 percent in 1996. In other words, construction unemployment averages are double the rate of all other major industries. The unemployment rate for construction laborers was 18.7 percent in 1995. (U.S. Bureau of the Census, 1997, p. 419). Thus, the high hourly wage of the construction man is partially offset by the high rate of unemployment in the industry. John T. Joyce, national secretary of the Bricklayers Union, commented on this aspect of construction work (Joyce, 1973, p. 10):

Just how affluent is the construction worker? Hourly earnings do not give an accurate picture. . . . According to Labor Department studies, the average full-time construction worker works only about 1,500 hours at his trade each year. . . . A major cause of underemployment among building tradesmen, is of course, the tendency to close down construction jobs in bad weather. But other liabilities of this kind of work not only curb a construction worker's earnings but also cause him many other problems. Since construction workers are only employed for a given job or project, they have frequent periods of unemployment between jobs. Unemployment rates in construction are historically double the national figures—even when the economy is strong.

Mike Cherry, an ironworker, tells what weather can do to a construction man's income (1974, p. 78):

In 1970 I worked in New York City from March 1st on. That was a famous year among construction people, because the winter was virtually snowless and the spring was almost without rain. In those ten months I lost a day and a half to the weather. The following year I lost forty-three days, which comes to about $3,400. Thus, in spite of the fact that I worked two months more, I earned about the same.

Unemployment in construction has been a source of concern to the industry as well as to the government. A number of proposals have been offered to control the fluctuations of activity so characteristic of the industry. One suggestion has been to subsidize firms that accelerate rather than reduce their building programs during the winter months (H.U.D. Report, 1973). This is the practice in Norway and Canada. Another proposal is the scheduling of contract awards for the spring of the year so that construction projects can get a good start and maintain high levels of activity and employment (U.S. Bureau of Labor Statistics, 1967). There have been suggestions to help construction workers find other jobs during the winter months. Another idea has been to use operating engineers to run snow-removal equipment in the winter (U.S. Bureau of Labor Statistics, 1970). One suggestion is to steer government construction contracts to officially designated labor surplus areas—those with unemployment rates 30 percent above the national average ("Seasonal Unemployment Remains a Labor Problem," November 7, 1977, p. 3). Some of the suggestions to combat construction unemployment involve technological changes to permit work to continue through winter. Some ideas are: the use of rust-resistant steel that does not require paint; additives in concrete so it can be poured in below-freezing weather; and special methods to heat concrete or masonry.

Job insecurity is a major source of job dissatisfaction among construction workers and should be viewed in combination with all the other factors that make for high job satisfaction in construction. While it is a source of worry and concern, I do not believe it overshadows all the other positive factors that foster satisfaction on the job for construction men and women.

In conclusion, it might be instructive to look at one of the most comprehensive study's on job satisfaction—the 1971 University of Michigan Survey Research Center study, *Survey of Working Conditions*. This study contains the best comparative data assembled to date on job satisfaction. It contains comparisons by age, occupation, personal income, industry, race, occupational group, education, and sex. In the study, "contract construction" had the lowest percentage of "workers expressing negative attitudes toward work"—only 5 percent. The data, by industry was as follows (1971, p. 408):

Industry	Number in Sample	Percent Dissatisfied
Contract construction	123	5%
Manufacturing	381	17%
Wholesale, retail	274	23%
Services	397	12%

8

Overview of the Construction Industry

The behavioral patterns and cultural views of construction workers have been examined. We will now examine these factors within the context of the construction industry, which will show that construction workers' behavior is appropriate for the social organization and technology of the industry.

IMPORTANCE OF THE CONSTRUCTION INDUSTRY

The construction industry employs 5,108,000 tradesmen and tradeswomen. This number represents 40 percent of the skilled workers in the United States listed in the "precision, production, craft, and repair" category, located in the U.S. Statistical Abstract (U.S. Bureau of the Census, 1997, p. 412).

The construction industry is of major importance to the functioning of the United States economy. It is one of the 10 economic indicators that is tracked by the U.S. Commerce Department in predicting the present and future state of the United States economy. Variations in the level and rate of investment in construction is significant in determining total economic activity. In the long run, the volume of investments in buildings, roads, dams, housing, and other structures affects the capacity of our national economy to produce and distribute the goods needed by consumers. Construction accounts for a large percentage of the output of lumber, stone, structural steel, clay, windows, roofing, concrete, blacktop, piping, electrical, plumbing, and heating and air-conditioning supplies and equipment in the country. While construction demand is a derived demand based on decisions outside the industry by government and private industry to invest, investment in construction may be the great harbinger of an impending economic expansion.

Gerald Finkel has singled out certain materials and equipment as key elements in the history and development of the construction industry—wood, steel, concrete, elevators, and falsework (Finkel, 1997, pp. 11–20). Wood has been an important builder's material because it is strong and durable, light, and can readily be cut to fit the requirements on low-rise structures. Wood is used in buildings in the form of timber posts, boards, planks, and decks. It is also used to make ladders, supports, and scaffolds. The bending strengths of wood are powerful and adequate up to six stories. However, wooden beams and joints are not capable of withstanding the stress of high-rise buildings that must resist wind, settling, and heavy weights. Exposure to the elements is also a problem with using wood as a building material. Flammability and the depletion of our forests are both issues regarding the use of wood in modern building and this has led to a substitution of other materials, such as steel (Finkel, 1997, pp. 12–13).

The durability, strength, and fire resistance of steel made up for the differential in the costs of erection compared to wood. Steel provides greater support than wood and can be used in buildings over 100 stories—the Empire State Building and the Twin Towers in New York City are two examples. Steel can be integrated into the core construction of buildings with steel girders supporting concrete flooring and the vertical steel rails for elevators. Steel as a material gave rise to a body of workers as riveters, erectors, and welders (Finkel, 1997, pp. 13–14).

A third key material singled out by Finkel is concrete. Concrete is produced by mixing stone with a cementitious binder such as a mixture of silica and lime. The development of portland cement, which is mixed with stone was an important part of the development of the modern concrete industry, along with the use of reinforcement rods, which are placed in the concrete to give it tensile strength. The hardening of cement around the rebars produces a powerful finished product that can sustain massive weights over wide expanses. The building of concrete plants and the organization of trucking concrete to the job site became an integral part of the construction industry. Contractors sought out concrete laborers, cement finishers, and drivers for skilled and semiskilled positions that provided hundreds of thousands of jobs for men in the concrete end of the construction industry. The industry was also aided by the development of reusable plywood forming systems that enabled floors to be poured on two- or three-day cycles that sped up the erection process of superstructures of buildings (Finkel, 1997, pp. 15–16).

The erection of high-rise commercial and residential structures would not have been possible without the development of the electrically-powered elevator. High-rise construction was useless without vertical transportation. As building heights increased, elevator technology advanced. The 102-story Empire State Building was constructed with elevators capable of moving people skyward at the rate of 1,200 feet per minute, while elevators in the 110-story World Trade Center climb at a rate of 1,800 feet per minute, or nearly three floors per second. Other mechanical and equipment developments were also important along with the elevator—ventilation and air-conditioning systems, electrical power equipment and lighting, plumbing systems, and instrumentation and temperature control systems, as well as others (Finkel, 1997, pp. 17–18).

Falsework is another area that has had to develop as construction advanced. Falsework refers to the temporary construction needed to build a final structure. It consists of scaffolding, ladders, and formwork, and it requires its own special skill requirements and engineering (Finkel, 1997, p. 18). One can see the hoists on the sides of buildings going up that are used to raise materials and personnel. The scaffolding of buildings are giving rise to more efficient and safer systems that are tied together and into the buildings to prevent them from collapsing. Sidewalk bridges are also used to protect the public, as well as providing a platform on its roof for workers to operate from. Then there are the flying forms that are bolted together that can be moved from area to area in the pouring of foundations and concrete floors and walls.

Finkel also singles out other aspects of the construction industry, namely the localized nature of the construction industry, the hand-tool technology, and the nonbureaucratic form of job management and control (Finkel, 1997, pp. 18–19). These aspects have been discussed in detail in previous chapters.

MAIN CHARACTERISTICS OF THE CONSTRUCTION INDUSTRY

Summarized below is an outline of the main technological and organizational characteristics of the construction industry. These characteristics provide the basis for the culture and behavioral patterns that are found on construction projects.

Uncertainty

Risk and uncertainty are major factors in the construction process. These factors are so widespread that the various organizations in the industry such as the general contractors associations, the Civil Engineering Society, architects and construction consultants, and real estate boards, are continually holding conferences on the subject of "Construction and Housing Risks" and how they can be controlled. Every construction project is beset with uncertainty. Will the owner go ahead? Will he receive his financing? Will the labor and materials needed be available during the entire course of the project? Will the project receive zoning board approval? Will the drawings be approved by the local building department? Will the project be opposed or even thwarted by a citizens' lobby, or by a legislature or local city or town council? If the project goes ahead will it be financially successful? Will the project be completed on time?

It takes so long to build most major projects that something unexpected is bound to happen, and it usually does—a strike, a material shortage, an economic recession, inflation, the cutoff of funds, a rash of bad weather, a labor shortage, and even a revolution, as many construction firms in Iran and South America found out.

Even if the project gets through all the preliminary uncertainty, there are the pitfalls in the design process, the bidding process, the awarding of contracts, and the difficulties of completing the project on time. Contractors start projects often without knowing what is in store. Conditions may be quite different from what they saw on the drawings. Contractors may be the low bidder and think they have secured a job only to find out that all the bids are thrown out for one reason or another.

Every construction worker lives with uncertainty because he or she knows that the job has a limited time period, on average one to three years. Construction workers also know that their craft or trade is not needed continuously. They are called to work on a job, perform work, and then asked to leave and return later when the craft is needed again. He or she may or may not then proceed to another project. Flexibility, mobility, and constantly changing job assignments are the way of life for most construction workers.

On any given day when he comes to work, a construction worker may or may not work because of weather conditions. Even if he starts working he may be rained out during the course of the working day. There is also the unpredictability of work assignments. If a machine breaks down he may find himself in another crew, at another location, doing a different task. Often a construction worker does not know what his assignments will be from day to day. If he is a bricklayer, he may be on ground-level one day and 10 stories high on a scaffold the next day.

There are very few repetitious tasks in construction. Flexibility and changeability are the norms; construction workers come to expect it. They accept it because they deal face-to-face with their foremen and superintendents, and changes are explained to them. In addition, they can see how the overall project is progressing and they understand how their work fits into the total pattern of a project. They have a strong notion of where they and their skills fit, so the constant movement and change are things they can understand and to which they can adapt.

Hand-Tool Technology

Construction is one of the few industries in the United States that still relies heavily on hand tools and a handicraft technology. Where else in a major industry do workers own many of their own tools? This does not mean that there are no machines in construction, but most of them are power tools that are held in the hand, like a skill saw. There are pipe cutting and threading machines and power tools like the Hilti, used for shooting fasteners into structures. These are all basically hand tools. The aspect of construction that utilizes engine-driven machines are earth-moving machines, hoisting equipment like cranes and telescopic cherry pickers, and pile-driving machines. There are also machines used for pouring concrete, such as concrete pumps, vibrators, compactor jumping jacks, and troweling machines. All of these, except the concrete pumps, are operated by hand. Most craftsmen are required to provide their own hand tools. They do not own the heavy construction equipment or material-handling equipment, or power tools, but whatever hand tools are needed they provide themselves.

The handicraft technology relates to the craft organization of labor in the construction industry, whereby about 50 skills are organized into 20 craft unions. These skills that are mastered by construction workers are very old, some of them going back to ancient times. A mason from ancient Egypt or medieval Europe would be quite at home on today's building projects. He would be impressed by some of the material-handling equipment, like the Lull used for loading bricks on to scaffold planks, but the actual laying up of masonry units would be quite familiar. The same would be true of the ancient carpenter, who, like his modern counterpart, used saws, planes, hammers, and rulers.

Anyone on or near a construction project will quickly notice the high percentage of pickup trucks owned by the workers. Many of these trucks have custom-built tool boxes, or racks to carry pipe and lumber. Some have small compressors or an oxyacetylene burning and welding outfit. The trucks and tools reflect two things about construction workers—they own their means of production and they can easily go into the contracting business—indeed, many of them do. There are 1.48 million self-employed construction workers in the United States (U.S. Department of Commerce, 1997, p. ii).

Ownership of tools and skills by the craftsman lead construction management to rely on the skilled worker to create the product. Skilled tradesmen assert that they know better than anyone how to perform their work. For its part, management expects the craftsman to perform his job with a minimum of supervision. Management tells the tradesman what, where, and when to produce, and allows the tradesman and tradeswoman to figure out how to do the work. Engineers and architects rely on the craftsman to interpret their plans and carry out their intent. This is in sharp contrast with factory work, where management and the industrial engineer aim to "tell every worker in the corporation exactly how to do his job down to the last detail" (Walker, 1962, p. 136).

The Informal System

Construction management, especially in the home office, is increasingly becoming formalized, with a stress on documenting decisions, writing letters, keeping financial and cost records, and estimating work based on computer programs. This is reflected in the almost three million administrative and office workers in the construction industry. While construction contracting home offices may be formalized, the dominant mode of operations at the job site is still informality. Face-to-face relationships and acceptance of verbal decisions without formal procedures are normal methods of operating a construction project. The formal system assumes that everything is absolutely clear on the plans and specifications, and in the contract. This is hardly ever the case. Every construction project inevitably has extras stemming from the fact that various items of work are not shown on the plans. It is impossible for architects and engineers to put everything on the plans, and contractors will perform items of work without additional cost when the intent of the drawings and specifications clearly indicate that certain work not shown must be done. There are many items that are simply missed because architects and engineers cannot think of everything. They try to cover themselves by using catchall phrases, but contractors are smart enough to qualify their bids or list their exclusions. Projects would never get done on time if every change had to be channeled through formal procedures, or if mistakes were not caught in the field and on-the-spot solutions were not worked out. In addition, many compromises are worked out between workers and management, or workers and architects, to perform the work in a practical way, if not exactly how if was designed by the architect. On one of my projects the architectural firm that designed the drawings did not spell out the proper head details to receive the specified windows. When the windows came in and carpenters began to install them they saw the problem and brought it to the attention of the architect. A meeting was held with the project architect, who said that it was going to be a source of great embarrassment to him personally if the contractor brought out the mistake and asked for an extra to reframe the window heads. Since there were about 500 windows in the building, it was a substantial cost. The architect told the contractor to go ahead and correct the window heads and that he would make sure the contractor would make up the cost by granting him a series of extras. This was not the way to do business, and the contractor had to trust this man to be as good as his word, since he couldn't document the agreement. Call it an informal compromise. As it turned out the architect was a man of his word and the contractor's costs were made whole. Many such compromises are settled on projects, most of them not as big or as risky as this one, but there are a lot of deals made on big projects between contractor and owner, contractor and subcontractor, and contractor and architect. Some architects draw plans that are just plain wrong and cannot be built, then, the tradesman has to solve the problem of how to do the work and achieve the planned result ("Listening to Contractors," 1998, pp. 54–57).

In construction, there is a need for crisis-oriented workers, particularly those directing work in the field. Things happen that require quick decisions—equipment breaks down and men have to be shifted to other work; a wall may start to shift or give way and has to be quickly shored up; a trench in which pipe is being installed collapses; the concrete plant or asphalt plant that was supposed to deliver material breaks down; someone gets hurt; structure steel is the wrong size; windows and elevators are late; a torrential downpour wipes out site work or roofing work for the day; the temperature drops below freezing and concrete for a bridge deck cannot be poured, or a key subcontractor didn't show up. All these things require shifts in plans and decisions that do not permit time to follow formal lines of communications. Supers and foremen have to act on their own. The most difficult decision is when field managers must decide to send all the workers home—they lose a day's pay and the job falls behind.

Construction work is, by and large, an informal, flexible, by-the-seat-of your-pants operation. Managers can draw up impressive bar charts and flow diagrams showing how the work is supposed to progress. These charts are helpful to organize a manager's thinking, but deviations are usual and managers try to prevent such deviations from being massive. Still, jobs get done and most of them finish close to the completion date, but it takes a lot of turning, twisting, and manipulation of plans, and lots of luck with the weather. Projects come close to completion dates because many people are willing to do a lot of bending and compromising. A formalized, regular, step-by-step process is out-of-step and unworkable on most construction projects.

The Subcontracting System

The subcontracting system is an integral, and appropriate, part of the construction industry. It permits the kind of flexibility required for various mixes of contractors and crafts to be mobilized to suit the unique requirements of a particular project. When the project is over, the contractors disperse. Subcontractors make possible the rapid mobilization and demobilization of crafts as changes in the kinds and volume of construction activity varies.

The general contractor cannot do everything. He doesn't have the know-how, the manpower, or the supervision. He must rely on subcontractors. There are far more specialty subcontractors—twice as many—as there are general contractors. The general contractor shares administration and supervision with his subcontractors, which diffuses project administration and causes the network of responsibility to be more horizontal than vertical. The general contractor deals with subcontractors who are independent and involved in other projects. The general contractor must, therefore, request, and sometimes threaten, a subcontractor to get him to perform, but he can't fire a sub as he can his own employees. The subcontractor has a contract and can sue the general contractor if the latter breaks the contract arbitrarily. The general contractor can enforce the terms of the contract, which includes a cancellation clause, but it must be for a good reason, like failure on the part of the subcontractor to prosecute the work or pay his material suppliers, which could cause them to encumber the property with a lien.

Subcontracting fosters a sense of democracy on the job. Every trade maintains its individual importance and standing. Trades must respect each other (since they depend on others) before they can do their own jobs. Even if a contractor is small, he still receives the respect of his associates because his trade is essential to the total construction process. On the Elm-Oak Buffalo road project, the sidewalk subcontractor was so small and weak financially that the general contractor had to buy all his materials and put his men on the general contractor's payroll. The boss worked along with the men in his crew. All the other trades, as well as the inspectors for the New York State Department of Transportation, had the highest respect for this contractor because of the excellent quality of his work, despite the small size of the company.

Subcontracting also leads to family-like relationships between the general contractor and his "family" of subcontractors. Many general contractors use the same group of subcontracting firms over the years. General contractors like to use good subs again. If the relationship is continuous over a protracted period, the general contractor and his subs will often develop a close personal relationship. They will socialize and engage in recreational activities together. Similarly, the workers for each firm will come to know each other and will work well in the field. Many of them will also become close friends. This makes for a trusting and responsible relationship on the project. Good friends do not let each other down, in their private or their work lives.

The Localized Nature of the Construction Industry

Every locality in the United States has its own construction industry. This stems from the nature of the construction product. It is bulky, costly, and uniquely fixed to a particular construction site. Structures are designed to fit on a particular piece of land. No factory can produce office buildings, power plants, schools, dams, or bridges, and then ship the finished project to a site. All large building projects must be constructed where they are fixed in place by a foundation in the ground. No two buildings are ever exactly the same because even if the design is similar they are located on different parcels of land. This is particularly true of commercial structures.

Construction is an industry of small firms. In 1994, there were 620,852 firms in the industry. Only 7 percent of these firms had more than 20 employees. Sixty-five percent of the firms had only one to four employees. Eight-five percent of receipts from contracting originate in the contractors' own home state. Most of these are from the home town or city (U.S. Department of Labor, 1998, pp. 16–20).

Since construction is an industry of small, local firms, almost everyone in the local industry in small towns and small cities knows each other. This includes the labor force, the contractors and subcontractors, the local supply houses and equipment rental companies, and the architects and engineers. The grouping of firms and workers, suppliers and equipment renters, and professionals take on the characteristics of a community. Outsiders are often kept out of the area because there is a limited amount of construction work in every locality and the local community of contractors, workers, and professionals naturally wish to maintain it for themselves. It is in the interest of all parties to do so—the labor unions, contractor employers, suppliers, banks, local architects and engineers, supply houses, and the construction workers.

One of the aspects of the localized nature of the construction industry is that reputation, either good or bad, becomes crucial in the ability of a firm to get business. Most contracts come to contractors through referrals and construction contractors rarely (or never) have to solicit business. They are either bidding on jobs publicly announced in industry newsletters like *The Dodge Reports* (an industry-wide informational newsletter that announces all the jobs going out for bid or being started in each region of the country), or they are getting repeat business from previous clients. Getting a bad reputation for not paying one's suppliers or subcontractors, not finishing a job on time, or doing shoddy work, can be disastrous in the construction industry. A firm that has that kind of reputation is not going to last in the industry. Some contractors are "change order specialists," that is, they spend their energies figuring out ways to wrangle changes out of the owner or general contractor rather than working conscientiously to fulfill their contracts. They, too, become known as con artists and usually do only one job for a general contractor or construction manager. (For a discussion of reputation in relation to minority contractors, see Waldinger, 1996, pp. 278–279.)

THE PRICE OF STRUCTURES

Commercial and industrial construction is unique, differing significantly from the manufacturing, service, and transportation industry. Unlike manufacturing where the producer decides what to make, construction products are determined by the customer. Pricing in construction is also unique. Unlike many industries, which issue a catalogue of their products with accompanying prices, there is no catalogue of buildings or structures. In construction, it is only when the nature of the desired product is determined through designed plans and specifications that it can be priced. Each commercial and industrial building is priced separately and distinctly in the form of a bid for that particular project. Bidding arrangements can vary, depending on whether the contract is let on a lump-sum, cost-plus, upset figure, or construction management basis. Many projects have select bidders' lists prepared by the owner's architect. Contracts let on a competitive basis have provisions for extras and credits and other contingencies that might arise during the construction period. Pricing is different for home construction. In home building usually there are prepared catalogues of products with a range of pricing before the homes are built. Developers perfect their products to the point where they can pinpoint all the costs that go into their homes, with all the alternates and changes that might be desired by the customer. Home building also differs from commercial and industrial building in that the producer often creates the product and then tries to market it to consumers. In most industrial and commercial buildings, customers are lined up in advance and they determine the layout of the buildings to suit their requirements.

Estimating construction jobs are now done with the help of computers. For example, Lotus has a software program that can spit out an estimate based on simplified inputs such as square footage of floor area, room sizes, exterior construction, square footage of walls, cubic footage of building, type of heating and air-conditioning system, electrical loads and numbers of light fixtures, outlets and switches, and types of finishes. There are also manuals, such as the Means Estimating Guide, that provide detailed information on labor, material, equipment, and overhead costs for any type of work or material that goes into buildings and structures. There are also separate manuals for commercial, industrial, and residential buildings.

A project in New Haven, Connecticut, was planned to build a new structure for the Travelers Insurance Company. I was sent there to find a general contractor and I finally settled on an old-line firm that had built the Yale Bowl. I sat down with the president of the company to go over his bid and compare his take-off with mine. His price was higher than my estimate and I wanted to see if I could negotiate him down to our budget. My take-off was based on each trade—an amount for concrete, masonry, structural work, and carpentry. I used the 16-part breakdown of all buildings that has become a standard in the industry, including the same divisions that architects used in drafting their specifications. When I sat down with the older gentleman (he was 25 years my senior), he removed a legal-sized yellow pad out of his briefcase. His estimate was contained within the pages of that yellow pad. Unlike my estimate based on trades and the 16-part typical breakdown, the New Haven general contractor had taken off the job sheet by drawing sheet. There were about 100 drawings, including the mechanicals, so he had 100 estimates, which he collated. He looked at each item on each drawing and assigned a value to it. He picked up every little detail and note on every drawing, something that I did not do, so naturally his estimate was higher than mine. But it was miraculously close to my estimate, close enough so that we both adjusted our numbers and I gave him the job.

What impressed me about the New Haven gentleman was the hands-on, almost loving care that he took to figure the work. He built the structure as he figured it, which is what every good estimator does because in order to estimate labor you have to determine how they are going to do the work, then you add a factor for difficulty for those items that are special or difficult to execute. Something must then be added for impossible-to-build items that architects sometimes include in the plans. I had great admiration for that New Haven contractor. The way he produced that estimate showed the knowledge and skill that he had accumulated in the industry. It may have been old-fashioned, but it retained the spirit of craft and workmanship that no computer print-out could match, no matter how superior the efficiency and time-saving aspects. I gave the job to that contractor and he produced the building on time and within the agreed budget. We moved Travelers Insurance Company into that building when they wished to move in, and I gave the contractor another job in New Haven a year later.

STAGES OF THE CONSTRUCTION PROCESS

The construction process passes through various stages. Assuming that all of the preplanning and financial arrangements are accounted for, there are four main stages in construction:

1. First there is the client, public or private, who decides he wants or needs a particular structure built. In rare cases, the client acts as his own designer and contractor, but normally, he will hire such services.

2. Next, the client retains an engineer or architect to design and estimate the cost of construction. The engineer advises the client on what the structure must contain to meet the client's needs. If the project is particularly complex or specialized, the architect will use his own consulting experts. These, in turn, will help design those aspects pertaining to their specialty. The engineer, architect, or specialty consultant will usually oversee the construction to make sure it is in accordance with his intended design.

3. Once a proposed project is set forth in plans and specifications, it is advertised for competitive bids. Some contracts are negotiated, but this is not common. Competitive bidding usually takes 30 to 60 days. In some cases, such as sewer and utility work or road building, general contractors can undertake the entire job themselves and formulate bids on their own. Most other construction does not conform to this pattern. Some

general contractors might account for 30 to 40 percent of the work if they do their own carpentry, concrete work, masonry, and structural steel. General contractors must secure bids from other trades and suppliers before they can submit their own bids. Some specialty subcontractors in turn subcontract some of their work, and they too must take bids from others. For example, a heating, ventilating, and air conditioning subcontractor will usually have to take bids from equipment suppliers, sheet metal subcontractors, temperature control subcontractors, and insulation subcontractors. All of this solicitation of subbids extends the time period necessary for the bidding process. At every level, careful estimates must be made before the final figure is submitted. Bidding costs are high and must be included in the annual costs of doing business in the construction field.

Competitive bidding can have its drawbacks. The pressures of competition depress the bids and may lead a contractor to substitute an inferior product for the one specified. He may try to avoid union labor. A contractor with a low bid may turn to fly-by-night subcontractors who are willing to work at any price but are unqualified to perform the work. This can lead to subcontractor failures, which happened once to a hospital job in Florida that I worked on as project manager. The company I worked for had bid the job way too low, about $1 million too low. In order to make up the money the company shopped all the subcontractors and selected the lowest bid, even if the contractors were not the most responsible or the most qualified. We used up three roofers on the job and each one was worse than the next. We finally ripped up the entire roof and started from scratch because the roofer we used (from Tennessee) did not take Florida weather into account and trapped moisture under the roof, ruining it completely. That error cost the company a bundle. We then pushed the concrete work, demanding impossible production each day in the pouring of the floors and columns. The columns and floors were flawed. The floors had to be flash-patched, which cost hundreds of thousands of dollars, and the columns had to be dressed to make them look square, costing even more money. Bid bonds keep out unqualified bidders, but it does not prevent a successful general contractor from shopping for unrealistically low prices. Contractors try to protect against these practices by forming associations, but many firms do not belong to them. Fly-by-night contractors spring up constantly since it takes little capital and it is relatively easy for small specialty contractors to get into the construction industry. Ultimately, it is the construction worker, through his trade union, who have established some uniformity through the imposition of uniform labor rates and standards of workmanship for a particular trade in a particular locality in the country (Slichter, Healy, and Livernash, 1960).

4. The fourth step in the building process is to build the structure for the price stipulated in the contract. The owner will designate an engineer or architect representative to oversee the project in the field to make sure work is performed in accordance with the plans and specifications. The general contractor will assign a project manager and a staff to run the construction work and coordinate the activities of all the subtrades. Monthly payments are made to the contractor to permit him to pay his subcontractors and suppliers and to meet his own monthly labor and overhead costs. At the conclusion of the project, the engineer or architect prepares a punch list of incomplete or faulty items of work that the general contractor and his subcontractors must complete or rectify. The owner withholds a certain percentage from each payment to guarantee that the contractor will have an incentive to complete all work properly since he will not collect his final payment until he satisfies the owner and his representatives. If contractors have

a lot of these 10 percent retentions outstanding it can cause him to go bankrupt. When the structure and all of its systems are accepted by the owner, and the contractor has secured from the local building department a Certificate of Occupancy that attests to the suitability of the structure for occupancy, then a date is selected for the owner or tenant to move in. Final payment then is made to the contractor. Most contracts have a one-year guarantee clause that requires the contractor to repair or correct any defects that may show up during that period. At the end of the first year of occupancy, if all corrections have been made, all contractual obligations are deemed to have been met. Some components of the building, mostly equipment like boilers, air-conditioning equipment, or electrical switchgear may have a longer warrantee period on material only. If everything goes well and the owner is satisfied, this is a plus for the contractor, since he depends on reputation and letters of recommendation from clients in order to convince other owners to give him work. A general contractor or a specialty contractor with a reputation for bad work or being late in delivering a building is not likely to last very long in the construction industry, which is localized and in-group oriented and where good and bad reputations are known to the major players in the local construction community.

THE LABOR FORCE

Eighty percent of the labor force in construction are blue-collar workers. The building construction labor force is composed of more than 20 crafts and many more specialties. Many contractors directly hire only one or two of those crafts. The number of workers and crafts hired depend on the type of work and the geographic area in which the contractor operates. A number of new specialties have appeared in the construction industry in recent years. A number of new products and new materials have been introduced in the construction field, particularly in the finish trades, and these have led to new specialties: examples include raised computer floors and electronic telephone systems.

Finding a job in construction is relatively simple when construction activity is high. Some projects usually are starting as others are finishing, and some contractors are hiring as others are laying off. The amount of time off for the worker between jobs may be large or small, depending on the amount of construction in the area. Seasonal unemployment, however, is ever-present in certain trades, even in years of high construction activity. As the rate of activity declines between November and March, workers are being hired for new projects at a slower rate than other workers are being laid off from projects approaching completion.

Workers are ordinarily hired by supers and foremen, who select applicants either at the job site or by contacting the office of local unions who represent the needed crafts. Construction workers are subject to layoffs when jobs are completed, or temporarily when their work is interrupted on a project and they are told to return at some future time when their services will again be needed. Each trade group comes to the job, performs its portion of the work, and leaves, as certain trades peak while others decline at varying rates. The use of the labor force requires constant adjustments and jockeying of the supply of men to mesh one trade with another. If subcontractors do not respond in time with sufficient men when they are required it can hold up and adversely affect an entire project.

Many construction workers do not expect to work permanently for one contractor. Compared with industrial workers, almost twice as many construction workers will be likely to work for more than one employer in the course of the year (U.S. Bureau of Labor Statistics, 1990, p. 6). They are more attached to their trade than to any employer. Knowing the nature of their industry, they take it for granted that they must be prepared to move, not only from site to site, but from city to city. Construction workers sometimes feel it necessary to migrate to areas with better long-term employment prospects, areas such as large cities like New York, Chicago, and Los Angeles. For union members such a move involves transfer of membership. Like other unions, building trades are organized through locals, each having jurisdiction over a designated geographical area. A member moving elsewhere usually can exchange his membership card for a card in a local union. Thereafter, he is a member in the new local union. Should he return to his previous place of work, he must obtain another transfer. Sometimes when a contractor has a need for a certain trade that is in short supply, he must go to the local and ask for permission to bring in men from outside the jurisdiction. I was project manager on a large project for a New Jersey pharmaceutical company. The windows were designed with limestone lintels and sills and we could not find enough masons skilled in setting limestone. The local union refused to let us bring in men from outside New Jersey and we were forced to seek the help of a non-mason building trade union leader who had the political clout to convince the mason's local to let us bring in men from Pennsylvania.

A construction worker usually leaves an area as a matter of choice, although there are exceptions. When a construction project is undertaken in a distant locality, comparatively few of the needed workers may live within reasonable commuting distance. When general construction activity is high, employers have difficulty manning isolated construction projects. When general construction activity is low, men with family responsibilities must choose between unemployment at home or a relatively steady job in a distant area.

The construction labor force is characterized by a high degree of trade specialization. This creates the need for a substantial degree of interdependence between crafts, requiring a constant shifting of the labor force on and off the projects. Employers greatly value the ability to hire and layoff men as job conditions demand. Equally important is the ability to hire men at a predetermined wage scale, which prevents the profit on a job from being eaten up by wage changes after a bid price is established. The flexibility that the contractor requires translates into job insecurity for the construction worker. Thus, he turns to his union to limit the effects of job insecurity.

Construction workers have a reputation for stealing. Every construction site is filled with materials and supplies that are tempting to anyone doing work in their homes. There are such items as floor tile and carpet, paint, hardware and locks, electrical receptacles, switches and fixtures, faucets, fans, bricks, and blocks and many other items useful to the homeowner. Contractors keep these items under lock and key in various trailers or in rooms provided by the general contractor, but trailers and rooms can be broken into. Some contractors try to control the thefts by using spot checks of the trunks of cars of workers leaving the job site. The problem with thefts is not so much the cost of the stolen items as the lost time in reordering new materials.

On our New Jersey transit job in Newark, New Jersey, someone stole a supply of aluminum window mullions that affected the windows on three floors. No one could have had any use for these mullions since they were custom-made for large office windows, so the thief apparently stole them to sell them for scrap. It was a critical item that held up the completion of the window installation for a whole month. We never knew whether there really was a theft. The contractor told us that the window mullions were found "missing" when the men went to install the windows. Whether they were really missing or whether the contractor was using the so-called theft to buy more time for himself we never found out. He might not have ordered enough mullions to complete the job. For an extended discussion of stealing among construction workers, see Riemer (1979, pp. 112–114).

Two cases of stealing follow. We were working on a road job in a major city. We had to install a storm water system in the streets in a location where the power company had its underground cables. The power company was paid to move their cables, but before they could remove them, four men working for our company in the road gang had their own ideas about disposing of the cables. One night these men backed up a bulldozer to one of the power company's manholes, attached a chain to the cables, and pulled out a bank of cables that stretched one full block from one manhole to another. Next, they cut up the copper and sold it for scrap. The power company estimated that their loss was in the neighborhood of $10,000. The power company confronted our boss with the theft. He did not argue and immediately wrote a check for $10,000 to the power company. He summoned the four men he suspected to his office, and with little difficulty got them to admit to the theft. He couldn't fire them because, after all, one of the men was his own brother, and another was the brother of the local "godfather." All he could do was dress them down and make them feel stupid for what they did. He did not make them give back the money. When he talked about the incident later he usually had a smile on his face.

Another incident of stealing concerned a carpenter who was one of the best craftsmen around. This man was a prolific gardener and he needed some bricks to edge one of his gardens. He took some bricks off the job in his trunk without asking the super's permission. The super was a stickler about men stealing and when he found out he blew his top. He immediately fired the carpenter and never spoke or had anything to do with the guy, someone he knew for at least 20 years. The super allowed no exceptions, even among friends or for a man he had known a long time. That was one of the reasons why he enjoyed the highest respect among the men he led, as well as the company that employed him.

CONSTRUCTION UNIONS

The peculiar economic and employment conditions in construction have brought contractors and unions into a more intimate relationship than that found in many other industries. Collective bargaining agreements are area wide, covering contractors and workers in a particular locality or region. This guarantees a continuing relationship between union and employer that is sometimes more long-lasting than the one between workers and employers.

As previously noted, flexibility is of critical importance to the contractor's need to expand or contract rapidly as conditions change on construction projects, or as the local market for construction expands or contracts. The craft union functions to support this flexibility of labor supply to the contractor and thus helps to stabilize the industry. Unions enforce standards of work and compensation, run the apprentice training programs for the crafts, and refer workers to contractors upon the latter's request. At the same time, it allows the employment relationship between contractors and construction worker to remain flexible and variable in response to changing market conditions. The craft union allows flexible employment relationships to exist for the skilled work force while maintaining stability of the industry through its enforcement of uniform wage rates and standards of workmanship. In today's political climate, unions have been criticized for restricting the rights of workers and for interfering with the prerogatives of employers. But in the construction industry, lack of unions in many areas can be detrimental to the pursuit of construction work. On a hospital project in Florida, the lack of unions in the area was a serious obstacle to finding competent contractors.

In an unstable industry subject to wide swings in activity during the business cycle, construction unions function to provide a stable source of skilled craft labor for contractors while preserving job opportunities for workers. One of the mechanism through which this is achieved is the union hiring hall. Craft unions provide a placement service through their hiring halls that benefit both contractors and workers. When a construction worker is looking for a job, he or she visits former employers at job sites and contacts supers or foremen he has worked with before. If this does not lead to a job, he resorts to the union hiring hall. The hiring hall serves as a central pool of labor for each craft or trade. The craft union acts (through the hall) as a clearinghouse for craftworkers in their jurisdiction. To secure their central place in the industry, unions strive for a monopoly position through the closed shop and an exclusive hiring hall arrangement. This has been met with employer resistance in many parts of the country, particularly in the South, and large portions of the construction industry today carry on work with nonunion workers.

As stated previously, construction operations involve the movement of firms and the hiring of qualified workers from project to project as new work is undertaken. The flow of any firm's work may not be continuous, since the securing of new jobs may involve periods of inactivity. Once a contract is awarded, the general contractor hires labor and subcontractors to perform work as required by the successive stages of construction. The subcontractors involved must plan their work to mesh with other trades and the overall schedule of the general contractor. When each stage is complete, the labor force leaves for another job or is laid off. The general contractor seldom maintains more than a small permanent crew of key men. Contractors depend on the unions to supply the skilled craftsmen as needed on short notice. The union functions to collect information about projects in the area and employment requirements, and dispatches men to projects. Unions try to distribute work fairly when work is scarce. Contractors find that hiring from the union hall is a distinct advantage. In most cases, the skills and experience of men sent by the union will meet the necessary standards. If men are sent who are not competent the contractor has the right to reject them and ask the business agent to send others. There is no requirement to retain a particular worker if he proves unsuitable or unqualified.

There are risks for employers who use a closed-shop, hiring-hall setup. The unions may not, in fact, have qualified men in the hall. They may not give the contractor an opportunity to ask for men he has employed previously to his satisfaction. Unions often employ a system of rotation, which serves to protect their less qualified members. They may use a system of favorites such as workers close to or related to the incumbent administration. Contractors who give the union trouble may get all the "butchers." The union may try to strengthen its bargaining position by limiting entry of new members into their ranks. In 1998, there was a strike of pipe fitters affecting jobs in New Jersey. The issue was that the union refused to take in qualified men off the street, whereas the contractors wanted to get men into the union (and into their employment) they knew were qualified. For all of these reasons, many contractors, while agreeing to the closed shop, insist on the right to do their own hiring or use the union's hiring hall as an option.

Whether contractors accept the union hiring hall or not, the closed-shop principle is a benefit to contractors and workers in regions where it is the rule. By placing a wage floor under the competitive forces at work in the industry, it prevents competition from getting out of hand and leading to low-ball prices among competing contractors. It also lends an element of stability to the industry which might otherwise be lacking. A uniform wage rate throughout a local market area is advantageous. Each contractor can submit only one bid and is presumably ignorant of the bid prices submitted by others. A major factor in the costs of each competing contractor is the total of wages paid for each trade. If all contractors know that their competitors must pay the same wage rate, this removes a large item from the sphere of competition. In the absence of unions, there is little reason to believe a uniform wage rate for a particular skill would prevail. Contractor competition based on differential wage rates could become intense, and the resulting instability would work to the detriment of all involved in the construction industry.

Not all crafts, sectors, or geographic areas in the United States are unionized. Union membership in the construction industry has fallen between 1983 and 1996 from 27.5 percent of the employed wage and salaried workers to 18.5 percent. A comparison of the median weekly earnings shows that union workers average $742 per week, while nonunion workers averaged $464 in 1996. Most of the nonunion construction workers are employed in the housing portion of the construction industry and most of the unionized members work in the commercial and industrial sectors of the construction industry. However, the numbers of unionized workers in the building trades have shown a steady decline since 1975. For example, bricklayers fell from 143,000 to 84,000; carpenters from 700,000 to 378,000; electrical workers from 856,000 to 679,000; laborers from 475,000 to 352,000; plumbers from 228,000 to 220,000; sheetmetal workers from 120,000 to 106,000. (For these figures see U.S. Bureau of the Census, 1997, pp. 440, 442).

The construction unions in the United States still have the Davis-Bacon Act, something they consider an important protection to their wages and conditions. The 65-year-old Davis-Bacon Act was sponsored by Republican members of Congress and signed by Republican President Herbert Hoover. Its philosophy is to prevent the eroding of the living standards of millions of construction workers and is as valid today as it was when the law was enacted in 1931. Local conditions are the touchstone of prevailing wage laws. On each government project subject to the act, successful contractors must pay their workers the prevailing wage and benefit norms in the area. Contractors submit their bids, knowing their competitors must also pay at least these minimum wage and benefit levels. Davis-Bacon uses the existing private construction market as a yardstick for setting wages and benefits. It requires that federal contractors live up to these standards. The prevailing wage is not the same as the union wage. The U.S. Department of Labor determines the prevailing wage rate for each job classification required for a construction project by surveying current wages and fringe benefits paid in the locality. Union construction workers point to the act as an important factor in protecting their wages and benefits, stimulating training, providing opportunities for minority employees, and boosting safety and health in the industry. In the face of the decline of unions in the construction industry, Davis-Bacon remains as an important law that construction unions support with all their will and resources. Besides fighting to preserve the act, unions are trying to create and protect union jobs by using their pension funds to finance private construction. By investing their union funds in mortgages for private construction, the unions achieve two things. First, they can make a 10 percent return on their investment. Second, they can use the leverage of their financing funds to insist that the construction that uses their funds be performed with union labor. Since construction unions, like many other unions, have enormous sums of money in their pension fund treasuries they can begin to use these monies to help create and preserve union jobs. It is a new concept and one that may spread throughout the country as construction unions seek new and creative ways to preserve jobs and invest in their own industry ("Unions Finance Construction," 1998, pp. 41–42).

Masons at work on brick wall

Vibrating concrete

Setting reinforcing bars for concrete pour

Pouring concrete with concrete pump

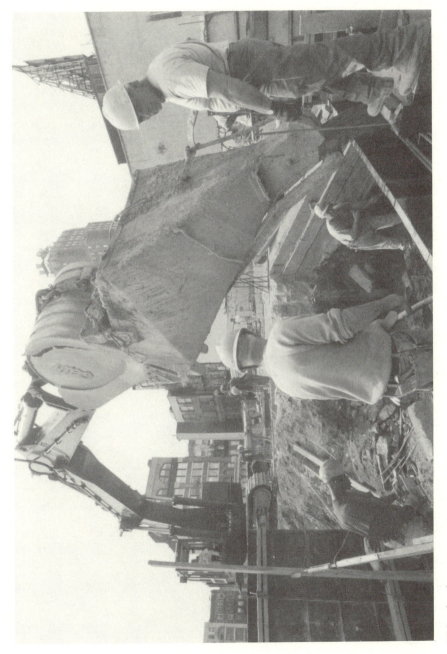

Using bucket to pour concrete

Screeding newly poured concrete

Troweling concrete with power trowel

Building forms for a building foundation made of concrete

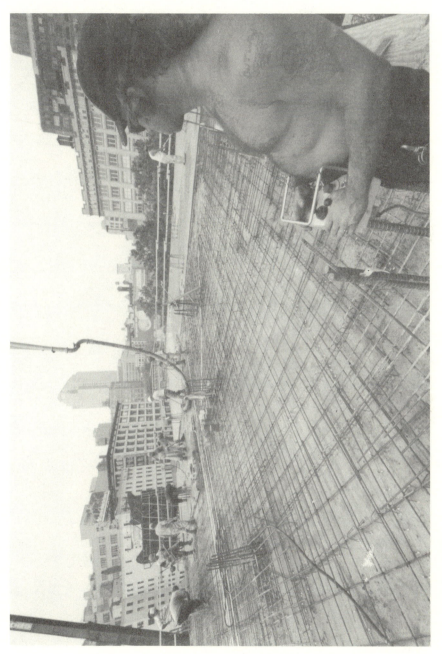

Rebars in a floor slab

Welding steel

Woman worker using concrete vibrator machine

Woman worker using power chipper

9

WOMEN IN CONSTRUCTION

Men and women rarely work in the same jobs in the same workplaces. Most men work in jobs only with other men; this is certainly true in construction. Most women work in jobs only with other women. This pertains to offices, schools, hospitals, and other places that women have traditionally been a majority. Job-level segregation by sex, although less common now than in the past, continues to be the norm rather than the exception in workplaces (Tomaskovic-Devey, 1993, p. 3).

Sex segregation at work is linked to sex inequalities in the labor force. Women tend to earn substantially less than white men and white men tend to have advantages in their access to the most desirable jobs. In the construction industry, where family connections are the key to access into the industry, white men usually have fathers, brothers, and uncles who are already in the trade or the union and are instrumental in getting them into the apprenticeship program or the union. Women normally do not have these relationships, which makes it extremely difficult for them to get into the industry. Their only access usually is through some kind of training program that is associated with affirmative action regulations that force the contractor or the union to hire a certain percentage of women because of the equal opportunities regulations associated with public works. Jobs that have high prestige and power over other workers, that are relatively autonomous such as crafts in construction, are more likely to be filled by white men. Although there has been some erosion of white men's advantages in the workplace over the last two decades, they still remain substantial. If sex segregation and the resulting inequalities in the workplace is to be challenged, it will require reeducating the behavior of employees, managers and employers who perpetuate the segregation, as in the construction industry (Tomaskovic-Devey, 1993, pp. 3–4). In the construction industry it will also require changes among contractors and unions, and within the public and private organizations that give out construction contracts.

In the last 20 years women have broken the barriers to their entry into the domi-
nantly male construction industry. Women have entered the construction industry
both as employees and as employers and contractors. While their numbers are still
small as a percentage of the total, their absolute numbers are significant. In 1996,
there were 796,000 women in construction (U.S. Bureau of Labor Statistics, 1996).
The breakdown of women in construction by employment are as follows:

- Administrative support: 412,000, or 51.8 percent
- Managerial and professional specialty: 227,000, or 28.5 percent
- Precision, production, and craft: 97,000, or 12.2 percent
- Operators, fabricators, and laborers: 49,000, or 6.2 percent

Women constitute 3.8 percent of the construction workers engaged in productive work on the job site, and they are only 2 percent of the well-paid construction
trades such as plumbers, electricians, carpenters, and so on, despite federal
legislation and regulations designed to increase their numbers. Thus, there is still a
long way to go before women become a significant factor on the construction job.
The Chicago Women in Trades organization has proposed as a goal for construction projects with budgets over 75 million that the number of work hours of
women laborers reach 30 percent, apprentices 25 percent, and journey-level 10
percent (Chicago Women in Trades, 1992, p. 26).

Why should women want to enter a field like construction, which is a traditionally male-dominated field where the worst male chauvinist behavioral traits are
present? Bad language, naked female pictures, sexual harassment, and mean-spir-
ited attitudes toward women on the job are regular features on most construction
projects. Why should any woman want to subject herself to work in such a bad environment from her point of view?

One answer is that construction work is well paid, even for the unskilled laborer;
it is highly paid for the skilled craftsperson. For women trying to raise a family, this
is a very attractive feature. Cynthia Long, who worked as an electrician for over 19
years, including two years as electrical superintendent on the World Financial
Center in New York City, said that when she looked at the possibilities for various
careers, she saw women spending a lot of money getting an education to become a
teacher or a nurse and all of them were very low-paid. The wages in construction
was one of the attractions for her (Eisenberg, 1998, p. 10). Another factor that
would attract anyone to the industry is that it is a place where one can learn and
practice an interesting craft. For anyone who likes to work with his or her hands,
construction is a rewarding experience. A third factor is that construction work
provides the satisfaction individuals gain from seeing material, objective embodiments of their efforts. When a building is completed almost every construction
person who worked on it takes pride in its new existence. Lorraine Bertosa, a carpenter, put it this way, "Carpentry is concrete—it's so tangible! There's something
good about that. . . . You have this thing you can touch and see and experience"
(Eisenberg, 1998, pp. 10–11). It was the collective efforts of the tradespersons who

brought it into being. Summing up, it is high wages, the chance to learn an interesting craft, and the job satisfaction of creating that make construction work attractive to women who desire to enter the industry. Thus, it is not surprising that many women wish to find work in the industry and have entered it.

There are two competing theories regarding why women wound up in certain occupations. One theory is that job and occupational segregation of women results from job queues, that is, women's preferences for certain kinds of jobs. The other theory is that employers' preferences for particular types of workers has resulted in women being segregated or concentrated in certain occupations like teaching and nursing (Reskin and Roos, 1990; Tolbert and Moen, 1998, pp. 168–194).

We can see both factors operating in the construction industry. In the past, women have avoided the construction industry because they identified it as a predominantly male province and they would have to deal with men dedicated to macho behavior and male dominance. They were not wrong, unfortunately, as the following experiences show. The second factor was even stronger, that is, the concerted effort of construction employers, unions, and construction workers to keep women out of the industry. In addition, employers, unions, and construction workers have driven women out of the industry after they had entered it. It was only when the federal government got into the act with affirmative action legislation, requiring contractors who were doing public work to hire a certain percentage of women, that females entered the construction industry, though the numbers are still small.

Are there drawbacks or unpleasant features for women in construction work? Yes, there are. Construction work is often dirty, dangerous, and physically exhausting. Strength plays a role in productivity and safety. The physical capability to handle the job is a serious issue for tradeswomen. Pre-apprenticeship programs designed for women have often included a component on building physical strength and endurance. Many women work out to make sure they are in shape to do the job. However, the increased use of prefabricated and new materials, such as plastic pipe replacing cast iron, and the increased use of improved mechanical lifting devices, have reduced the relative importance of brawn (Eisenberg, 1998, pp. 129–130).

The unions have always fought against making workers lift overly heavy weights or working unsafely. But once women entered the industry they used heavy lifting chores to pressure women into leaving the industry, instead of protecting their own male backs along with those of females. Paulette Jourdan, an apprentice plumber on her second day on the job, was assigned to work with 10-foot lengths of four-inch cast iron pipe. When she went to one end to pick up the pipe, her journeyman partner said that he was picking up a length by himself and she had to do the same. Normally, plumbers will carry four-inch cast iron with a man at each end. Paulette weighed 105 pounds and the pipe weighed 90 pounds, but she got it up on her shoulders, and over the next four months, she got stronger. By the time they had her up before the apprenticeship committee and tried to claim that she couldn't handle four-inch pipe, she was already carrying it down basements and told them so. Later, she found out that plumbers are not required to carry four-inch cast iron by themselves (Eisenberg, 1998, pp. 133–134).

Women in construction must like working outdoors in all kinds of weather. Construction is not steady work since everyone gets laid off when a project is completed, and it requires mobility and constantly looking for new work as each job is completed. It also requires a long period of training before a worker is ready and able to perform as a craftsperson and command high wages. Add to this the entire range of special problems that women find in construction (detailed below), and it is not surprising that women make up only 3.8 percent of construction workers in the field. Their numbers are kept down by the push of some in the industry who try to keep them out, and by the pull of women who drop out (or do not want in) because of the problems they face. Many women become tired of coping with all the hassles and not being allowed to just do their work.

There is an organization in existence, the National Association of Women in Construction (NAWIC), that was founded in 1953 to advance the causes of all women in construction, from the skilled trades to business ownership. NAWIC has a membership of 6,000, with chapters in 47 U.S. states, three Canadian provinces, and Australia and New Zealand. NAWIC provides a quarterly magazine for its members that details the activities of women in construction in all parts of the country. The existence of such an organization is a reflection of the rising strength of women in construction that carries the prediction that their influence and numbers should grow in the future. However, women must overcome many obstacles before they find a strong place in the construction industry. Women can, however, make their own contribution to the industry. Gay Wilkinson was told by her instructor in a welding training program that he found that women were assets as welders because they were more patient and more skillful in the long run than most men. Gay was able to prove to her partner that she was willing to take chances and that she could squeeze into places working on boilers that he couldn't. Finally, he asked her to go for coffee. For three weeks before that no one except the general foreman spoke to her (Eisenberg, 1998, pp. 15–18).

Entry into the Industry

Women who enter the construction trades encounter difficult working conditions. Tradeswomen in surveys, questionnaires, and interviews describe discrimination in hiring, layoffs, training, and treatment by construction unions. They speak of hostile work environments and isolation from other women. They relate as almost routine incidents of sexual harassment ranging from unwelcome sexual remarks to sexual touching and even assaults. Racism represents additional burdens for African-American women in construction. Conflicts between work and family present problems for tradeswomen, as they do for many other women in the workplace. In interviews and focus groups women who have left the trades point to a combination of factors such as isolation from other women to sexual harassment as the most likely influences in their decision to leave their trade. Many women leave because they become tired of working in a world that was traditionally reserved for men. Still, many women have coped with the hostile construction environment and enjoy the work itself, as attested by the 150,000 women on construction sites today. These women believe that they should not have to develop strategies for coping, but should be judged on their ability to perform the work they are assigned to do.

Women who have tried to enter the skilled, well-paid construction trades have run up against tremendous resistance. Despite federal programs that prohibit gender discrimination and set goals for hiring tradeswomen and recruiting female apprentices (6.9 percent in 1981), women make up only 3.8 percent of the construction work force in the field. Although there are federal guidelines that prohibit sexual harassment and unequal treatment on the job, the working life of tradeswomen remains difficult. Women have tried to get into the unionized sector of the construction industry because it offers higher wages, safer conditions, and better benefits packages than the nonunion sector. In the skilled trades, unions are more highly regarded for the quality of their training programs, which are funded by members' dues and the contributions of contractors. It was the union jobs and apprenticeship slots that were targeted by efforts of the government to bring women into the industry (Eisenberg, 1998, p. 22).

Many women state that without federal affirmative action they would never be able to get into construction. Since contacts are essential to entry into construction, women are at a disadvantage as their previous absence in the industry has left them with none of the networks possessed by male relatives of men working in the industry and having positions in the construction unions. Male relatives find out about positions in advance, and before a woman has a chance to apply the jobs are gone (Eisenberg, 1998, pp. 26, 33, 36, 56, 200).

SEXUAL HARASSMENT

Sexual harassment in various forms is a fact of working life for many construction tradeswomen. Women's complaints include sexual assault, being touched in sexual ways, working around pictures of naked and near-naked women, and unwanted sexual remarks. Women tell of pranks, the spreading of rumors, threats of physical harm, and more subtle forms of sexual harassment such as staring at their breasts. Women have had condoms put on their car aerials, oil poured in their coat pockets and their tools welded to their work benches. In a survey of tradeswomen in Chicago, 88 percent reported pictures of naked and partially-naked women on the job; 83 percent experienced unwelcome sexual remarks; and 57 percent were touched or asked for sex (Chicago Women in Trades, 1992, pp. 6, 12).

Women working on construction jobs face the dilemma of constant sexual harassment in subtle or crass ways, and then having to deal with it. Many women complain but their complaints are either ignored or they are considered troublemakers. Other women try to deal with harassment head-on by confronting their tormentors and trying to "tough-it-out." But when the men on a project gang up on a woman or play mean tricks there is not much a woman can do about it individually. If the union or the construction company refuses to make it clear that sexual harassment will not be tolerated and threaten to discharge men who practice it, tradeswomen will have a difficult time coping with sexual harassment. Many women quit in the face of constant intimidation; some try to transfer to another job. Those who stay hope that with time and patience the harassment will cease and the male construction workers will accept them on their merits and for their work.

Yvonne Valles joined the painters union as a first-year apprentice. She was hanging vinyl wallpaper at a hotel in Los Angeles, and within the first two weeks on the job she was sexually harassed by her foreman. The foreman and a couple of other painters would talk explicitly about women all the time. They also left magazines of naked women in the bathroom that Yvonne had to use. They harassed her from day one and they thought it was funny. There was also an 18-year-old apprentice who stuck a Polaroid picture in front of her face—a picture of a young woman laying down with her legs open. She told him to get lost and later told the head of the apprentice school what was going on, but nothing ever happened. She was told, "You know, Yvonne, I can report this but it might not be good for you." Yvonne came to the conclusion that women that file lawsuits against their companies wind up getting blackballed (Eisenberg, 1998, pp. 74–75).

Harassment is not only sexual. Men try to frighten women into leaving by injuring them. Karen Pollak, a carpenter, had a sledge hammer dropped on her. The journeyman responsible for her safety not only dropped a sledge hammer and other objects on her, but he failed to nail down the scaffolding planks they were working on without telling her, which resulted in her falling and breaking her nose. Rather than bringing him up on charges in the union, the super accommodated the journeyman's wishes and transferred her. Women who are constantly transferred from situations where they face hostility and humiliation, find it hard to build self-confidence and gain their bearings as developing mechanics (Eisenberg, 1998, p. 81).

SEXIST ATTITUDES AMONG CONSTRUCTION WORKERS

The construction industry is overwhelmingly male and women are viewed by construction men as unwanted intruders. Tradeswomen must face hostility as outsiders, plus the additional burden of sexist attitudes from male coworkers. In one survey, more than half the women reported that men refused to work with them (Chicago Women in Trades, 1992, p. 13).

Women on construction projects work in an environment that is uncomfortable because construction men like to swear and talk about sex. The men do not behave this way when they are with their wives and children. Many men are uncomfortable working with or near women in construction and find it almost impossible to deal with them simply as coworkers. Some men resent the presence of women in construction because they believe women are taking jobs away from their friends or family members. Some men take out their anger toward women by sabotaging their work. Karen Pollak, assigned to put in insulation at the edge of a building, was given a safety belt that was too large for her. Later, her partner, who was none too happy about working with her and did everything he could to drive her crazy, destroyed her Volkswagen with a sledge hammer, explaining,

"We don't drive Communist cars onto union parking lots" (Eisenberg, 1998, p. 73).

Men will place women in a dangerous situation hoping to scare them off the job. As a last resort, some women are even threatened with physical harm. Maura Russell, a first-year apprentice plumber in Boston, was sent to a new building under construction. There was a very sick man on the crew. One day she and the man were carrying a length of 8-inch cast iron pipe, she on one end and he on the other. They were carrying it toward a trench, walking by a large pit that had reinforcing bars sticking up in various patterns because they were going to pour a floor and columns. The man gave her a shove with that pipe so that she went down into the pit with the heavy pipe. She was lucky she landed on her feet, still holding the pipe. She could have landed on her back or stomach with the rebar sticking through her. He told her, "You gotta watch out, you could get killed around here." One time she was pouring lead for joints (it was before plastic pipe when lead and oakum joints were used for cast iron waste lines). He leaned over to her and said, "Watch out that you don't get any water in that lead. It could pop up and you'd get a face full of lead and that wouldn't be too pretty, would it?" (Eisenberg, 1998, pp. 72–73). When water falls in hot lead, the lead explodes.

PROBLEMS FINDING WORK

Given the nature of the construction industry, which is based on projects of limited duration, finding steady work is a problem for both men and women. Most workers, except superintendents, are laid off when a project is completed, so tradespersons may work from a few weeks to a year or two on a project. No one remains steady even on a long-term project, as trades come and leave as they are needed. Masonry and steel stay for a limited time and then they are gone. Finishing trades like drywall and painting do not start until the building is well advanced and enclosed. Men and women expect to work only part of the year. Construction people spend more time looking for work than in most other kinds of jobs. Since there are so many occasions when tradeswomen are laid off and when they are looking for work, the discrimination in hiring and firing is very significant to tradeswomen.

Finding steady work is significant for women since moving from the apprentice level to the journey level cannot take place if a tradeswoman does not have a specified number of hours of work. If a tradeswoman cannot find work she will not advance through the apprenticeship stage.

Tradespeople find work in several ways: through the union that refers workers to jobs through the union hiring hall, or through individual contacts. Since women are new to the industry they have fewer contacts and are at a disadvantage. Unions have not been supportive of tradeswomen and many women leave the trades because of a lack of work. To find work on their own, tradeswomen need a network of contacts. In the Chicago survey of tradeswomen, 26 percent of survey respondents reported leaving the trades because of lack of steady work; many reported discrimination by employers. Thirty-eight percent of those surveyed said they felt they were not hired because of their gender; and 44 percent reported they felt they were laid off unfairly at some point in their career. While unions have been important in improving the welfare of workers, 23 percent of women reported that unions have withheld job referrals. Some women reported that unions are supportive only part of the time and usually on issues that affect men as well as women (Chicago Women in Trades, 1992, pp. 15–16).

PROBLEMS WITH TRAINING

Problems with training seems to be common among tradeswomen. The Chicago survey shows (a) women did not receive proper training, tools, or equipment; and (b) they are given the dirtiest and heaviest work, which are significant factors in why some women leave the trades. Many women in focus groups report being assigned menial tasks and not being allowed to learn all aspects of their trades.

Hostility and harassment are part of nearly every tradeswoman's classroom experience. Getting proper on-the-job training is an even bigger problem. In principle, apprentices work with a journey-level worker on a series of difficult tasks to learn the trade. In practice, however, women are given routine, unskilled tasks like cleaning up and sorting tools. Instead of progressing to more complex tasks they do the same task over and over. One apprentice carpenter caulked windows for six months, while another stuffed insulation for a year. The result is that women leave their apprenticeships without learning the trade, which in turn results in difficulties getting a job. Men get mad at the women for not holding up their end. One female pipefitter reported that all she was assigned to do was sort fittings, get what the guys needed, load and unload trucks—anything but piping work. Some supervisors are overprotective and only give women the easy jobs, which also prevents them from learning their trade.

The heart of apprenticeship training is learning on the job from the journeyman partner. Helen Vozenilek, an apprentice electrician, found that she was told to do certain things with individual wires, but never told why. Diane Maurer was lucky. Her foreman made sure she learned everything from switchgear to main feeders, but another woman apprentice was told by the journeyman, "Ain't got to show you shit." Still, some men were willing to teach and many women succeeded because there were men who had the courage to break ranks and assist women apprentices (Eisenberg, 1998, pp. 49–67).

INADEQUATE TOILET FACILITIES

Tradeswomen complain about toilet facilities on work sites. Most construction projects use portable toilets. At many sites these toilets are dirty health hazards. Some sites have no facilities so men urinate on the ground and women have no facilities at all. On many sites, sinks for washing hands are nonexistent.

Privacy is often a problem. Women report finding peepholes in toilets. Some toilets have no tops so women can be seen from above. In a high-rise building toilets may be several floors below where women are working. The best sites have clean, locked, separate, and accessible toilets and changing sites for women. Eighty percent of tradeswomen in a survey have been on work sites with no toilets or dirty toilets (Chicago Women in Trades, 1992, p. 18).

Sanitation facilities are the general contractor's responsibility. The question of toilet facilities challenges contractors in the construction industry to accommodate the needs of women, which are different from that of men. Women must sit to urinate, they have menstrual periods, they get pregnant, they need more time to use the bathroom. Karen Pollak, was told that her bathroom was on the top floor of a job that had 17 floors. She was also told that the elevator could only be used to move materials. She had to climb ladders from floor to floor to get up to the bathroom, and then she was yelled at for taking too much time. Some women wait until lunchtime and then find a place to eat that has toilet facilities. But for a woman having her period, and starting work at 7:00 A.M., that is too long a wait. Women construction workers rightfully feel that their dignity as workers should be respected, and that includes having decent bathroom facilities (Eisenberg, 1998, pp. 124–128).

MULTIPLE DISCRIMINATION

Some tradeswomen have to cope with multiple discrimination. In addition to sexism, women of color face racism. Lesbian women report hate language about lesbians. Many supervisors take the attitude that black women can't learn. Many white supervisors take the attitude that whether women work or learn is a matter of indifference to them. Women want to learn and perform work with pride and satisfaction. Many women face the charge of being lesbian just because they want to work in construction. Many white men in construction reason that if a woman is in the trades and doesn't want to go to bed with any of the men they must be lesbians. Black women have the most trying conditions as far as men not wanting to work with them or being laid off unfairly.

Minority women are used by contractors to meet both their minority and women quotas on government projects. Karen Pollak, a Cherokee Indian, faced discrimination not only on the job but at apprenticeship school. Once she got so mad over her treatment she kicked a door right off its jambs. Yvonne Valles, a Chicana painter, noticed that all the fine, interior finish painting or paperhanging was given to white women, while the rough work on the exterior was given to female minorities. Carpenter Irene Soloway observed that more liberties were taken with black women who faced more sexual harassment, particularly from white men. Also, black women are put on heavy construction more than white women. Diana Sukiel, a white woman, who got into construction through her cousin, received fair treatment from the union when she became pregnant. She was told to stop working after her third month, and she collected weekly disability pay until six weeks after she delivered her son. But another apprentice who was African-American, was asked to leave school when she became pregnant, which meant the end of her apprenticeship (Eisenberg, 1998, pp. 142–145).

ISOLATION FROM OTHER WOMEN

Women who work in construction find the isolation from other women a burden, and many leave the trades for that reason. Being the only woman on a construction project is very lonely. It makes such women conspicuous and vulnerable. In such a situation many women not only work alone, but take breaks alone and eat lunch alone. In the Chicago survey, 22 percent of the respondents said they had never worked with another woman. The early tradeswomen in the 1970s seldom worked with other women (Chicago Women in Trades, 1992, pp. 19–20). Conditions have changed in the 1990s, but women are still clearly outnumbered. Women who work alone get tired of standing out and being seen as a woman rather than as a worker. Support groups like coalitions of labor union women do help to provide outlets for women to get together for drinks, meals, and conversation. If there is only one woman on a job it is very hard to make complaints, but if there are two or more women making complaints then it is difficult for supervisors to ignore them.

It is hard to convey the feeling of isolation that a woman feels when she is the only woman among 86 men who don't want her there, which is why women form caucuses and groups to get together when they're out of work. Together, women can cry, scream, holler, bitch, laugh, tell jokes, and complain to their heart's content (Eisenberg, 1998, pp. 111–113).

SAFETY PROBLEMS

Construction work is physically demanding and dangerous. Many women report being placed in a dangerous situation. Some women are "tested" by male co-workers and asked to lift and carry materials that men would not be able to handle alone. Some women leave the trades because of the danger. In the Chicago survey, 17 percent reported leaving the job because of injury and 9 percent left because of dangerous working conditions. Five percent left because of the physical demands of the work (Chicago Women in Trades, 1992, p. 20). Women stress the need for physical conditioning and for training in handling heavy objects. They emphasize that women need to respect their physical limits. Some men drop things on women or they make fun of women who show fear or fright. Many women, like many men first starting in construction, have to get used to working at great heights. Men carry each other, especially when they get older, but no one wants to carry a woman.

PROMOTIONS

In construction the positions of superintendent, general foreman, and foreman are desirable because of higher wages, but also because they offer intellectual challenges. When a worker is asked to hold a supervisory position it is a sign that the superiors have confidence and respect for the worker's abilities. Even a working foreman of a small crew spends time going over blueprints, planning, and ordering materials. It's a high compliment for a woman to be asked to be a foreman. She has to be sure of herself and she has to know at least as much (or more) than any of the members of the crew she will be leading.

One woman said, it was like *Mutiny on the Bounty* when she made foreman, as she had to cajole, threaten, and get in the face of members of her crew to get them to perform. Another woman, Lorraine Bertosa, a carpenter, split a crew with another foreman and they each led their group with a challenge to see which crew could put up walls the fastest. She got a great deal of satisfaction by being urged to compete (Eisenberg, 1998, pp. 166–168).

Diane Maurer became general foreman on two multimillion dollar projects because of the strong affirmative action program in the Seattle area. The Seattle local union of the International Brotherhood of Electrical Workers (IBEW) was unique in putting women in positions of leadership, and was helped by the affirmative action of county and state programs. Diane went way beyond what any male foreman would do, as far as planning ahead, arranging for equipment and supplies, and letting the general contractor know when and where her crew would be working so he could have the area cleared for her. Despite all her credentials she was passed over for a male foreman when another opening came up (Eisenberg, 1998, pp. 169, 172, 179).

WOMEN WHO LEAVE THE TRADES

Women who leave the trades tend to be older and to have started in the earlier years when women first entered construction. Women who leave tend to have been more isolated from other women. Women who leave often want to go back to school or get more training. Sexual harassment is a major factor leading women to leave. Other factors include not being given proper tools or training or being given dirty, heavy, or one-dimensional, boring jobs. Whatever reasons given, many women simply leave because they become tired of working in a field traditionally reserved for men.

Women who get into construction do so for the good hourly wages. When they work steadily they can make $40,000 per year. But tradeswomen find that all jobs are short-lived and when the project is over they have to find other work, sometimes outside the industry. Many are out of work for months. For single women with children, that is a great hardship. Thus, the unsteady nature of the work drives many women out of the industry. Some women try to stay in construction by getting a civil service job with a government agency so they can work steadily. Women have not been in construction long enough for them to have built up a strong network of contacts from one generation to another, so steady work is still a rarity. There aren't many women who have started at 30, worked steadily, and retired with a fairly decent work life and a good pension (Eisenberg 1998, pp. 151–164).

HOW TRADESWOMEN COPE

In spite of the difficulties, many women do stay in the trades and learn to cope; and some women even thrive. Many women state that they enjoy the physical work and the sense of accomplishment that comes with construction work. They also enjoy the good wages that are paid in construction. More than 50 percent of those surveyed in Chicago were the main wage earners in their family. Women have different coping strategies—some are quiet and reserved, while others are outgoing. All women must have courage and determination.

Many women try to be themselves and do not try to act like men. Many women are laid back, not approaching others if they don't approach them. Most women realize they are breaking into a man's world, but they do not try to change men's attitudes. At the same time, they object to dirty jokes and pictures of nude women. Women who stay on the job know they have to be strong, or complain when an injustice is done to them.

Maura Russell, an apprentice plumber, never had an opportunity to work with another woman in her trade. On one job with several hundred workers building apartments for the elderly, there were two other tradeswomen, an electrician and a taper. They hung around together and Maura joined them and one time the three of them were having lunch in K's car. One guy, an asphalt contractor, came over to where they were eating and pissed on the side of the car. K confronted him and he denied it and the super backed the guy. At which point K took out her Swiss Army knife and told the guy that she would slash his tires if he didn't apologize. He'd been laughing at the incident, which is what really enraged her. He finally did say, "Oh, I'm sorry, I'm sorry." She said, "No, you got out of the car to piss on my car, and now you have to get out to apologize." So he did. The super tried to get her fired, which he was not able to do (Eisenberg, 1998, pp. 82–83). Sometimes women cope by acting tough.

POSITIVE PASSIONS

In spite of these problems, many women have had positive experiences in the construction industry. For example, Barbara Henry, an electrician, said that she did not know anything about being an electrician, but once she learned her trade she could go into any house, open an electrical box, and understand where the power came from and what switch and what wire was doing what. She liked to look at blueprints that told her what was going on electrically. It was unbelievable to her that she got a high from her knowledge and her skill (Eisenberg, 1998, p. 87).

Lorraine Bertosi, an ironworker, said she was in heaven working on the Sohio Building in Cleveland. The building was 45 stories in the air, and she could feel the excitement and vibrations of the workers putting the building together. As she said, "everything was cooking." She liked being around ironworkers, walking the beams with a great deal of pride. Working up high, with guy lines and safety belts, she and the other men were in their own world. She found herself walking taller after being around the ironworkers. She got respect from them, even if they were not afraid to hand it out if she deserved it. When she was up there she forgot everything, except for her safety and her partner's safety. It took a special breed of person to walk those beams (Eisenberg, 1998, p. 88).

Mary-Ann Cloherty recognized from an early age that tools had a magical appeal. They were special and only certain people got to use them. She was aware that her brothers got the tools or a chemistry set, while she got a toy broom, but going into construction changed her outlook (Eisenberg, 1998, p. 89).

Maura Russell said that most women she's known who did some welding were surprised at how much they liked it. There was something about the rhythm of it, and to do it well the welder has to have all her senses working. The sound, the smell, the look, seeing the color and the liquid puddle changing, all that has to be observed to do a good job (Eisenberg, 1998, p. 91).

Paulette Jourdan took great pride in her work as a plumber. To her, big two-inch and three-inch copper water lines, smooth and wiped clean and assembled, look like artwork. It has to be plumb because if it goes in crooked someone is going to spot it. She had to crawl under houses to do her work, but when she finished she knew that the people in the house had a new water system that was not going to move or leak and that it was installed properly (Eisenberg, 1998, p. 92).

What Gayann Wilkinson liked about construction work was solving problems. Being able to identify a problem and figure out how to repair it or how she could make it work was a challenge. She had to figure out what materials she needed, how she was going to do the work, and then how to achieve the final product. That gave her special satisfaction (Eisenberg, 1998, p. 92).

Randy Loomans worked on high-rises in Seattle as an ironworker, installing various kinds of facing on buildings. On one job she worked installing all the glass for the building, making sure all the pieces fit and looked right. When she was finished working on a building, she could drive by and say, "I put the face on that building." There was something there for her to look at and see (Eisenberg, 1998, pp. 93–94).

Irene Soloway looked at her job as a carpenter this way: "I mean you get to carry tools. You get to hit people, you know, if you have to. You have so much more personal freedom than you would in so many other jobs. Good pay, good hours, pretty much equal rights as opposed to a lot of white-collar work.... I always say to the guys, You are so lucky to have me on the job, you know. You all agree with each other all the time, it's so boring" (Eisenberg, 1998, p. 94).

Gloria Flowers said it was an exhilarating feeling once she got used to climbing up high and plugging into the camaraderie that men experience with each other. It opened her up as a female. She learned to joke around, tease, and have a good time. She was not the kind of person who could be confined to an office eight hours a day. She had to get outside and feel the wind in her face. She liked fresh air, even in the winter (Eisenberg, 1998, p. 94).

Angela Summer said one thing she liked about working with men was that a lot of them are trained to work together. She commented, "There's a team-type thing that you do together, if you can find a guy who can get beyond the bullshit" (Eisenberg, 1998, p. 95).

Melinda Hernandez said she loved her work. She loved learning it, doing it, bending pipe, and pulling wires. She felt the craft itself was wonderful and she got to use her brains. It was always a thrill to go on to a new job site and a new project. Everything was exciting, a new adventure. She still likes her work, but she used to have a real love for it. Now she has lost heart in the work because of the harassment, disrespect, and inconsideration (Eisenberg, 1998, p. 193).

Jean Schroedel interviewed women in the trades, including construction women. (Schroedel, 1985, pp. 7–24, 34–40, 53–64, 143–163, 190–202).

One of the women who told her story to Jean Schroedel was Laura Pfandler, a pipefitter. Laura liked the wages in construction, starting out at $5.06 an hour as a helper; after two years she earned $10.22 an hour. Laura was scared being a woman and working with so many men and she realized that the men were not overjoyed at her being there. At first they ignored her, but then she started speaking up, telling them she did not like the manner in which they referred to women. For a long time she was not allowed to do certain jobs because many of the men could not stand the idea that women could do the same work as they could. If a woman can do the same work it is not masculine and tough.

Laura was promoted to fitter, installing gas mains, and she came to like the work. Gas piping mains are out in the street, usually buried three to four feet deep. To run new mains the crews had to dig up the old mains, which meant using a 90-pound breaker to tear up concrete and blacktop. Laura found this kind of work demanding, heavy, physical labor. She also learned to use a jumping jack that tamped down the earth. It was hard on her back, but she was proud at being able to lift it and she felt that she had become a lot stronger since she started working in construction.

As a fitter, Laura did a lot of gas welding using a torch connected to oxygen and acetylene tanks. She found gas welding hot and slow because she was actually melting the pipe with heat. At first it was hard for her to control the puddle of liquid metal, but later she learned how to angle the tip of the welding rod to control the way the puddle of metal moved. She learned to be confident and steady, finding that different sized pipes melted at different rates. All together, she found it was a complicated skill that she had mastered. She also learned not to take crap from the other men while she did her job. She liked her job best when there were other women working for the gas company because she felt working with other women in the trades gave her the support she needed.

Another woman who told her story to Jean Schroedel was Elaine Canfield, a carpenter. Elaine knew nothing about carpentry, not even how to use a hammer or a saw, but she liked the idea of working with wood and thought there was a lot of independence in a trade. The money was excellent and she worked from job to job, not necessarily full time. She also realized that there was a lot of danger in being a carpenter and she worried about fatal injuries, high work, losing an arm or a hand, or having something explode in her face and losing her eyesight.

Elaine was accepted into a program run in conjunction with the local carpenters union. During the six-week program she was taught how to use the basic tools— hammer, handsaw, tri-square, crowbar, and skillsaw. She was amazed at how much there was to learn, especially mentally. Carpenters were not people who just worked with their hands. When she got into carpentry she was amazed by the amount of intellectual work involving math and mechanics. She found out that she had to visualize what she was going to build. She had to know how she was going to connect things, why she was cutting wood in certain dimensions, as well as mechanics, leverage, how things worked for her, and how to do her work in the fastest way possible. She learned a lot of things at the training school, especially how to survive in the trade and look for work.

On her first job she didn't use a hammer for about a month and a half, since she was assigned to a steel form crew involved in cutting and stripping concrete forms. She was given an electrical impact wrench and her job was to tighten nuts and bolts on the wood forms built to pour concrete columns. She was disturbed because she didn't get to use her head, asking herself, "Is this carpentry? Where's the wood? Where's the nails?" She was disappointed at first but the other carpenters assured her there would be other work for her.

Elaine learned that in construction she had to work in dirty conditions and be exposed to the elements. She learned to work in the snow and with the wind blowing 40 miles an hour. But she found that at other times, construction was the best thing going. On a beautiful day she thought about people in offices and factories and wouldn't trade with them for the world (Schroedel, 1985, p. 37).

As a first-year apprentice, Elaine was mostly a "gofer." She was told to get tools, plug power tools in, set up work areas, get sawhorses, and assist the best way she could. By the time she was a third-year apprentice she had a lot of responsibility. Journeymen kept telling her what to do, but she learned to do the work herself. By the time she became a fourth-year apprentice she was doing lots of form work on her own and functioning on a journey level.

Elaine had to learn how to psyche out the men on the job and stand her ground. She had to be tactful, not hostile, and above all she had to learn her skills because the men felt threatened by her being on the job. Elaine was able to work with a crew where she was accepted and was treated like one of the guys. She was paid compliments and treated like an equal, which was a real breakthrough, but the most important thing was that she was recognized as a fairly good carpenter. Before she joined her present crew she did have to stand a lot of nastiness like dirty jokes, and men burping and farting to see if they could get a reaction from her. At first the men didn't talk to her and one time she was laid off when she couldn't do high work. But she stuck with it and now belongs to a group called Women in the Trades, where she gets support, sympathy, and understanding, and where she can share the feelings of accomplishment at work (Schroedel, 1985, pp. 39–40).

Angela Summer went into construction to become a plumber. At first, like many other women, she thought about carpentry, feeling that she would like to work with wood and make beautiful things, but she was scared of the math. So Angela took up plumbing and found out that it had more complicated math than carpentry.

The attraction of going into construction was being able to use her body and be physical, which she loved to do, plus being able to use her mind. The money she could earn was also an attraction. She did have fears, especially about being qualified and being able to do things as well as the men.

Angela was in a training program for seven months, learning the vocabulary, the names of tools, and how to use them. She also learned how to make diagrams, but not much practical, hands-on work. The training did help her when she got into the union, as compared with other men starting out who didn't know anything. She felt comfortable with tools like crescent wrenches, screwdrivers, pipe wrenches, and basic wrenches. She learned to use a threading machine and a cutting machine, and she also learned how to solder pipes together.

After leaving her training school, it took three years for Angela to get into the union. She applied twice, had to file suit, and was finally accepted. She was lucky because she was hired as a first-year apprentice and the journeyman/foreman who was to train her was a nice guy, as well as being the first black man to get into the union. She already knew how to do lots of things and she was on her own quite a lot. She worked with her journeyman like a team, changing around toilets, using sledge hammers, using drills and saber saws, and heating up lead to pour in joints for showers. Angela found out there was no such thing as a typical job. She might work with one other man or with a small crew of four or five, or on big jobs with 15 or 20 men. But she never got to work with another woman in the crew. Some of the men were decent and others were not so. The whole time she was with the men she was made to feel different, and often excluded. She worked with one man who was decent and with another man who told jokes that were either racist or sexist. The men stood up for each other against her, while the union wasn't much better since they didn't want her in the union and did not give her support.

Angela hung out a lot with women that were in her union. She needed the support of women who did the work that she did. She also found her body changed a lot from the work. She felt really strong, but she learned not to try to lift very heavy pipe alone, like four-inch cast iron, and asked for help.

Finally, she was almost a journeywoman and was getting more positive feedback about her work. It's not something that the men did often, but she had the feeling, even if the men didn't tell her, that they were happy with her work because sometimes she would get into a rhythm, really producing with her partners. Angela believes plumbing is a good field for women, with good wages and lots of security (Schroedel, 1985, pp. 53–63).

Ann Johnson started out in nursing, but then switched to construction to become a painter. She found that painting could be dangerous because she worked on ladders all the time, and worked in some really high areas. If there's a ladder that is not high enough, she had to use one that was a little short and it was hard for her to handle. Spraying was also hazardous because she had to use nose and eye protection and the paint got all over her eyes until she learned to use goggles. Once she stepped back into a hole and broke a bone in her foot. She found the job very hard and she did not get much help from her husband in taking care of the house (Schroedel, 1985, pp. 148–149).

Marge Kirk became a concrete-truck driver in the construction industry, and in telling about her experiences she presents many insights into the nature of construction work. Marge was a waitress before she got into construction. She left because working with the public wore her out. She took a truck-driving class at the South Seattle Community College. She wanted to have a skill that would give her independence. She wanted to learn things that she would have to do in an emergency, like lower gears plus light braking going down hills, and using a little throttle going around curves. Marge also wanted practice driving a truck to gain confidence. Marge and the other woman in the class were perfectionists. The men seemed to feel if you jammed the truck into gear it will go, but the women tried to get it right. They had higher expectations than the men.

Marge said that the illusion about going to school is that she would get a job, but she found that getting a job was really hard. She went everywhere looking for work. She talked to dispatchers, went through the phone book, and walked around looking for out of the way places. All she got for her efforts was, "Well, why don't you make out an application." In reality, the trucking companies had no intention of looking at her application and nothing was going to make them hire a woman unless she was related to someone in the company or sleeping with somebody there.

Finally, one company had a friendly woman working in personnel who sent Marge to the superintendent. He said, "Come on down and ride with us and we'll see how you do" (Schroedel, 1985, p. 154). Actually, the company needed another woman on their list for minority quotas and she came at the right time. The drivers were all big, heavy-set men, like construction workers, and the office space was gray and depressing. It was full of men standing around, very much in charge of their world. She had a scary feeling about it. That was the beginning of 1978.

There were some disastrous moments while she was training. She was training on a concrete truck, learning to go forward and back up. The man who was training her got her right next to a car and she rolled into the car and made a little scratch. She got all shaken up and was convinced she would lose her job. She didn't think the man who was training her was out to get her. He just wasn't sure how to relate to a woman. If he related to her as a woman he would help out in a patronizing way, but when he had to relate to her as a truck driver he didn't know what to do (Schroedel, 1985, p. 155).

One time Marge was sent to a construction job and had to back up a narrow dirt road and then get around a corner. Every time she got the truck near the forms the front wheel would run into the form. She tried again and again and finally swung out wide, but she got the duals, the back wheels, too close to the side of the road and sank into a soft spot. Again, she said to herself, "there goes my job." There she was with this top-heavy truck leaning into a ravine. The big fear with concrete trucks is rolling them over. The load of concrete had calcium in it to make it set faster, so it was getting harder and harder. She called for a mechanic and another truck driver came down, and soon all the men working there, about 15 men, joined in. They kept adding water to the concrete because it was getting harder and stickier. Finally, they brought the concrete pump down and they got the load into the pump, which pumped it into another truck. They had a lot of trouble getting the concrete through the chute, but after all the hassle and all the help it worked out and she was able to drive out of the hole. When she got back to the plant she was really shaken but the dispatcher actually showed some empathy, took her to lunch, and calmed her down. It was definitely her mistake but he gave her a break.

A dispatcher wants drivers who will do whatever he wants, especially new drivers. As a woman it is even harder, since the dispatcher is the big cheese and she's the new woman. She felt she was in a male workplace where all the men were in competition to see who, if anyone, was going to "score." The worst part for Marge was that the dispatcher had been successful with one of the women that came before her. At the time she had no boyfriend she could use for protection, so it made her fair game according to the men. She wanted the job, she wanted to be a good truck driver, and she wanted to pull her weight as a driver. The years passed and she survived. The men are beginning to see her as a human, not just "a broad with legs and boobs." The dispatcher now sees her as a driver, not just a woman (Schroedel, 1985, pp. 156–157).

Marge learned to accept the construction field as it was. Sex, money, and macho toughness were the major topics of conversation. She had to figure out the best way to react—when to be rude and when to laugh it off. Marge found that sex was the central topic concerning her with her coworkers, even though she wanted to be thought of differently. She believes things are going to get more interesting in the years to come as women enter workplaces dominated by men. Marge believes there will be different norms. Just being friends with a woman will be a whole new way of life for men. Marge found she had to be realistic and one-sided because she was in the position of being a woman in an all-men's field, so she became cynical about men in a lot of ways. But she also learned to appreciate the men on the job. She recognized construction as hard and dangerous work that took a lot out of the men's bodies. She enjoyed their humor and stories and admired the camaraderie they shared. The women in construction can be cool to each other and yet understand and seem to know what's going on with each other (Schroedel, 1985, pp. 158–159).

It took a long time for Marge to think of herself as a woman and as a truck driver. At home she wanted to do beautiful things, look pretty, and have clean nails. She wanted to sew, have pretty flowers, and feel like a woman. The job made her feel hardened. She had to have her "guts up to par," she had to go for it, and she had to go fast. The job took a lot out of her physically. She damaged her back by lifting sacks of gravel weighing 100 pounds. The pounding of the trucks was hard and she was always in a rush. It was also hard on her kidneys and bladder because a lot of jobs have no places for women to go to the bathroom. What did she do? She waited. She was tired for a long time and had to cut back on her social life, going to bed early so she could get up the next day, especially in the summer when there was lots of overtime (Schroedel, 1985, pp. 160–161).

Marge asked herself if it was worth it, given the hard times and changes she had to go through. Some days it seemed perfectly normal for her to have such a job, driving, being outdoors, being physical, and meeting different people on the job sites. She liked the never-boring challenge of the new situations in construction. Then again, it was such a male world, why should a woman bother with it? She felt there was a lot of nonsense that should be done away with, but that there was much women could learn from working with men, and certainly a lot that men could learn from working with women. The major thing Marge would say to a woman going into her kind of work is forget the romantic idea and realize "it's hard work. Period" (Schroedel, 1985, p. 163).

Anna Brinkley, an electrician, is the final trade to be described here (Schroedel, 1985, pp. 190–202). Anna chose electrician's work because of the money. Money meant independence, being able to support her family without having a man around if she couldn't find a decent man to relate to her family.

Anna Brinkley worked as a maintenance electrician. She got to work many different jobs. When she worked on cranes she was on top of a building in the crane barn. She liked the work and found it exciting to work on big machinery. Sometimes she worked in a motor shop or on a factory floor, taking repair calls when something in the factory broke down. When something would break down she would be given a dispatch card with a building number and a supervisor's number. She would try to troubleshoot the machine, which meant fixing it, ordering parts, deciding if it needed to be junked, or sometimes just tagging it for a day or two while she thought about the problem (Schroedel, 1985, pp. 195–196).

A lot of men were afraid of her because if they acted a certain way they thought she might file a sex-discrimination charge. The whole thing about discrimination confused them and they didn't realize how difficult it was for a woman to prove a harassment case. Anna thought a lot of nice men were confused and didn't know how to act around a woman in the workplace. The older male workers were good electricians, highly skilled workers who felt absolutely no threat from Anna, believing she could not take their job nor would she ever attain their level of skill. They taught her many things and many saw her almost like a daughter (Schroedel, 1985, pp. 196–197).

Anna felt that supervisors sometimes did not have confidence in her ability and therefore did not give her the hard jobs. She believed that was a form of discrimination. They would give her things that they thought she could handle, which meant that she would not learn the entire trade. She fought against that attitude because she wanted to be a full-fledged electrician capable of tackling any job (Schroedel, 1985, p. 198).

GOOD WORKSITES FOR WOMEN

Where there is a genuine commitment to have women on a work site, conditions are much better. The commitment can be informal, involving an owner or a foreman who wants women on the job. One owner in Chicago told the men that if they didn't want to work with women they could leave. This owner checked up on the women to see how they were getting on with their work and their conditions. He threw men off the job for making derogatory remarks to or against women.

A very structured commitment to women is found on construction projects of Stein & Co., a Chicago developer with a female president. Stein & Co. works with contractors, affirmative action specialists, and community-based groups to recruit, train, and retain women on their work sites. At times there are as many as 35 tradeswomen on their construction projects. One project had 85 women. Stein superintendents are trained to create an equitable workplace. Women workers receive support services, including counseling, intervention, and mediation to deal with workplace issues. Pornography and sexual graffiti are not tolerated. Women have separate, locked, clean toilets and changing areas. The number of women working compared to the goals are checked. All women who leave are interviewed. When there are as many as 30 women on a Stein project, the men must accept their presence and treat them primarily as workers. When there are women of all trades, they blend in with all other workers (Chicago Women in Trades, 1992, p. 24).

CONCLUSION

Women in construction face problems including sexual harassment, sexist attitudes, finding work, training, hygienic facilities, racism, and unsafe conditions, besides the normal job problems that exist for all workers in construction. While women learn to cope with these problems (and some women are very successful in spite of a hostile environment), individual strategies should not be necessary. Success or failure should be based on a woman's ability to do the work, not on her ability to cope. Changing job conditions in construction does not mean special treatment for women. Tradeswomen wish only to work beside men in an environment that treats all workers with respect. They want to do their own jobs well and be accepted for the quality of their work. Women also want to be treated decently and equitably while they are working on a construction site to support their families.

Melinda Hernandez had this to say about women in construction:

Women have to take a stand and say, Look, this is not acceptable. Stop hitting on me. I'm here to do a day's work. I'm not here to go out with you. I'm not here to boost your ego. We should get along as colleagues, but we don't have to get along as men and women, because that's not what this is about. Two people working, that's what we are. Work is work. (Eisenberg, 1998, p. 194)

Eisenberg concludes that in the end, it is the unions that will be crucial in getting women into construction. Unions have the structure, funds, training programs, and self-interest in diversification and growth to want to recruit women. Unions can establish child care centers. They can apply the same resourcefulness they use in building to overcome the obstacles to getting women into the trades (Eisenberg, 1998, pp. 207–208).

10

MINORITIES IN CONSTRUCTION

AFFIRMATIVE ACTION IN JERSEY CITY, NEW JERSEY, 1998

Hartz Mountain recently built a new hotel in Jersey City, New Jersey. Hartz was granted a tax abatement that was approved by the Municipal Council of the city. In exchange for the granting of a tax abatement on the property, the city stated the following:

The City wishes to assure continuing employment opportunities for City residents, particularly residents who are Minorities and business opportunities for Local Businesses, especially Minority and Women Owned Local Businesses, with employers located in or relocating to the City who are the recipients of Economic Incentives. The City has determined to accomplish that goal by requiring the Recipient of an Economic Incentive to act in Good Faith, as defined herein, and discharge its obligations under this Agreement. To the extent mandated by State and Federal law and so long as the Entity discharges its Good Faith obligations under this agreement, the City acknowledges that the Recipient and its contractors are free to hire whomever they choose. (Agreement between Jersey City and the Hartz Corporation, 1998, p. 3; agreement is in this author's possession.)

The city also set forth certain goals that they expected Hartz to meet, namely:

1. Employment: The Recipient (Hartz) shall make a Good Faith effort to achieve the goal of a work force representing fifty-one (51%) percent City residents, fifty-one (51%) percent of whom are residents who are minorities and, in Non-Traditional Jobs, six point nine (6.9%) of whom are residents who are women, it being understood that one employee may satisfy more than one category.

2. Business Contracting: The Recipient shall make a Good Faith effort to achieve the goal of awarding twenty (20%) percent of the dollar amount of its contracts to Local Businesses, fifty-one (51%) percent of which shall be Minorities or Women Owned Local

Businesses, it being understood that one contract may satisfy more than one category. (Agreement, p. 3.)

Minorities were defined as African-American, Hispanic, Asian, and American Indian. In effect, based on these percentages, Hartz was required to try to hire half of its work force from Jersey City, of which half (or 25 percent) would be minorities. Also, 20 percent of the total cost of the project was to be awarded to local contractors, half of whom were to be minority or women-owned businesses. Hartz had no trouble meeting the worker requirements since workers were recruited from the Jersey City area, but did have trouble finding minority and women-owned contractors. Hartz made a good faith effort to comply with the agreement that was accepted by Jersey City, and submitted monthly reports on the percentages of workers on the job in the various trades. Jersey City specified that as long as a good faith effort was made to hire minority workers and contractors, Hartz could hire "whomever they choose."

I interviewed the drywall contractor on the hotel project about how he made out in conforming to the Jersey City affirmative action plan. He said he had no problem with the carpenters' local—they sent him 50 percent residents of Jersey City and 25 percent of those were minorities. He did have problems with the laborers' local union and the spacklers' local union, who told him that they had minorities on other jobs that they were not going to take to supply the Hartz hotel job. The boss of the drywall company said he was given a letter from the two local unions stating that they could not supply him with minorities and he was then free to hire whomever he wanted for those two trades. He had 60 men on the job and one woman. He would check his percentages every week, then call the hiring hall (he said it was like ordering sandwiches in a deli). He would say, "I need two blacks and one white; or I need one white and no minorities this week." He said there was no difference as far as output or skills between the minorities and the white workers that were sent to him by the hiring hall, but he did have his own men that were regulars in his company and there was a big difference between them and the workers sent from the hall. He expected 30 sheetrock boards installed each day by each worker and if a man did not give him that output, he would give him a warning. If any man failed to give him 30 boards after that, he would lay him off and replace him. Some men, minorities and white, gave him 40 boards a day. His regulars, who had worked for him before, were given the harder tasks like framing and cutting openings. Some journeymen came in off the street. He would ask them if they lived in Jersey City and what their last names were to see if they were Hispanic so he could use them to meet his quotas. He would try them out and if they were okay he'd call the business agent and have them checked in for the job. All in all, the job went well for him. He kept up with the schedule and made money, but not as much as he anticipated. I interviewed the painting contractor on the same hotel job and he told me he did not make any money. The painters' union would not let him hire anyone who worked for him the previous two years, even though some of them were minorities, and they forced him to only take men on the list at the hiring hall. He had to hire men who knew they were there for only one job and they did not produce the work he needed in order to make a profit on the job.

In spite of the fact that affirmative action as a policy is being challenged through-out the country, it is still in force in most of the country and still being applied in public works. In 1997, 13 state legislatures questioned the validity of affirmative action measures. Seven of those states, California, Colorado, Florida, Illinois, Massachusetts, Oregon, and Washington, tried to place the issue on the ballot. Only California actually voted on the issue, as the other six states failed to get enough signatures to put the issue on the ballot (Issues and Opportunities Report, 1998). In 1998, the state of Washington in a referendum, voted to eliminate affirmative action in education and public works.

THE CONSTRUCTION INDUSTRY AND THE EMPLOYMENT OF MINORITIES

The construction industry has been a target for attempts to create jobs for minorities for a number of reasons. First, it is an industry that is affected by governments at all levels, since federal, state, and local governments all have public works projects for which they award contracts to construction firms. These are projects for roads, office buildings, schools, sewage treatment plants, waterworks, dams, bridges, parks, airports, jails, courthouses, monuments, and other public works that are financed by bonds, government funds, and other means paid for by taxpayers, locally or nationwide. Through their power to award contracts to construction firms, cities, states, counties, townships, and the federal government can impose certain rules as a condition for doing public works. If a township or city grants favors like tax abatement, they too can impose certain rules. One of these rules, which has now become commonplace, is that contractors must hire minority workers and also employ minority contractors as subcontractors. Most government contracts also require affirmative action programs and cite certain goals for hiring a certain percentage of minority workers and minority businesses.

Another reason why construction gets lots of attention from advocates for minority hiring is that it is visible and easily viewed by the public. A third reason is that when construction takes place in inner-city neighborhoods, local advocacy groups can see if there are minorities working on the project. There is no doubt that the affirmative action provisions of the public works contracts forced contractors to hire minorities and they began to be visible on the construction projects in the 1970s, 1980s, and 1990s. Minority workers are still scarce on private construction jobs, and minority contractors even rarer though the national figures show that there is a minority presence in the industry. According to the U.S. Bureau of the Census, in 1996 blacks made up 7.5 percent of the construction trades, while Hispanics were 11.7 percent; and blacks consisted of 6.2 percent of carpenters, while Hispanics were 9.9 percent. Since blacks are 12 percent of the general population, they are far from achieving parity in the construction industry, while Hispanics, who are 10 percent of the general population, have achieved parity. It is interesting to compare the figures between 1983 and 1996. The black percentage in the construction trades rose from 6.6 percent in 1983 to 7.5 percent in 1996, an increase of just over 15 percent. Hispanics, however, rose from 6.0 percent to 11.7

percent of construction workers, a near 100 percent increase. It is interesting to note that female employment in the trades rose by 70 percent, of course the numbers for female tradeswomen were small to begin with. Female tradeswomen rose from 107,000 to 125,000, which was only 2.5 percent of all tradesworkers in the construction industry in 1996. Blacks numbered 375,000 workers in 1996 and Hispanics numbered 585,000 in 1996. (For these statistics, see U.S. Bureau of the Census, 1997, p. 412.) Hispanics now have a higher percentage of construction workers than African-Americans. Is this attributable to the fact that they are considered closer to being white than blacks and that they are more acceptable to the unions and contractors? Have Hispanics been more active in trying to break into the construction industry and its high wages, while blacks have concentrated more on gaining entry into jobs in the public sphere of government work? Is the pool of skilled workers among Hispanics higher than among African-Americans? For whatever reason, Hispanics have achieved parity in the construction industry while African-Americans have a long way to go.

In the 1950s and 1960s, there weren't many black union contractors. It was hard for them to get financing, find black union men in their trade, and solicit contracts from white businessmen. I went into the sprinkler business for a short time in the 1960s. It was a relatively easy trade, but like all construction work the biggest problem was getting paid since we were working for private owners of buildings, not public agencies where the money is safe. What was easy about sprinkler work was the relatively simple rules for laying out a sprinkler system that is based on so many square feet in a room or area and then figuring the coverage for each sprinkler head. There are manuals that tell you what size pipe carries what volume of water under what pressure. Pump manufacturers will engineer the fire pump for each system. In the 1960s, New York City had a big push to get building owners, especially owners of loft and warehouse buildings on lower Broadway, to put in sprinkler systems. Most of the buildings did not have these system and therefore were in violation of the fire code. To put in a sprinkler system was an additional expense for many owners that they could not recover by raising the rents, so many tried to get away without doing it. But many owners did have sprinklers installed when they were hit with violations and could not sell their buildings. I was able to sign up a number of these owners to install sprinkler systems in their buildings.

I found a nonunion minority contractor whose name was Conrad, to run the work and install the systems. He was more knowledgeable about sprinkler systems than I was and he taught me how to lay out the systems, and where to go to get the pipe cut and threaded, have the proper fittings supplied, and have the pipe marked based on my drawings. I was able to get credit to buy the sprinkler heads and the fire pump and financed our operations. City water pressure in the street was not sufficient to raise the water to the top of a six- or eight-story building so we had to furnish and hook up a fire pump. Conrad provided the men to do the work and I brought in the business. Conrad also supervised the work. He always wore a jacket and tie, no matter how dirty or sweaty the job. I figured it was his way of differentiating himself as the boss. We lasted in that business for about one year. When Conrad got sick and couldn't work we had to quit. We both did well but without

Conrad I was in no position to get the work done and I was not about to go union with Local 638 steamfitters. This was a case where a minority contractor was really competent to do major jobs, but he lacked the contacts with the local union. He could not get business from owners without a white front man like me, and he could not buy supplies and equipment because he had no credit or standing with white suppliers. So while it is relatively easy to go into business in construction, it is a whole different ballgame for minority contractors. It is not an even playing field and those who squawk about special treatment like set-asides and providing financial aid, have never had to face the real world of the marketplace, which has always favored the white male.

THE HISTORY OF EMPLOYMENT OF MINORITIES IN THE CONSTRUCTION INDUSTRY

The history of the U.S. working class and the U.S. labor movement is a history in which the ethnic and racial dimension was a crucial factor. After 1850, immigration from Europe accelerated and swelled to enormous proportions during the last decade of the nineteenth century and the first two decades of the twentieth century. By the end of the nineteenth century the U.S. working class was an immigrant working class full of Irish, Italian, Germans, Jewish, Slavic, Greek, Russian, and East European blue-collar and manual workers. European immigrants exercised great influence within organized labor which began to organize larger proportions of the working classes after the Civil War. Miners, railroad workers, steel workers, shoe workers, textile workers, and building trades workers were all swept into the various national trade union organizations—the National Labor Union, the Knights of Labor, the Industrial Workers of the World (IWW), the Railroad Brotherhoods, and finally, the American Federation of Labor. The building trades department became an important sector of the AFL, which was founded in the 1880s. Immigrants came to hold important positions in the labor movement, especially in the northeast and in cities. By 1900, Irish immigrants or their descendants held the presidencies of more than 50 of the 110 national unions in the American Federation of Labor. Many other unions were led by Germans, Jews, Italians, and Slavs (or their sons). These immigrants and their followers were dependent on the communal advances of their ethnic group and participation in organized labor was part of the process. Also part of the process was the exclusionary and racist policies that kept blacks, Asians, and other minorities out of the unions. Racism united white workers and was used as an organizing instrument by labor unions (Hill, 1989, pp. 190–191).

Race and racism were crucial factors in determining the characteristics of organized labor in its formative years, during a period of white supremacy that continued from the late nineteenth century until the civil rights acts of the 1960s, and left a permanent mark on the development of U.S. society. White supremacy as ideology and practice was a strategy for assimilation by European working-class immigrants of the white ethnics who constituted a major part of the membership and leadership of organized labor in the United States. While white ethnics experienced much hardship economically, and had to struggle to make a living, they also benefitted from the far more brutal discrimination against African-Americans. The occupational patterns of discrimination suffered by generations of minorities were different from those experienced by European immigrant workers. One consequence is that current opposition to affirmative action is based on perceived group interest. What appears to be philosophical arguments about quotas and reverse discrimination is in reality an extensive effort by white ethnics to maintain their preferential position. Wages and status derive from steady work and can only be obtained by entering the permanent labor force, and labor unions were important in providing access to the job market for many groups of immigrant workers. In contrast to the white ethnics, generations of black workers were systematically barred from employment in the primary sectors of the labor market and thereby denied the economic base that made possible the celebrated achievements and social mobility of white immigrant communities. Nowhere was this process more pronounced than among the building trades, which shared the assumption of the early American Federation of Labor that non-Caucasian workers could not be assimilated and therefore they should be denied union membership on a racial basis and denied employment in unionized occupations. Thus, blacks and other minorities were assigned to a permanent position as marginal laborers in unskilled and menial classifications at the lowest wages. The unions were leaders in the exclusionary laws against the Chinese and other Asians on the West Coast. The construction unions were among the most vociferous in their prejudices and exclusionary practices against blacks and Asians (Hill, 1989, pp. 197–198).

Whatever difficulties white immigrants initially experienced, they could eventually become naturalized and gain full participation in the society. White immigrants sought assimilation and acculturation, a process that required establishment of ethnic identity groups. For European immigrant workers, class consciousness was based on ethnic group consciousness and not identity with blacks or other nonwhite workers. Over time, the ethnic and racial divisions within the working class reinforced labor market segmentation and led to the development of a dual racial labor system. Contemporary racial patterns of employment are the consequence of the white working class establishing its turf and unwilling to give it up or sacrifice any of it to advance the interests of minority workers. This is why changes in racial employment, as represented by affirmative action and other programs, is so bitterly resisted and why job inequality is so deeply rooted in certain industries, particularly the construction industry. In 1971, for example, in the building trades only 4.3 percent of the operating engineers were African-Ameerican and Puerto Rican, whereas at that time they accounted for 39.3 percent of the laborers' union (Foner and Lewis, 1989, p. 625).

During the antebellum period in the South, blacks, both slave and free, were prominent in the skilled and unskilled building crafts. Some of the best buildings in the South, including Monticello and a large number of buildings in Washington, D.C., were built with black labor. Schools, courthouses, public buildings, and many of the mansions of the south were constructed by black construction workers. After the Civil War, blacks were pushed out of the crafts and marginalized in functions to that of laborers, hod-carriers, and other menial occupations. In 1898, John Stevens Durham, a white social reformer, described how African-American participation in industrial organizations and in the building trades was checked by the interference of labor organizations. He noted how blacks were restricted to the lowest-paying menial jobs as a result of labor union practices in many industries and among the building crafts. Durham found that this practice went on in both the North as well as the South. In Philadelphia and other northern cities at the turn of the century, where work opportunities were in general expanding, blacks experienced severe job curtailment and were increasingly limited to menial and service occupations (Hill, 1989, pp. 206–207).

After 1900, black workers were admitted into some AFL unions, but they were usually limited to segregated or auxiliary units, a policy sanctioned by Article XII, Section VI, of the Constitution of the American Federation of Labor as revised in 1900:

Separate charters may be issued to central unions, local unions, or federal labor unions, composed exclusive of colored workers, where in the judgment of the Executive Council it appears advisable.

Building trades unions, like the sheetmetal workers, engaged in similar practices. Article IV, Section I of that union's 1918 constitution, provided that separate charters for black sheet metal workers would be granted,

[O]nly with the consent of the white local union established in the locality . . . where there are a sufficient number of Negro sheet metal workers, they may be organized as an Auxiliary Local and shall come under the jurisdiction of the White Local Union having jurisdiction over said locality. Members of Auxiliary Locals composed of colored sheet metal workers shall not transfer except to another Auxiliary Local composed of colored members. (Hill, 1989, p. 210)

Another construction workers' union, the International Brotherhood of Electrical Workers, in 1903, stated in its official publication that "we do not want the Negro in the International Brotherhood of Electrical Workers, but we think they should be organized into locals of their own." A major result of creating segregated locals and auxiliary units was to prevent blacks from protecting their own interests in the collective bargaining process (Hill, 1989, p. 210).

Eric Arneson states that in some cases blacks expressed their preference for all-black unions, which, in the context of Jim Crow, afforded them control over finances, allowed them to elect their own leaders, and provided them with a greater degree of protection. This is not to say that blacks accepted a second-class status. To the contrary, many saw their own racially distinct union locals as vehicles to protect their members and advance their own agendas. They did not seek integration but equality of status with the local union of their white counterparts. This was especially the case with biracial unions—those in which blacks and whites organized racially distinct locals—in the longshore, coal mining, timber, and occasionally, building industries (Arnesen, 1998, pp. 157, 171).

In a 1930 study of the racial practices of labor unions, Ira De A. Reid noted that even though some unions, and this included construction unions, had removed racial exclusion provisions from their constitutions, they continued to exclude nonwhites by tacit consent. He stated:

Tacit agreement, examinations and local determination of eligibility for membership serve as deterrents to Negro inclusion in many unions. The Plumbers have never made an issue of the question of admitting Negroes, though it is generally understood that they are not admitted. Despite persistent efforts of Negro plumbers in Philadelphia, New York, and Chicago to secure membership, they have not succeeded. . . . In Philadelphia, the licensing board will not grant licenses to Negro plumbers. (Hill, 1989, p. 212)

Many construction unions had lobbied successfully in state legislatures and city councils for the enactment of statutes requiring that craftsmen such as plumbers, steamfitters, and electricians be licensed by state or municipal boards on which union representatives would sit. A 1905 letter from C. H. Perry, secretary of Local Union 110 of the plumbers union in Virginia, to the editor of the *Journal*, official organ of the plumbers union, revealed the purpose of such lobbying to "entirely eliminate the black artisan . . . from the craft, especially in the southern district, as the Negro is a factor there" (Spero and Harris, 1931, pp. 477–478). By 1925 more than 30 states required licensing boards, which included union representatives, thus providing labor unions with the legal means to eliminate nonwhites from many construction trades (Hill, 1989, p. 213).

Data from cities, north and south, reveal the consequences of organized labor's efforts to remove nonwhite workers from many crafts and industries. According to Kenneth L. Kusmer (1976, pp. 68–73), in Cleveland, Ohio:

Union policies, both national and local, effectively kept most eligible Negroes out of the trade union movement. The Boilermaker's Union, the International Association of Machinists, and the Plumbers and Steamfitters Union had a national policy of excluding blacks. Other union locals in the city such as the Metal Polishers and the Paperhangers, barred Negroes on their own initiative. . . . In 1870 fully 31.7 percent of all black males in Cleveland had been employed in skilled trades; by 1910 this figure had dropped sharply to 11 percent. . . . The 1910 Census listed only five black plumbers in the entire city. (Hill, 1989, p. 214)

Craft unions in the construction trades were a most important factor in the process of racial job displacement during the post-Reconstruction period. Prior to emancipation, there had been a concentration of black workers, both slave and free, in the building trades. The construction unions converted these jobs to "white men's work" and forced African-Americans out. This process occurred in many cities along the eastern seaboard and throughout the southern states. In New York City, between 1890 and 1910, when the percentage of total immigrant white population reach 76 percent, black occupational eviction was intensified among painters, brickmakers, and other trades. White immigrants did not have an easy initial passage into all labor organizations. Hostility toward white foreign-born workers characterized some craft unions, especially in the building trades. A number of unions required citizenship or a declaration of intent as a condition of membership; others imposed high initiation fees, or required approval for admission by officers of the national organization or the presentation of a membership card from a foreign union. Nevertheless, unions eventually admitted them. In time, these immigrant groups achieved control of certain trades and established an "ethnic lock" on jobs and union jurisdiction within their respective crafts. Locals of the bricklayers union were either Irish or Italian, and the painters union was largely Jewish (Hill, 1989, p. 216).

Whatever problems experienced by European ethnic groups, they were white in a society acutely conscious of race. European immigrants and their descendants contributed to the development of discriminatory patterns, just as they were the beneficiaries of such practices themselves. The idea that the suffering of white people was more important and worthy of attention than the suffering of black people, and that it was acceptable to obtain advantages at the expense of blacks, permeated much of U.S. society. European immigrants benefited from the exclusionary racial pattern since it gave them preferential status and treatment in gaining access to training and jobs reserved for whites only. This preferential treatment made possible the economic gains of ethnic communities, in contrast to the declining condition of black workers. The elimination of traditional patterns of discrimination required by the Civil Rights Act of 1964 adversely affected the expectations of whites since it compelled competition with black workers and other minority group members where no competition previously existed. White worker expectations had become the norm, and any alteration of the norm was considered "reverse discrimination." The primary issue in the affirmative action controversy is the removal of the preferential treatment traditionally enjoyed by white workers at the expense of blacks as a class (Hill, 1989, pp. 232–233).

Until the 1960s, New York's building trades were virtually impenetrable to African-Americans. Blacks made some gains in construction jobs after World War I, but the impact of the 1930s depression reversed them. Craft union policies became more rigid. Powerful Local 3, an electrical workers union, simply refused to admit blacks. Plumbers' Local 2, George Meany's home union, used control of the licensing requirement to keep blacks out. The carpenters' union segregated its membership by race. The District Council assigned all black members to Local 1888, a mixed local based in Harlem. White members gradually transferred to other locals. Finally, the Carpenters' District Council made Harlem the sole jurisdiction for which Local 1888 members could work. Predictably, black membership in the carpenters' local union fell from 440 members in 1926 to 65 in 1935.

Although World War II helped redress some of the damage of the 1930s, African-Americans remained on the margins of the construction industry, mostly confined to rough, laborers' work and the trowel trades. Until the 1960s, each carpenters' local union had its quota of two blacks who were allowed to do finish work. Plumbers Local 2 had three black members who were rarely allowed to work with other journeymen. Sheetmetal Local 28, a strictly father-son local, had no black members at all. But once protest engulfed New York's African-American community in the 1960s, it was inevitable that civil rights advocates would turn to the construction industry. In those days of urban renewal, when the black ghettos of New York and other cities contained numerous construction sites, everyone could see the persistence of an all-white work force. Pickets, demonstrations, and violence spread to construction sites throughout the city. These conflicts have remained a part of the construction scene and have resulted in a number of responses by the industry, the unions, and the government (Waldinger, 1996, pp. 182–184). In the building trades in the 1960s in New York City (where most of the construction unions were concentrated), blacks actually lost ground in jobs in proportion to their presence in the city's population. From 1960 to 1970, blacks increased 60 percent in population but black construction workers increased only 33.3 percent (Foner and Lewis, 1989, p. 669).

Two court cases, one in 1969 and the other in 1973, illustrate how the preferential system for whites was maintained within two construction craft unions. The first case involved the asbestos workers, Local 53, in New Orleans. The court found that Local 53's practice was to refer white persons of limited experience and white journeymen of other trade unions to become mechanic asbestos workers. The same local union refused to provide the same treatment for "Negroes or Mexican-Americans for membership in the union or for employment," and even admitted this at the trial. The other case, from New York City, involved the construction lathers Local 46. The district court found that there was a pervasive practice in this union of handing out jobs on the basis of union membership, kinship, friendship, and "pull." The hirings at the construction site, the by-passing of the lists, and the use of the hiring hall as a formality, all reflected the practice of preferring Local 46 members, relatives, friends, or friends of friends in job referrals. Since the membership of Local 46 had for so long been almost exclusively white, the jobs, especially the more desirable jobs, had gone disproportionately to whites rather than blacks. Commenting on the union's practice the court commented that the U.S. Government has shown in case after case the preference of whites over blacks on grounds of nepotism or acquaintanceship. The union called the court-ordered affirmative action remedy "reverse discrimination," but the U.S. Court of Appeals for the Second Circuit rejected the union's contention (Hill, 1989, pp. 233–234).

After the passage of the Civil Rights Act of 1964, with its Title VII, which "bars employment discrimination because of race, color, religion, sex, or national origin" (Sobel, 1980, p. 2), the construction labor unions and the AFL-CIO became most active in leading a national campaign against affirmative action. They lobbied extensively in Congress against affirmative action requirements imposed by federal agencies on government contractors and used their political influence to cripple enforcement in the construction industry. The AFL-CIO building and construction trades department joined with employer associations in the legal attack against the Philadelphia Plan to provide jobs for minority workers in federally subsidized construction projects and filed amicus curiae in other cases against affirmative action programs. George Meany, who was president of the AFL-CIO and the business agent for the New York plumbers union, stated that he was opposed to the idea that people are to be employed because their skin is black, which he said is "discrimination in reverse and we don't buy it." A significant factor in the resistance of building trades unions to the requirements of civil rights laws and affirmative action, is that it cuts into the traditional seniority rights provisions of their contracts that state that layoffs shall be according to seniority. Thus, construction unions oppose any attempt to reduce the work force in a way that would not disproportionately victimize newly hired women and black workers. This came up in a case involving the International Brotherhood of Electrical Workers and Jersey Central Power and Light in 1975. The Third Circuit Court of Appeals ruled that the union seniority system would be sustained even if it operated to the disadvantage of females and minority groups as a result of past employment practices. Another factor in the resistance of building trades unions to affirmative actions is that many unions are based on ethnic communities and the leaders and members of those unions believe that the jobs they control belong to their ethnic group and they are not ready to share those jobs with outsiders, that is, minorities or women (Hill, 1989, pp. 235, 237).

The events leading to the first lawsuit filed by the Department of Justice under Title VII tells much about the racial practices of the AFL-CIO unions in the building trades. In response to repeated civil rights demonstrations during 1965 at the Gateway Arch, a federally-funded construction project in St. Louis, the U.S. government required each contractor to employ a minimum percentage of minority workers. When the general contractor engaged three fully qualified black plumbers who were members of an independent labor union, all workers belong to the AFL-CIO construction unions walked off the job. In February 1966, the U.S. attorney general filed a Title VII suit against four of the unions involved in the walkout—electrical workers, sheetmetal workers, plumbers, and steamfitters. The AFL-CIO Building and Construction Trades Council of St. Louis was also named as a defendant. The government charged that the unions refused to admit blacks and operated their respective hiring halls on a discriminatory basis. Prior to trial the plumbers and steamfitters agreed in a consent decree to some remedial action in the future. Similar work stoppages by the building trades unions to prevent the employment of blacks on other publicly-funded construction projects took place during this period in Cleveland, Philadelphia, and New York City. The construction unions repeatedly resisted, evaded, and in some cases, defied the law. Instead of complying with the federal executive orders to eliminate discrimination in the construction industry, the AFL-CIO and its affiliated building trade unions proposed voluntary "hometown plans," based on a variety of training activities, the so-called outreach programs under union control. These plans were intended as a substitute for federal contract compliance and enforcement of civil rights laws in the construction industry. They were pressed by the AFL-CIO as the alternative to government-imposed plans containing mandatory hiring goals and timetables (Hill, 1989, pp. 237–238).

In New York City, civil rights groups made opening up skilled construction jobs for minorities a top priority in the 1960s and 1970s. But 30 years after the Civil Rights Act of 1964, blacks have not received their fair share of construction jobs, though construction grew by 63 percent between 1980 and 1990 in New York, out-pacing every other industry. Blacks had less of a share in the industry in 1990 than they did in 1980. In 1970, New York's construction sector employed 11,600 Afri-can-American men, which represented 95 percent of parity (the proportion of jobs in relation to the proportion of blacks in the population). But by 1990, there were only 7,200 black men in construction and the parity index had fallen to 72 percent (Waldinger, 1996, pp. 177, 352). Two factors, the informal hiring and training practices, and the political power of construction unions, have prevented Afri-can-Americans from achieving parity within the industry. The industry's reliance on informal social networks for recruitment and training make it difficult for new-comers to break into the industry. In the United States as a whole blacks are grossly overrepresented among laborers and underrepresented among the skilled trades where they are 60 percent of parity, with lower levels of participation among the most highly paid crafts like electricians and plumbers. Ownership is common in construction where firm size is small. Journeymen go from craftsman to owners and back again, making the level of self-employment a good indicator of the acqui-sition of higher-level skills and contacts. Despite two decades of efforts to spur black business in construction, with set-asides and financial assistance, the owner-ship in 1990 by African-American businesses in construction is more under-represented among the ranks of the self-employed than they were in the discriminatory skilled crafts (Waldinger, 1996, pp. 277–278).

THE HIRING OF MINORITIES, THE HOMETOWN PLANS OF THE 1970S, AND APPRENTICESHIP PROGRAMS FOR MINORITIES IN THE CONSTRUCTION INDUSTRY

The apprenticeship system in the United States is based on a set of legal relations that binds the construction industry to the state. Modern apprenticeship was born under the New Deal, a product of the National Apprenticeship Act of 1937, known as the Fitzgerald Act, that established standards for apprenticeship programs. It set up a Bureau of Apprenticeship Training in the Department of Labor to oversee standards, and also gave states the option of establishing their own state appren-ticeship councils. About 30 states set up such councils. Another New Deal pro-gram, the Davis-Bacon Act, also had an influence over apprenticeship programs. The act tried to set a floor under wages in the construction industry and stated that all workers on jobs funded by the U.S. government must be paid the prevailing wage in the region where the construction took place. The only class of worker ex-empted from the prevailing wage requirement for journeyworkers were appren-tices enrolled in government-approved, registered programs. This was a way for unions to provide contractors doing government work with a source of cheap un-ion labor. Thus, there was a linkage between Davis-Bacon and apprenticeship that the government could use to pry open apprenticeship doors for minorities. In the 1940s and 1950s, the government resisted efforts to force unions to increase mi-nority participation in their apprenticeship programs. In the 1960s, the regulators bowed to pressure from protesters, legislators, and the courts, and in 1964 closed apprenticeship programs were prohibited. While regulators are charged with increasing minority participation in apprenticeships, very little has changed with this approach. In New York, for example, in Local 3 of the electrical workers union, there was a decline in the minority share of blacks and Hispanics at a time when minority population expanded. In 1986, only 140 minorities in New York completed apprenticeship programs, compared to 130 who dropped out prior to completion. This dismal record elicited a resounding silence from the New York State Department of Labor (Waldinger, 1996, pp. 184–188).

A new approach was tried. Instead of calling for compliance with civil rights laws and federal executive orders to eliminate the nationwide pattern of discrimination in the construction industry, the AFL-CIO and its affiliated building trades unions proposed voluntary "hometown plans," based on a variety of training activities and so-called outreach programs under union control. These plans were intended as a substitute for federal contract compliance and the enforcement of civil rights laws in the construction industry. They were vigorously pressed by the AFL-CIO as the alternative to government-imposed plans containing mandatory hiring goals and timetables (Hill, 1989, p. 238).

The outreach programs boosted the proportion of apprenticeships provided to minorities a little, but the number of apprentice slots was severely limited. In September 1969, the Nixon administration launched the so-called Philadelphia Plan, requiring government construction contractors to commit themselves to goals in six trades—ironworker, plumber, steamfitter, electrician, sheetmetal worker, and stationary engineer or elevator construction workers, in which minority participation was less than 1.6 percent. In March 1970, a district court upheld the Philadelphia Plan. Earlier, Judge Weiner rejected a suit by the Contractors Association of Eastern Pennsylvania requesting an injunction against the plan, calling it unconstitutional. Weiner said that it did not violate the Civil Rights Act, which forbade quotas, because it did not require a contractor to hire a definite percentage of a minority group. The Philadelphia Plan, however, did require contractors to make a good-faith effort to hire specific percentages of blacks on projects of more than half a million dollars. Later, reports on the results of the Philadelphia Plan by the Office of Federal Contract Compliance Programs, stated that contractors were abusing and disregarding the plan by not hiring additional minority employees (Sobel, 1980, pp. 20–21; Waldinger, 1996, p. 191).

This approach of voluntary hometown plans preceded federally imposed plans in five other cities—Atlanta, San Francisco, Washington, D.C., St. Louis, and Camden, New Jersey. To avert a similar fate, and moved by federal persuasion and dollars, unions and contractors in 70 other localities developed hometown plans or negotiated hiring plans. Like the imposed plans, the hometown plans specified minority hiring goals. These goals were agreed on after negotiations among unions, contractors, minority groups, and local political officials. Negotiated plans met the satisfaction of officials in the Office of Federal Contract and Compliance Programs, who saw money-savings potentials and the possibilities of great commitment from unions and contractors as well as more administrative flexibility (Waldinger, 1996, p. 191).

A plan similar to the Philadelphia Plan was upheld in Ohio. In Chicago, a plan was negotiated in January 1970, after African-American community groups forced the shutting down of several state construction jobs. The agreement called for 4,000 blacks to be trained as skilled construction workers and admitted to the Chicago unions. The unions offered to train 1,000 blacks and accept 3,000 blacks for apprenticeship positions. Under the agreement, 1,000 blacks who could qualify as apprentices or journeymen would be put to work immediately. A second 1,000 would start on-the-job training as soon as possible, and another 1,000 would be slated to begin journeyman training leading to full status as skilled workers. The other 1,000 would be given a specialized pre-apprentice training program for rudimentary construction skills. On June 4, 1971, the U.S. Labor Department said that it was withdrawing its support of the Chicago voluntary equal hiring plan for federal construction projects and would impose mandatory racial quotas on federally-assisted projects throughout the city. The Chicago Plan collapsed after 18 months. It had pledged to hire 4,000 minority group members, but by June 4, 1971, only 885 African-Americans and Hispanics had been taken on for apprentice training, only a few had obtained membership in Chicago's construction unions, and only 150 minority workers had been placed by May 1971. The plan was disbanded when its director, Hubbard, was arrested in Los Angeles and charged with embezzling $100,000. A new plan was launched in October 1972, run by the Chicago Urban League and funded with 1.7 million by the U.S. Labor Department. The 1972 plan also collapsed when the U.S. Labor Department withdrew support because of poor performance. The department noted that only about 200 minority workers had been hired under a first-year federal grant of 1.7 million, compared to the goal of training 1,700 such workers. The U.S. Labor Department announced that it would impose its own hiring plan and set goals and timetables, which was greeted with skepticism by Herbert Hill, labor director of the National Associations for the Advancement of Colored People (NAACP) (Sobel, 1980, pp. 21, 30, 105).

The New York Plan was announced on March 21, 1970, and called for recruiting and training minority group members as skilled construction workers. Peter Brennan, president of the Buildings and Construction Trades Council of Greater New York, said the plan would go into effect as soon as the funds became available. The Workers Defense League, an organization led by Bayard Rustin was to aid in selecting and preparing blacks and other minority group members for construction trades apprenticeship programs. Governor Rockefeller, Mayor John Lindsay, and industry and union representatives signed the job plan accord on December 10, 1970. On January 12, 1973, New York City announced that it was withdrawing from the plan, since according to the city, only 537 trainees had been placed by June 1972. The city asked the U.S. Labor Department to impose minority job goals and timetables, as mandated by federal law in the absence of local voluntary plans, on all federally-aided construction in New York. Thomas J. Broidrich, a construction company executive and head of the New York Plan, said the city's charges were unfair, since the city had not supplied its $100,000 share of the costs until June 1972, and the federal government had decided not to fund a central training facility. Broidrich said 610 trainees were currently in the plan, 480 were actually in jobs and 34 were journeymen. In August 1974, a state supreme court justice ruled that New York City had gone beyond its authority in imposing the mandatory standards and the U.S. Labor Department said it would not appeal the decision. A new plan called for hiring one minority on-the-job trainee for every four experienced workers on each project, but that plan never materialized as a series of complicated lawsuits ensued and the whole affair came crashing down in 1976 when the New York State Court of Appeals ruled that the mayor had exceeded his authority in setting goals and targets in the absence of legislative consent.

When Koch became mayor, having received considerable African-American support in the 1977 Democratic run-off primary, he reinstated the one-to-four ratio. But the New York state labor department decided in the mid-1980s, that State Labor Law 220 recognizes only two classifications of workers—apprentices and journeyworkers, and not trainees. This decision left New York State and its municipalities without an affirmative action program in construction. As the 1990s began, the New York Plan limped along through a loophole, providing trainees to contractors working on projects enjoying a New York City tax abatement, and therefore not directly subject to State Law 220. Two decades of conflict yielded few journey-level jobs for minority workers. The New York Plan failed to supply support for the generally poor, generally unskilled workers it sent out to construction sites. Some workers did pick up a trade, but most were assigned "gofer" jobs by contractors who were mainly interested in moving the same black workers from job to job in order to meet government hiring goals. Consequently, the New York Plan has added few craftsworkers to the union rolls. Of the 5,000 trainees it placed in jobs between 1971 and 1988, only 800 were ever accepted into the unions. The history of the New York Plan is the story of an opportunity squandered. From the start, the unions and contractors froze out the minority groups pushing for minority employment. From the beginning, Peter Brennan, head of the New York Building Trades Council signaled to building trades unions throughout the country to dig in their heels. In the 1980s, with support from the electrical workers, the New York State department of labor moved against the New York Plan, leaving New York State without any training or affirmative action program in construction. Unlike the political leaders, the union leaders had the staying power and commitment to see their goals through. Long after Rockefeller and Lindsay were gone, the union officials remained in place (Sobel, 1980, pp. 22–23; Waldinger, 1996, pp. 191–195).

At the end of the day, the evidence in Chicago, Pittsburgh, San Francisco, New York, Boston, Atlanta, and many other cities reveals that hometown plans and apprenticeship outreach programs did not eliminate or even diminish discriminatory job patterns in the construction industry. After a survey of the Washington, D.C. plan, the *Washington Post* concluded that "the white men's unions of 1970 remain the white men's unions of the 1980s" (Hill, 1989, p. 239). Apprenticeship outreach programs, after more than 20 years of operation, have failed to eliminate the discriminatory racial pattern in the building trades. They have served the interests of restrictive labor unions, but not the interests of African-Americans and other minority workers. Data reveal that the present system of apprenticeship training constitutes an additional and formidable barrier to minority workers. In *United States v. Local 638, Steamfitters*, the district court stated: "This practice of admitting whites by informal standards and without reference to apprenticeship programs while denying such admission to non-whites is discriminatory and unlawful." While there has been an increase in African-American participation in the construction industry, there has been little change in the percentages of black journeymen admitted into unions controlling employment in the skilled occupations. Black construction workers remain concentrated in unskilled laborers' jobs, among carpenters and in the trowel trades. Apprenticeship training is not an end in itself. It is meaningful only if it leads to skilled employment and union membership, and it has failed to do so for most African-Americans seeking to enter the crafts (Hill, 1989, pp. 239–240).

Established workers in the construction industry have an enduring interest in restricting hiring to the members of the incumbents' core network. Construction's position in the job hierarchy make it a target for civil rights groups, with its high wages for many of the trades like ironworkers, carpenters, electricians, and plumbers, and even for laborers, as compared with other blue-collar workers. In good times and bad, the building trades enjoy a plentiful supply of new recruits. In New York City, the electricians' union received an annual average of over 4,000 applications for about 500 apprenticeship slots between 1986 and 1989. Whites dominated the electricians' pool, with 4 whites to every 1 nonwhite applicant. Historically, exclusion results from the formal and informal arrangements that connect craftsworkers to one another and their employers through which construction workers and their unions control access to the trade. Those practices came under intense scrutiny in the 1960s as blacks began agitating for access to skilled, unionized trades. Although white dominance was rooted in informal processes, the government was a potentially important player, owing to its role as a consumer of construction services and the prevailing wage policies it used when awarding contracts. By the late 1960s and early 1970s, shifts in the power of African-American protesters relative to white-dominated construction unions led governments at various levels to open up apprenticeship programs and impose minority hiring goals on public jobs. Though 30 years of protest over discrimination in construction have produced progress, the gains are disappointing and severe barriers remain in place. To the extent that African-Americans made inroads into the union sector, they did so under conditions of intense community mobilization and alliances to other white interest groups. The history of affirmative action policies in construction bears witness to the unions' ability to control those policies to meet their own ultimate ends. Unions were highly political entities, embedded in the political parties, with long-established strategies for controlling those state policies that affected their industry (Waldinger, 1996, pp. 199–201).

COURT-IMPOSED REMEDIES

The building trades unions have been involved in much litigation regarding discrimination in hiring of minorities. New York City's construction unions have been particularly involved in such litigation. Numerous actions were brought against New York locals in federal courts, including Steamfitters' Local 638, Sheetmetal Workers Local 28, Wire Lathers' Local 46, Ironworkers' Locals 40 and 580, Operating Engineers' Locals 14 and 15, Elevator Constructors' Local 1, and Local 3 of the International Brotherhood of Electrical Workers. The action against the sheetmetal workers highlights not only the crafts' tenacious resistance to integration, but also the nexus between formal and informal training systems in impeding minority access to construction jobs. In 1948, the New York State Commission against Discrimination ordered Local 28 to desist from excluding blacks. The "Caucasian only" clause was removed from the union's constitution, but 15 years later, 1963, not a single African-American worker had been admitted into membership. On March 4, 1964, the state commission ruled that Local 28 had excluded blacks during the entire 78 years of the union's existence and ordered them to admit blacks. When Local 28 refused to comply the commission took the local to court. In 1971, the federal government began action against the sheetmetal workers' union. Following a trial in 1975, the district court found that the union had selected friends and relatives for apprenticeship examinations, it refused to admit blacks, and in its organizing drives it extended union status to white employees only. The district court then established a membership goal for the local of 29 percent, to be met by 1981. Noting that the goal had not been met the district court cited the local for contempt and fined them $150,000. The city brought a second contempt proceeding, which led to a 1983 district court proposed Employment, Training and Recruitment Fund financed by the $150,000 fine imposed by the court. The deadline for the 29 percent minority membership goal was extended to August 1987. It also ordered a quota of three minority apprentices for every one white apprentice. When the union appealed this ruling to the Supreme Court, the court upheld the lower court's ruling. However, despite the existence of a court-appointed administrator empowered to increase the number of minority apprentices, minority enrollment in the program was difficult to sustain because the minority apprentices lacked access to the informal support system. The apprenticeship group had a high number of whites with relatives in the trade.

Furthermore, the union found time was on their side. It took almost 40 years for white workers in the sheetmetal union to desist. Those unions that prolonged their resistance into the 1980s found that time was not an enemy but a friend. With the advent of the Reagan administration, monitoring the behavior of construction unions under consent decrees from the court no longer took high priority (Waldinger, 1996, pp. 195–197).

MINORITY BUSINESS IN THE CONSTRUCTION INDUSTRY

In October 1996, the Urban Institute in Washington, D.C., prepared a report on minorities share of government contracts that included the construction industry (Enchautegui, et al., 1996). The Urban Institute analysis revealed substantial disparities between the share of contract dollars received by minority-owned firms and the share of all firms that they represent. Based on their number, minority-owned firms received only 57 cents for every dollar they would be expected to receive. Government contracting provides governments with a potentially powerful tool for promoting minority opportunities and counteracting discrimination. In 1990, procurement at all levels of government represented approximately $450 billion, or almost 10 percent of Gross National Product (GNP). State and local government spending accounted for more than half of all procurement, or approximately $250 billion. In 1995, federal spending on contracting exceeded spending for federal employment. (Enchautegui, et al., 1996, pp. i–ii).

There are two types of barriers faced by minority firms: (1) barriers to firm formation and growth, and (2) barriers to participation in the government contracting process itself. In general, minority-owned firms are smaller in size and fewer in number than majority-owned firms. Major barriers to the formation and development of minority-owned businesses include:

- *Lack of financial capital*: minorities have lower incomes, fewer assets, and diminished access to business loans.
- *Lack of social capital*: minorities' access to business networks is limited, and their own family networks may be smaller or less valuable than those of their majority counterparts.
- *Lower human capital endowments*: minorities have less education and professional training, and their access to union and other apprenticeship programs is more limited.
- *Residential segregation:* minorities' access to lucrative, nonminority consumer markets is comparatively limited, due in part to historical patterns of residential segregation.

Each of the barriers has been produced and perpetuated, at least in part by discrimination. Minority-owned businesses turn to securing government contracts to offset some of the limitations imposed by the private market. But barriers embedded in the contracting process itself can impede minority firms from winning government contracts. These barriers include:

- Failure of government to break large contracts down into smaller projects so that minority firms, which tend to be smaller, can compete.
- Extensive granting of waivers from minority subcontracting requirements to majority contractors.
- Ineffective screening for false minority fronts.
- Limited notice of contract competitions.
- Bid shopping on the part of majority prime contractors, who disclose minority firms' subcontracting bids to their majority competitors so they can be underbid.

Federal, state, and local governments addressed these barriers with a wide range of affirmative action programs. These programs fall into two broad categories. One category uses race as a factor in the award of contracts. Examples include the use of sole source contracts, set-asides, price or evaluation advantages, and the use of goals for prime or subcontracting. These policies are intended to directly increase the number of contract and subcontract awards received by minority firms (Enchautegui, et al., 1996, pp. ii–iii).

A second category of procurement-related policies seeks to expand the number of minority-owned firms contracting with government by increasing their financial, social, or human capital. These initiatives are sometimes referred to as affirmative action programs and sometimes as race-neutral policies. The goal is to put minority firms in a better position to compete as either prime contractors or subcontractors. These policies include lending and bonding help, technical assistance programs, expanded notice requirements, and imposing prompt payment directives on government agencies. In general, these policies are intended to enlarge the pool of potential minority bidders for public contracts. They do not directly affect outcomes in the contractor selection process. Affirmative action programs in contracting have been directed primarily at assisting minority-owned businesses and not, for the most part, at increasing minority employment. The future of affirmative action is being defined in large measure by the rulings of the Supreme Court in two cases that deal with government contracting.

In a 1989 case, *City of Richmond v. J. A. Croson,* the Supreme Court held that state and local preference programs would be subject to the Court's rigorous "strict scrutiny standard." Under this standard racial classifications must serve a "compelling interest" and be "narrowly tailored" to suit that purpose. The program adopted by the Richmond city council was instituted in the light of gross disparities between Richmond's black population, which was 50 percent of the total population, and the percentage of city contracts awarded to minority-owned businesses, which was less than 1 percent. Richmond's majority black city council believed that this situation was not the result of the market but a reflection of substantial discrimination. They adopted an affirmative action program that required 30 percent of state and city contracts be set side for minority firms. The Supreme Court decision, written by Justice Sandra Day O'Connor, stated that the disparate numbers were simply the natural result of some undetermined market force and not the result of some past discrimination. Richmond had been before the Supreme Court in a number of cases involving questions of discrimination in voting, housing, and schools. Virginia actually closed its schools rather than integrate them, yet the Court took none of these examples of de jure discrimination into account. O'Connor said that minorities simply didn't choose to become contractors in proportion to their percentage in the population. The philosophy in Croson was that the state must treat blacks and whites the same by not considering their race. Kimberle Crenshaw comments that treating different things the same can generate as much inequality as treating the same things differently. She cites Anatole France who noted that the law in its majestic equality prevents the rich and the poor from sleeping under bridges, showing that the law results in inequality when the rich will never seek that worldly pleasure, and the poor have no other choice. A similar denial of social power differentials between racial groups reproduces and insulates that very power disparity, reinforcing the system and insulating it from attack (Crenshaw, 1997).

It was in response to Croson that many state and local governments commissioned the disparity studies analyzed by the Urban Institute for its report. The disparity studies document differences between the share of all firms that minorities own and the share of government contracts they receive. In addition, they often document the role that state and local governments and the private sector have played in perpetuating historical patterns of discrimination through their contracting practices.

In June 1995, the Supreme Court decided *Adarand Constructors v. Pena*, apparently making all federal race-conscious, affirmative action programs subject to the same strict scrutiny standard announced in *Croson*. The impact of applying strict scrutiny to affirmative action programs is profound: proponents of race-based policies intended to help minorities must meet the same high standard of proof required for proponents of race-based practices that disadvantage minorities (Enchautegui, et al., 1996, pp. iii–v).

The Urban Institute report examined whether there is disparity in the receipt of state and local government contract dollars between minority-owned and majority-owned businesses. The Urban Institute researchers combined the results of 58 studies. Following the Supreme Court decision in the *Croson* case, the percentage of all government contract dollars received by minority-owned businesses was then compared to the percentage of all businesses "ready, willing, and able" to carry out government contracts that are minority-owned. Where these percentages are similar, there is no disparity in government contracting. For example, if 5 percent of all "ready, willing, and able" firms are minority-owned and 5 percent of government contracting dollars are awarded to minority-owned firms, there is no disparity. If only 2 percent of government dollars went to minority-owned firms, there would be disparity. The Urban Institute found substantial disparity in government contracting. Minority-owned businesses receive far fewer government contract dollars than would be expected based on their availability. Minority- owned businesses as a group receive only 57 cents of each dollar that they would be expected to receive based on the percentage of all "ready, willing, and able" firms that are minority-owned. The study included government contracting for construction, goods, professional services, and other services. In construction the disparity was 61 cents for each dollar they would be expected to receive, and in construction subcontracting, the disparity was 95 cents. (Enchautegui, et al., 1996, p. vi).

The study found that disparity was greater in jurisdictions where no goals programs were in place and their findings indicate that overall, affirmative action programs may reduce disparity. The disparities documented in government contract awards can result from government or private discrimination or can be the product of minority-owned firms being, on average, less qualified to win government contractors than majority-owned firms. In the latter case, being less qualified (e.g., having less experience, fewer employees, or lacking access to bonding) may or may not result from past or present discrimination. Due to data limitation, the Urban Institute could not determine the degree to which the findings of disparity result from discrimination. The problem of linking disparity to discrimination is one that is being grappled with by the courts (Enchautegui, et al., 1996, p. ix).

The Urban Institute report drew the following conclusions:

1. Minority firms are less successful than their majority counterparts in obtaining procurement dollars at the state and local government levels. This is not necessarily proof of discrimination on the part of state and local governments. At a minimum the findings suggest that barriers remain to minority firms' participation in the government contracting process.

2. Disparities indicate that adoption of affirmative action and other programs designed to assist minority firms has not led to broad displacement of majority firms in the award of government contracts. That is, the results do not support claims of widespread reverse discrimination in contracting at the state and local government levels.

3. Disparities are greater in those areas where no affirmative action program is in place. While a causal relationship between these facts cannot be established on the basis of this report alone, the results may indicate that affirmative action programs help to reduce disparities. Repealing affirmative action policies would limit the tools available to government to rectify these disparities. (Enchautegui, et al., 1996, pp. ix–x).

Construction is one industry where it is relatively easy for journeymen to go into business. Its competitive structure and low capital-to-labor ratios has made it a time-honored ethnic pathway into business. Construction has the further virtue of being an industry in which black entrepreneurs have a significant presence, in part due to public policies that have sought to leverage government resources to increase opportunities for black entrepreneurs. The record of black business growth in construction still reads better than it does in the economy overall (Waldinger, 1996, pp. 267–268). Many minorities are among the 1.4 million self-employed in the industry, that is, skilled tradesmen with no employees doing contracting work. Many journeymen turn to going into business when jobs are scarce, and many go the other way and take jobs when they get tired of running around trying to pick up contract work. If they have a skill it doesn't take much capital to perform work—just their own tools, which they have anyway, and supplies which they can buy on credit if the supply house knows them.

In construction you have to do good work and build your reputation. Waldinger states:

Getting customers is akin to eliciting the cooperation of skilled workers, in that both depend on trust. Any one job is likely to differ significantly from the next, making price no more, and possibly less important than getting the work done right and on time. Since construction is "a very small world," developing a good reputation is essential. (Waldinger, 1996, p. 272)

Few other industries rely as much as construction on ongoing relationships between contractors, clients, key workers, subcontractors, suppliers, architects, and a host of other players. The industry has always served as a place where immigrant businesses could be set up and succeed. In 1990, 46 percent of all New York's construction personnel were foreign-born, and the same proportion held among those working for themselves. The constant round of the construction business cycle transforms workers into contractors because of the small size of so many construction firms. Journeymen turned contractors start small and do anything—small jobs, repair jobs, or taking work from other contractors. The biggest problem is getting paid. If they know the person who hired them for the work they have a chance. If they take work from strangers they are asking for trouble. Fledgling contractors often choose neighborhood work because these jobs are too small to attract larger competitors and if you do a good job, the word spreads and you get other work. Contractors in an industry as fragmented as construction have no choice but to be interdependent with workers, other contractors, suppliers, clients, and building inspectors. This interdependency provides a network for establishing confidence and assessing reliability, making every construction market a small town where good and bad news travels fast. It makes it hard for outsiders to break through this network and that is why African-Americans and other minorities, like Asians, have a hard time in many areas of the construction industry. White contractors, having survived for many years based on father-son businesses and networks of relatives in the unions and contracting firms, set up interdependencies and enclaves which serve to keep out outsiders. Thus, African-Americans and others have difficulty in the construction industry in going into business, in finding work, in getting whites to work for them, in getting credit from suppliers, in getting recognition from inspectors and public authorities, "The typical white contractor began from a milieu connected to, if not ensconced in the industry, which generated know-how and contacts. African-American builders, by contrast, were outsiders who had to pick up skills and knowledge without the social capital whites enjoyed. . . . Whereas white neophytes entered familiar terrain, surrounded by friendly, or at least familiar faces, the black contractors found that going into construction meant learning an entirely new world" (Waldinger, 1996, p. 274).

While access to formal sources is helpful, contractors rely on their reputation and their clients' wishes to maintain existing relationships. Thus, African-American contractors struggle to get business while the more established firms rely on reputations and existing contacts. Reputation reduces the need to seek out work or bid for jobs. The widespread preference for working with contractors that have a good track record and enjoy existing relationships makes it difficult for outsiders who lack these contacts.

Even the most experienced black contractors find that the problems of creating relationships with white general contractors and developers, combined with the greater opportunity in the public sector, leads them to shy away from private work. Black contractors find that transactions with the larger, white entities are unlikely to evolve into stable, mutually beneficial relationships. Furthermore, with private sector jobs come collection problems, which is true for all contractors, white and black. Public work has its own pitfalls, above and beyond greater exposure to unionization. In public jobs, the money is good (they don't go bankrupt), but public agencies are notorious for being slow to pay. Contractors who get into a dispute with a resident engineer or bureaucrat who supervised their work may run into an arbitrary and illogical reason for not getting paid. Authorities may sometimes use any excuse for not rendering payment, and if a contractor has a lot of retainages outstanding, it could put them out of business. While black contractors may be very active in bidding public work, especially in cities like Newark or New York, they have to worry about running into a hostile bureaucrat who will make their lives miserable (Waldinger, 1996, pp. 278–283).

Another minority, the Koreans, also found it difficult to break into the dominant construction network and had to create their own niche in the industry. Koreans arrived in the United States with high levels of skill, but many found there were few outlets for their prior training in small businesses of various kinds. Construction was an exception, since skills and experience acquired prior to immigration could be transferred to the United States. Many Korean contractors had an engineering or architects' degree and many had construction experience at high levels. Still, Koreans encountered problems in transferring their human capital to a U.S. setting, such as the language. Korean contractors had an ethnic market to which they could turn. The burgeoning Asian middle-class meant work for Korean builders. Not only did they build homes for middle-class and wealthy Koreans, but store renovations and remodeling of Korean businesses provided outlets for Korean contractors. Many contractors found the Korean church provided a means for making contacts. Capital flowed from Taiwan and Hong Kong, which generated new construction in the Flushing area of Queens and created markets for the emerging group of Korean contractors. Thus, the growth of New York's middle-class Asian community spurred the development of a Korean construction sector in two different ways. First, the prevalence of Asian property ownership created the ethnic demand for construction services, lacking in black communities. Second, ties to the ethnic clientele made this a protected market. The Koreans appear to be embedded in ethnic networks, through which they secure jobs and skilled labor. Ethnic solidarity operates less powerfully among black contractors, who are tied to a community where intraethnic diversity and internal competition have grown as a result of Caribbean immigration. Compared to whites, Korean and Hispanic contractors are more likely to employ relatives and co-ethnics. Considerations of trust and risk-aversion lead ethnic owners to hire their own kind. Outsiders fare poorly when immigrant entrepreneurs rely on their own kind. The variations among ethnic business communities aside, job opportunities tend to be withdrawn from the open market, a change that hurts low-skilled, native minorities who lack the networks needed to connect with an ethnic business niche. New York's new ethnic economies accentuate the city's segmented system, providing new incentives and mechanisms for contention over the ethnic division of labor and its fruits (Waldinger, 1996, pp. 276–278, 284–286, 294–299).

AFFIRMATIVE ACTION PROGRAMS AND BLACK EMPLOYMENT

One of the foremost researchers on affirmative action programs, Jonathan S. Leonard, has evaluated the impact of affirmative action on black employment (Leonard, 1990, pp. 47–63). Leonard points out that affirmative action has been one of the most controversial government interventions in the labor market. In recent years, two major criticisms of affirmative action argue: (1) that affirmative action does not work and therefore we should dispose of it, and (2) that affirmative action does work and therefore we should dispose of it. The question is, was affirmative action successful in increasing employment opportunities for blacks (Leonard, 1990, p. 47)?

Executive Order 10925, issued by President John Kennedy on March 6, 1961, was the first to require federal contractors to take affirmative action, and the first to establish specific sanctions, including termination of contract and debarment. Previous nondiscrimination regulations were voluntary and without teeth. The nondiscrimination clauses in government contracts was virtually unenforced by contracting agencies during the years preceding 1961. After the Civil Rights Act of 1964, with its Title VII section banning discrimination in employment, President Johnson's Executive Order 11246 was the first to be enforced stringently enough to provoke serious conflict and debate. Under Executive Order 11246, federal contractors had to agree not to discriminate against any employee or applicant for employment because of race, color, religion, sex, or national origin, and to take affirmative action to ensure that applicants are employed and employees are treated fairly during employment without regard to their race, color, religion, sex, or national origin (Leonard, 1990, p. 48). The part about how people are treated "during employment" is interesting, because in the construction industry minorities and women found that after they were employed they were isolated and treated badly, from being ignored or not being talked to, to harassment for women. In construction this is especially telling since learning a trade in construction is mainly on-the-job training based on instruction from seasoned journeymen. If minorities are being treated badly in construction and they are not going to be properly trained, their chances of success are reduced drastically and their chances of failure rise accordingly.

Federal contractors were required to develop affirmative action plans, including goals and timetables, for good-faith efforts to correct deficiencies in minority and female employment. They were also obliged not to discriminate. It is a measure of this nation's progress that no one argues against the second obligation not to discriminate, but it is another story with regard to affirmative action. Leonard quotes Lawrence Silberman, Undersecretary of Labor from 1970 to 1973, who wrote that the government was trying to avoid turning affirmative action into quotas because it introduced a group rights concept antithetical to traditional American notions of individual merit and responsibility. Silberman also said that affirmative action programs without measurable results invites sham efforts. Numerical standards in the quest for equal opportunity opened the door to an emphasis on equal results and raised the question whether discrimination and its remedy should be addressed in terms of groups or individuals (Leonard, 1990, pp. 48–49).

Studies of affirmative action in its first few years by the U.S. Commission on Civil Rights, the U.S. General Accounting Office (GAO), and the House and Senate Committees on Labor and Public Welfare, found that affirmative action had been ineffective. The GAO found that the almost nonexistence of enforcement actions conveyed to contractors that the compliance agencies did not intend to enforce the program. The ultimate sanction of debarment had been used less than 30 times.

Despite the weak enforcement in its early years and despite the ineffectiveness of compliance reviews, studies between 1973 and 1976 showed that affirmative action had been effective in increasing black male employment in the contractor sector. The effects were not large, less than a 1 percent increase in the black male share of employment per year, but it showed that even with weak enforcement, affirmative action under the contract compliance program did increase the proportion of black males in federal contractor firms in the early 1970s (Leonard, 1990, pp. 49–50).

Enforcement of affirmative action did become more aggressive after 1973, with increased incidence of debarment and back-pay awards. The contract compliance agencies were reorganized into the Office of Federal Contract Compliance Programs in 1978. The Office of Federal Contract Compliance Programs (OFCCP) is part of the U.S. Department of Labor's Employment Standards Administration. It has a national network of 10 regional offices, each with district and area offices in major metropolitan centers. It is charged with enforcing Executive Order 11246, a 30-year-old order signed by President Lyndon B. Johnson, that prohibits discrimination in hiring or employment opportunities on the basis of race, color, gender, religion, and national origin. It requires all contractors and subcontractors with a federal contract of $50,000 or more and 50 or more employees, to develop a written affirmative action program that sets forth specific and result-oriented procedures to which a contractor commits itself to apply every good faith effort. On September 18, 1997, the OFCCP revised some of its regulations to implement Executive Order 11246, which prohibits employment discrimination and establishes affirmative action requirements for Federal contractors and subcontractors. For a full description of the regulations and requirements for nondiscrimination and affirmative action on all federal contracts, see the following documents: *Equal Employment Opportunity, Title 41, Part 60 of the Code of Federal Regulations,* Chapter 60, U.S. Department of Labor, Employment Standards Administration, Office of Federal Contract Compliance Programs, October 20, 1978; *Pamphlet OFCCP 7, OFCCP at a Glance*, U. S. Department of Labor, Employment Standards Administration, September 1994; Part II, *Government Contractors, Affirmative Action Requirements, Executive Order 11246, Final Rule,* U.S. Department of Labor, Employment Standards Administration, Office of Federal Contract Compliance Programs, September 18, 1997. In spite of all the talk that affirmative action is dead, it is still part of the rules and regulations for doing business with the federal government as a contractor.

Leonard compared data on employment demographics reported to the government by 68,690 establishments in 1974 and 1980. These companies employ more than 16 million people. He found that between 1974 and 1980 black male and female employment shares increased significantly faster in contractor establishments that had an affirmative action obligation as compared with those that did not. Even controlling for establishment size, growth region, industry, occupational and corporate structure, employment of blacks grew significantly faster in contractor establishments with affirmative action obligations than in contractor establishments with no affirmative action programs (Leonard, 1990, pp. 50–51).

Leonard concludes: "Although affirmative action has lacked public consensus and vigorous enforcement, and has frequently been criticized as an exercise in paper pushing, it has actually been of material importance in prompting companies to increase their employment of blacks" (Leonard, 1990, p. 52).

Leonard cites four econometric studies (p. 50) that found while affirmative action increases total black male employment among federal contractors, it does not increase their employment share in the skilled occupations. These studies suggest that contractors have been able to fulfill their obligations by hiring into relatively unskilled positions. Before 1974, affirmative action appears to have been more effective in increasing employment than in promoting occupational advancement. By the late 1970s, affirmative action was more effective in increasing minority employment in skilled occupations. In a study that he conducted (Leonard, 1984, pp. 377–385), Leonard found that black males' share of employment increased faster in affirmative action programs than in nonaffirmative actions programs in every occupation except laborers and white-collar trainees. The lesson to be drawn from the evidence is that affirmative action programs work best when they are vigorously enforced, work with other policies that augment the skills of members of minority groups, and work with growing employers (Leonard, 1990, pp. 52–53, 54).

The goals and timetables for the employment of minorities and females drawn from the affirmative action plans of federal contractors stand accused of two mutually inconsistent charges. The first is that "goal" is really a polite word for inflexible quotas for minority and female employment. The second is that affirmative action has never been enforced stringently enough to produce significant results. The problem with enforcement of affirmative action programs is that the penalties to contractors is not very great. The ultimate sanction available to the government is to bar a firm from bidding on federal contractors, but fewer than 30 firms have ever been debarred. If the Office of Federal Contract Compliance Programs finds an establishment's affirmative action plan unacceptable, it may issue a show-cause notice as a preliminary step to debarment. But this step has been taken in only 1 to 4 percent of all compliance reviews. Of these, one-third to one-half involve basic paperwork deficiencies such as failure to prepare or update an affirmative action plan. The other major sanction is to award back pay as part of a conciliation agreement. In 1973 and 1974, $54 million was awarded in 91 settlements, averaging $63 per beneficiary. In 1980, $9.2 million was awarded to 4,336 employees. These beneficiaries represented less than two-thirds of 1 percent of all minority employees at the reviewed establishments. After 1980, back-pay awards were phased out because the administration found them undesirable and in excess of regulatory authority. The low penalties if caught are compounded by the low probability of apprehension. All of this suggests that contractors might well face (and perceive) only a weak threat of enforcement (Leonard, 1990, p. 54).

Black economic advance faltered along a number of dimensions during the 1980s. Affirmative action under the contract compliance program virtually ceased to exist in all but name after 1980. After 1980, fewer administrative complaints were filed, back-pay awards were phased out, and the already rare penalty of debarment was virtually nonexistent. Over the same period, staffing and real budget were reduced. This resulted in a reversal of black advances under affirmative action. Between 1980 and 1984, both male and female black employment grew more slowly among contractors. Affirmative action, such as it was, no longer aided blacks (Leonard, 1990, pp. 58–59).

Title VII of the Civil Rights Act of 1964, which made employment discrimination illegal, stands at the center of the federal antidiscrimination effort. The Johnson Executive Order 11246 has functioned within the backdrop of the Title VII congressional mandate and substantial legal sanctions. Title VII allows individuals to bring suit and this litigation has resulted in multimillion dollar remedies. The threat of costly Title VII litigation, largely private, has been of great importance to employers. The Equal Employment Opportunity Commission (EEOC) has helped to establish far-reaching principles of Title VII law in the courts which was used by private litigants. However, a 1976 General Accounting Office review of direct EEOC enforcement activity concluded that it was generally ineffective. Most individual charges were closed administratively before a formal investigation. Charges took about two years to be resolved, and only 11 percent resulted in successful negotiated settlements. There was little EEOC follow-up to ensure compliance with conciliation agreements, and entering into such agreements caused no significant change in a firm's employment of blacks or females. Between 1973 and 1975, among 12,800 charges for which the EEOC found evidence of discrimination and was able to negotiate settlements, fewer than 1 percent had been brought to litigation resulting in favorable court decisions (Leonard, 1990, pp. 59–60; Hill, 1983, pp. 45–72).

Leonard concludes that:

Despite poor targeting, affirmative action has helped promote the employment of minorities and women, and Title VII has likely played an even greater role. But has this pressure led to reduced discrimination, or has it gone beyond and induced reverse discrimination against white males? The evidence is least conclusive on this question. Direct tests of the impact of affirmative action on productivity find no significant evidence of a productivity decline, which implies a lack of substantial reverse discrimination (See Jonathan S. Leonard, "Anti-Discrimination or Reverse Discrimination: The Impact of Changing Demographics, Title VII and Affirmative Action on Productivity," *Journal of Human Resources*, vol. 19, Spring 1984, pp. 145–174). However, since the productivity estimates are not measured with great precision, strong policy conclusions based on this particular result should be resisted. The available evidence is not yet strong enough to be compelling on either side of this issue . . . while the impact of affirmative action on other groups is still open to question, the evidence reviewed here is that affirmative action has been successful in the past in promoting the integration of blacks into the American workplace. (Leonard, 1990, pp. 61–62)

THE CASE FOR AFFIRMATIVE ACTION

This section presents the case for affirmative action. I am a supporter of affirmative action because I have witnessed that without affirmative action, minorities and women would not have been able to enter the construction industry in any real numbers. There are a number of studies making the case for affirmative action. One of the better ones, which is well-reasoned and balanced, is by Christopher Edley, Jr. (1996). Edley's analysis is excellent, but in my opinion it is too complex in its presentation. For a simple, concise, and clearly argued logical case for affirmative action, I prefer Barbara B. Bergmann (1996). The material that follows is based on Bergmann's work.

Affirmative action is planning and acting to end the absence of minorities and women from certain jobs like construction. The government has taken the lead in pushing affirmative action, but the pace of affirmative action for the most part has been left to the discretion of managers and owners of individual workplaces. Private companies with fewer than 50 employees are exempt from affirmative action though they employ about one-third of American workers (U.S. Bureau of the Census, 1994, p. 546).

What are the reasons for employing affirmative action programs? First, it is based on the reality that exhortations and telling people not to discriminate don't do much good, and court cases against individual discrimination take years to work their way through the courts. Affirmative action programs seek to find qualified candidates for jobs and to break down barriers that prevent such qualified minorities from getting a job. Second, the goal of affirmative action is to achieve racial and gender diversity in the workplace, a diversity that is considered a positive value since it enriches work environments by permitting relationships between people of diverse cultures and values. A third motive for affirmative action is to reduce the poverty of minority groups, since the concentration of poverty (for example in the inner cities) leads to dysfunctional behavior and can lead to the disruption of the larger American social fabric (Bergmann, 1996, pp. 8–11).

Affirmative action has nothing to do with quotas. The typical plan calls for efforts to get applications for each kind of job in reasonable numbers from qualified people from previously excluded groups. Those administering the plan try to remove bias from the selection process for hiring candidates. Affirmative action tries to see that minorities who have been previously excluded from certain jobs are treated fairly and protected from harassment once they are on the job. The heart of an affirmative action plan is numerical hiring goals based on the availability of qualified minority people and women for each kind of job. The implementation of such a plan has to pay attention to the race and sex of candidates and to exert pressure on those who have previously controlled the selection process. Advocates of affirmative action argue that goals are not quotas because these goals are not hard and fast and can be reduced or abandoned if no suitable minority or white female candidates can be found. Those who argue against affirmative action say they want hiring and selection systems to reward merit that is fair to all candidates, but under present conditions the merits of black and female candidates are habitually overlooked. The absence of minorities and women from certain jobs is not due to their lack of competence but rather to discriminatory policies and practices of those selecting candidates for jobs.

Despite all the outcries that minorities are taking all the good jobs, minority representation is almost untouched in many workplaces. We continue to see white male monopolies in most of the high places and not-so-high places in U.S. society, including the skilled crafts in the construction industry. Change is occurring, but it is slow and halting. On many job sites where white males predominate, it is unlikely that a minority or a woman would be chosen for any of the important jobs over a white male. It is a fact that white men continue to predominate in the best positions by a wide margin and that blacks and women predominate in the boring, dead-end, ill-paid positions. In 1992, of children under six, only 8 percent of those with a white man in their family were poor, while 48 percent of those without a white man were poor (Bergmann, 1996, p. 16, citing the U.S. Bureau of the Census, 1994, p. 476).

Those who believe that affirmative action is necessary and desirable think that there are white women and African-Americans who could perform well in jobs that at present they rarely hold. They view the near-monopoly that white males maintain of many jobs as the result of custom, stereotypical thinking, old-boy networks, and plain discrimination. Advocates of affirmative action do not think that the command, "Just don't discriminate" will accomplish much, and they see little chance of any but the slowest progress in eliminating the white male monopoly without affirmative action (Bergmann, 1996, p. 17).

Some opponents of affirmative action deny that there is much discrimination in the labor market, which they believe is quite fair. Their diagnosis of the situation is that women and minorities are not as capable and do not strive as hard as white men, and so white men win out in the competition for the best jobs because they are the best applicants. These opponents of affirmative action feel blacks and women are already as successful as they deserve to be, given their abilities and the efforts they make. Other opponents of affirmative action agree that there is discrimination and they would like to see the domination of white males end. However, they believe that affirmative action is not the right remedy because it does more harm than good. Instead, they would rely on lawsuits to get rid of outright discrimination. An essential step in deciding whether affirmative action is a good or bad idea is making a judgment as to whether we presently have a system that is by and large fair. If it turns out, on examination, that the job market is still stacked against blacks and women, that they are slighted and overlooked, then both our laws and our values demand that something be done about it. Once we are at the stage of saying that something needs to be done, we can consider whether affirmative action should be part of the program we adopt (Bergmann, 1996, pp. 18–20).

Affirmative action plans will not operate properly or correctly 100 percent of the time. Poorly trained people may be hired, but many poorly trained white men are hired by mistake when there are no affirmative action programs. No human policy is immune to bad application. Thus, affirmative action programs should permit probationary periods in which employers can easily fire workers for cause. Most people believe that the most qualified candidate should get the job, but if blacks are excluded from certain workplaces regardless of their qualifications that is not fair, and that is what affirmative action is about. If a black candidate is better qualified than other candidates and that person is hired then there is no question of unfairness to any white applicant. The hard cases are those in which the best black candidate appears amply qualified but is not the one judged the best candidate. Is it fair, under the affirmative action plan, to hire that person and pass over a white candidate judged the best. Thus, a black candidate would not only have to be qualified, but he or she must be superior to all other candidates.

Violations of the merit system occur regularly in the workplace as managers hire a nephew or a friend, or take on someone who will help the sports team. As indicated, in construction friends and relatives are regularly hired and "outsiders" are never even considered with regard to their qualifications. The *New York Times* placed at their head the son of the majority stockholder and there was no outcry, but let them try to ensure that there will be blacks among its reporters and editors, then resentments arise. The sense of grievance about the supposed unfairness of affirmative action is partly based on the belief that it has produced a huge rise in the fortunes of blacks and a huge decline in the fortunes of whites. The facts are, however, that in the labor market white males retain largely intact the highly favored position they had in 1964, the year employment discrimination was made illegal. In 1994, the pay of white males was 49 percent higher than pay for other labor force participants. Opening access for all to the job enclaves that are now the preserves of white males would take a far more rigorous application of affirmative action than has yet occurred (Bergmann, 1996, pp. 22–27).

A study by sociologist Donald Tomaskovic-Devey (1993, pp. 24–28), who surveyed workers in North Carolina in 1989, found that jobs in which 100 percent of the incumbents were male or 100 percent were female, accounted for 70 percent of all jobs. In another 16 percent of all jobs, segregation by sex almost total. Segregation by race was less strict than segregation by sex. Still, 56 percent worked in jobs that were totally segregated by race. Only 15 percent of the jobs were shared by blacks and whites roughly proportional to their work force presence.

The U.S. Labor Department's Office of Federal Contract Compliance Programs, that visits government contractors to inquire about their compliance with nondiscrimination requirements, found that in 1994–1995, 75 percent of the employers it checked were in substantial noncompliance. Ending affirmative action would not put an end to the notice taken of race and sex in many workplaces when people are assigned to jobs. It would put an end to the effort to reduce segregation.

There are many workplaces where affirmative action has not been seriously implemented and where it has not been given a chance to work. The Office of Contract Compliance Programs is understaffed, has few effective ways of encouraging compliance, lacks vigor, and has been poorly managed. Its 1995 budget of $59 million and staff of 918 provides minuscule resources for its task of supervising nondiscrimination in the 150,000 workplaces of federal contractors that employ 28 million people, almost 20 percent of the nation's workforce. It makes about 4,000 compliance reviews a year, a rate at which it would investigate each of the 150,000 workplaces once every 38 years. Only 41 firms out of 150,000 have been debarred since 1972. Debarment virtually ceased during the Reagan-Bush era and those that were debarred only had it last for three months. As bad as the record of the large companies, the record of the small firms is much worse, and small workplaces employ 56 percent of those working for private employers (Bergmann, 1996, pp.

53–59). Construction is an industry of small employers so its record on affirmative action is very poor, except for the fact that many contractors do public works projects where they are required to have an affirmative action program.

People who are against affirmative action argue that in selecting candidates for jobs, recruiters should ignore gender, race, or ethnicity. But if people involved in the selection process do not take race, gender, or ethnicity into account they are not likely to select a candidate of a nontraditional race or gender, even if very promising candidates of this kind are available. One way employers stick with the kinds of workers they are used to is by filling their vacancies with people recommended by those already working there in the kind of job they are filling. There is considerable incentives for employers to fill jobs in this way, and the practice is widespread (Stinchcombe, 1990, pp. 243–244). It saves recruiting expenses and makes for congenial work groups. A worker who recommends someone vouches for that person as someone likely to do well. This seemingly innocent recruiting practice makes it particularly hard for African-Americans to improve their status. Relying on employee recommendations effectively excludes from good jobs those who do not have relations and friends with good jobs. This is particularly true in construction where contacts in the industry are the key to breaking into the industry.

Affirmative action is based on the belief that the groups who have been monopolizing the best jobs are not the only ones qualified to hold them. An affirmative action plan seeks people who can be expected to fill certain jobs competently. They need to reflect the availability of qualified people for each kind of job in each group. The use of numerical goals to spur managers into action has been used in all aspects of modern management. Modern businesses use numerical goals to manage production, sales, investments, and costs. Without goals it is difficult to determine whether managers have done a good job or not. When people know they will not be held responsible they are less likely to make significant efforts. In the absence of goals and a system of rewards for meeting goals, it is natural for managers to let difficult matters slide or to put them off (Bergmann, 1996, pp. 84–85).

The arguments about reverse discrimination can be made clear by looking at the Disabilities Act of 1990, designed to enable people with disabilities to find work. If a disabled person finds work does that mean that those who are not disabled have been discriminated against when a disabled person is given a job, even if the nondisabled person can do the job better? The idea that in hiring the manager should blind himself to a person's disability would be ludicrous if the purpose of the act is to secure employment for the disabled. Thus, the idea that we could break the pattern of race and sex segregation by ordering people doing the hiring to be sex-blind or race-blind is no less ludicrous (Bergmann, 1996, p. 91).

Affirmative action goals are not meant to last forever. When will it end in the United States? It should end when the justification for it no longer exists, when the country has achieved racial justice. Some critics doubt the good faith of those who promise that affirmative action is only temporary and transitional. But it is no more fantastic to promise that affirmative action is temporary than to promise that racial justice is achievable (Edley, 1996, p. 278).

The opponents of affirmative action argue that all candidates should be chosen on the basis of merit and that it is unfair when a black of less merit wins out for a job over a white. But the question of merit is very fuzzy and there is no one way or accurate way to measure it. In thinking about affirmative action these erroneous assumptions are frequently made:

1. That for each job opening there is only one person who is unambiguously the best among the candidates.

2. That the identity of that candidate is revealed by the employer's selection process.

3. That the evaluation is uninfluenced by the sex, race, ethnicity, age, or disability status of the candidates.

4. That the "best" candidate is head and shoulders above all the others, so that the substitution of one judged third or fourth instead of the one judged best would make a great difference to productivity.

It is wrong to assume that the candidate chosen in the absence of affirmative action is always better than all of those sent away or that those not deemed the best will not be able to perform the job as good as those thought to be the best. If it were generally agreed that it is ethically important never to consider anything but merit in the sense of the predicted ability to perform the major function for which the person is being selected, then we would not have veterans' preferences or the preferential admissions of the children of alumni to Harvard. These practices are tolerated and never protested. As a general principle, nobody seems to care very much; only its application to race seems to resonate (Bergmann, 1996, pp. 103–105).

In their talk of fairness, the foes of affirmative action focus on a black and a white person competing for a job. The black person is poorly qualified, the white person highly qualified. The white person is from a poor family and the black grew up in comfortable circumstances. Affirmative action is a contest between individuals in which the undeserving black person is the winner and gets 100 percent of the prize, while the white person gets nothing. From this scenario one gets the impression that the white male group has suffered from affirmative action. But the evidence of who gets the best jobs shows a different picture. There has been some desegregation, but jobs in many workplaces remain segregated with whites having the best jobs. In the wages they earn, black people and white women are still far behind white males of similar education and experience. Members of the white male group continue to win almost all of the contests for the best jobs in each of the major occupational groups in most workplaces, including construction. Affirmative action's removal of white men's privilege of exclusive access of high-paying jobs does inflict losses on white men. But foes of affirmative action pay no attention to the losses of those individuals who, in the absence of affirmative action, have been excluded because they are black or female. A local newspaper ran a photograph of the group of rejected white candidates across the street from the headquarters of a fire department. No pictures ever appeared in that newspaper showing the far larger group of blacks who for years had been rejected from firefighter jobs by a selection system rigged to exclude them. Able blacks had been excluded in favor of less qualified or equally qualified whites. The invisibility of the blacks excluded by discrimination promotes the topsy-turvy view that whites are victims and blacks are in a privileged position in our society—that blacks have been "given too much" (Bergmann, 1996, pp. 126–128).

The opponents of affirmative action constantly argue that hiring for employment should be race-neutral and colorblind. David Roediger, quoting other authors to support his own viewpoint, points out that a far more consequential issue than that of whether policies are "race-specific" or "universal" is how those policies come to be seen in "racial and pejorative" terms. Thus, welfare and job-training programs become "nonwhite." The tremendous benefits of federal housing administration loans, the home-mortgage tax deduction, and federal subsidy of highway construction for new suburbs meanwhile are typed as "race-neutral," despite their accruing overwhelmingly to the white middle class (Roediger, 1997, p. 53).

Does the existence of affirmative action plans have the effect of creating resentment among white workers, who would otherwise be fair and just toward blacks and women. Hardly. It is likely that many blacks and women fail on the job they get through affirmative action because of bad treatment, harassment, and not being given proper training on the job after they secure it. It is known that most learning about a job comes from on-the-job training and experience in working at the job. That is why this notion of hiring by merit is so ridiculous. You can't tell how well a person will adapt to and perform on a job until after they are hired, and so any candidate from number one to number ten could fail or succeed once they are on the job. If blacks and women are shut out from that avenue of learning how to do their jobs, then a large proportion of them are bound to fail. That result then gives the opponents of affirmative action the chance to say, "See, I told you they were unqualified and they shouldn't have been given the job in the first place."

There has been no research on the treatment of black employees in workplaces with and without affirmative action plans. Lacking research of this type, we cannot reliably distinguish instances of previously benign whites being turned ugly by affirmative action, from those in which whites were not benign to begin with. Thus, we have to conclude that this apparently potent accusation against affirmative action is not based on substantial information. Affirmative action may sometimes be hurtful in the way these detractors claim, but we do not know how often. It is often argued that blacks who get jobs through affirmative action (favoritism) would suffer in that people would believe they are not qualified. But we do not hear warnings to rich and well-connected people that they should refrain from using their influence to get their children into exclusive schools or hired for good jobs. Those against affirmative action suggest that they oppose it in the interest of fairness or that blacks who get jobs through affirmative action will be looked upon as "affirmative action babies." They never mention that they are opposed to affirmative action because they do not want to see the advantages of white males dismantled. That point of view is never openly articulated when affirmative action is debated, but it is out there (Bergmann, 1996, pp. 133–134, 141, 150).

Businessmen are aware that the composition of the labor force is changing and they want to train and hire more minorities. White males who were the mainstays of the economy a generation ago, will comprise only 15 percent of the net additions to the labor force between 1985 and 2000. Managers will need to increase the diversity of the work force. The share of white native-born men in the U.S. work force has been shrinking since 1950. By 1980 their share had dipped below 50 percent. By 1994, it was down to 41 percent. Government projections place the proportion of white men in the national workforce in the year 2005 at 38 percent (U. S. Bureau of the Census, 1992, p. 393).

Jacqueline Jones (1998, pp. 389–390), states that many of the largest U.S. corporations have reached a consensus that workplace diversity was good for business. Some companies instituted mentoring and internship programs for black employees, and provided managers with financial incentives to recruit and retain black workers. They also offered sensitivity training workshops for white employees. But Jones relates how Texaco's attempts at creating diversity in the 1990s was little more than a public relations play and that black employees did not receive promotions commensurate with their experience and performance. White coworkers at Texaco harassed blacks by scribbling "KKK" on their cars and referring to them as "niggers" and "porch monkeys." Jones states that faddish attempts at workplace diversity will falter as long as black and white people continue to live apart from each other and attend separate schools.

One alternative to affirmative action is to have programs that help people from disadvantaged backgrounds, regardless of their race or sex. There are black authors who have supported this position (Wilson, 1987). Since African-Americans suffer from high rates of poverty, those promoting this strategy hope that such a program would help many of the same people who are targeted by affirmative action. Some white males would presumably be included in the programs, perhaps making it less unpopular than affirmative action. In practice, a black person might get a job that a white person might have had in the absence of such a program. Displacement of the white for a black would be done in the name of helping the disadvantaged rather than helping blacks and might pass muster with those who claim their opposition to affirmative action is based on not liking any program that makes use of people's racial or ethnic identification. Whites already win most of the well-paying jobs that go to the low-skilled people of modest backgrounds— over-the-road truck drivers, house painters, and the like. To prevent the program from freezing out blacks, formal or informal quotas for blacks in the program would have to be set up. But if that happened, the programs would become race-based. A program to give special help to the disadvantaged might accomplish some good. While it would not do the job that affirmative action is designed to do, it would be a worthwhile companion program (Bergmann, 1996, pp. 167–168).

Among those who oppose affirmative action there are those who advocate training instead of affirmative action, but they ignore the fact that even now blacks and women with good qualifications do not do as well as white men in the labor market. Women college graduates earn little more on average than males with only a high school diploma. Representing the education-improvement strategy as a solution that does away with affirmative action puts off making improvements in the job situation for blacks until an indefinite future that may never come. The education improvement approach ignores the fact that it is difficult to motivate young people to undergo training and take education seriously if they have little hope of getting a good job at the end of it. It also ignores the fact that blacks and women are largely excluded from much of the work for which unskilled persons are hired and given on-the-job training. Apprenticeship programs, which could provide an excellent way to integrate crafts occupations by sex and race, continue to be egregious offenders in restricting their benefits to white males (Bergmann, 1996, pp. 177–178).

Regarding affirmative action, President Clinton said, "Mend it, don't end it." Affirmative action programs will remain controversial, like any policy that addresses a painful problem. The solution for America's color problem can be no easier than the solution to problems of poverty, environmental protection, the creation of jobs, and the preservation of a robust economy and a workable democracy. The continuing controversy is about values and visions for America in the twenty-first century (Edley, 1996, p. 278).

11

Summary and Conclusion

I have presented the idea that the social organization of the construction industry, as well as the technology and traditions of the industry, leads to construction worker behavior that results in the following cultural patterns:

1. Autonomy and self-reliance of the craftsworker.
2. Large measure of control over the work process by the craftsworker.
3. Decentralized decision making on the construction site.
4. Nonbureaucratic organization of construction work.
5. Loose supervision of craftsworkers by construction management.
6. Integrated and interdependence of work groups.
7. Enjoyment of work satisfaction by construction workers.

THEORETICAL ORIENTATION

The theoretical orientation of this book is based on the idea that construction workers develop a distinctive culture based on their work environment and the ideas and values they derive from performing construction work. Otterbein (1977, p. 1) has defined culture as "everything that a group of people thinks, and says, and does and makes." I have not dealt with everything that construction workers think, say, do, and make, but mainly what they do, say, think, and make as things in their work environment—the construction project. Based on the social structure they share in their work environment, construction workers constitute a distinctive subculture and form an occupational group. They have a set of ideas, values, beliefs, and behavior patterns that stem from their work, which they learn and transmit to new members of their group.

Another theoretical orientation of this book is that occupation is an important factor in modern society in the formation of beliefs and attitudes. An extension of this idea is the concept that occupational groups also develop distinctive and identifiable subcultures based on their work and workplaces.

THE SOCIAL AND TECHNOLOGICAL BASE OF THE CONSTRUCTION INDUSTRY

The technological base of the construction industry is mainly a hand labor and handicraft technology. There have been technological improvements in the past 40 years in the industry, mostly in lifting devices that now permit workers to use machines to get them to heights of 40 or 50 feet inside a cage at the end of a telescopic hi-lift. The latest device is the so-called "genie" that can not only get a worker up high, but also reaches out laterally 25 or 30 feet. These devices obviate the need to raise scaffolds for many inside jobs. But on larger tasks like installing masonry or precast on a large building, say 40 or 50 stories high, scaffolding is necessary. Other improvements have been made in earth-moving equipment, and there have been a number of prefabricated products such as windows, pre-hung doors and frames, floor plank, and prefabricated millwork that save time but still require journeymen and journeywomen to install them on the job. Hand-held power tools for fasteners and sheet-rock have sped up the work, but they too, still rely on the hand labor of the craftsworker. Labor, rather than machinery, is the key to production and output in construction work. For this reason, there is great reliance on the individual worker. Construction is a labor-intensive industry. Its growth means the growth of employment.

The social base of the construction industry is decentralized and locally oriented. This tends to limit the size of firms and with it, the growth of large bureaucratic organizations. There are about 621,000 construction companies in the United States and most of these establishments tend to be small, the majority employing fewer than 10 workers. About 8 out of 10 workers are employed by small contractors, those with less than 100 workers (U.S. Department of Labor, 1998, p. 17). Of those establishments in construction that have payrolls, 519,252, or 81.9 percent of all establishments, have from 1 to 9 employees (Construction Chart Book, 1998, chart 3). The nature of the industry tends to stress informality, personal relations, and community-like networks within the local and decentralized construction industry that exists in every locality in the country.

The construction industry is characterized by wide fluctuations of cyclical flows of investment in commercial, industrial, and residential building activity. As a result, the culture of construction workers is one where job insecurity is a way of life. The large degree of variability in the industry makes mass production unfeasible. Mass production of product is also not practical because of the reliance on craftsworkers and hand methods of production rather than automatic machinery. Reliance on craft methods engenders independence and autonomy among construction workers, many of whom supply their own tools.

The social organization of the construction industry is flexible and mobile, with constant shifting of workers from job to job, from work site to work site, and from employer to employer. This reduces the loyalty of employees to a particular employer. Ultimately construction workers rely on their own abilities and skills to make them employable, their unions where they are organized, and their contacts among friends and relatives who are in a position to offer them work. Of course, if a construction worker has been with a particular firm for a number of years, they are likely to show loyalty to that firm and sometimes have a patriarchal relationship with the owners (Silver, 1986, p. 160). When I worked for Elia in Niagara Falls, many of the key workers had been with the firm, 10, 20, even 30 years. Not only were they loyal to the Elias but they knew them socially and participated in many events with them, from dinners to golfing. Some of the men were second, and even third generation employees with the firm. But this applied only to the key workers who were never laid off. The general run of men that were hired for projects were loyal to their trade, their union, and each other, rather than the company.

I interviewed a group of construction men, asking about their loyalties—to their craft or to their employer. Not a single one said, "the employer." Most of them said, "both." One guy said, "to myself," and another said, "to myself and my family," and one man indicated the attitude of most by remarking, "look, my trade is my livelihood." Two men mentioned the union. The downsizing that has taken place in U.S. industry has resulted in a consequent decline in company loyalty throughout the country. It is hardly credible that construction workers, who are constantly laid off and transferring from one employer to another, and from one job site to another, would have stronger loyalties to their employer than to their trade.

Construction workers display a special loyalty to their craft. The craft organization is a subsystem in the social organization of construction and it fosters craft consciousness. At the next level is occupational consciousness that ties all construction workers together. At the higher level is blue-collar consciousness, in which construction workers identify with people who work with their hands or engage in manual trades. Ideologically, one find little class consciousness among construction workers regarding worker-boss differentiation. The high wages and life styles of construction craftsworkers is not conducive to hostility toward employers as a class or toward capitalists as a social group.

Construction is a complex industry, involving constantly changing environments and conditions. Its cyclical nature is in conformity with all of natural and human life in the ebb and flow of human circumstances, like the tides, the wheel of fortune, and the rise and fall of civilizations. Construction requires flexibility in its labor force and its contractors. Thus, the subcontracting system, which can adapt quickly to changes, is well suited to the organization and planning of construction work. Construction and building also rely heavily on worker skills and the human factor, which is more adaptable to changes than investment in large, fixed capital. These aspects of the construction industry fit in well with the culture of construction work that is carried on with loose, informal, and personal relationships between those managing and those carrying out the work tasks.

Uncertainty and imprecision are strong elements in the nature of the construction industry. Lack of precision is a factor in how well or poorly a production task can be controlled. As the data presented in this book has shown, uncertainty is high in construction because of environmental factors (weather and climate), the variability of the construction site, the long period of the production process, and the many interdependent steps involved in the building process. This reduces management control, and reinforces the kind of loose, day-to-day, decentralized, on-the-spot kind of administration of construction work that takes place on the job site.

CONSTRUCTION WORKERS' BEHAVIOR

One of the key elements in construction work is the pattern of personal relations in the work process. The use of small crews, hand tools, and skilled hand labor fosters personal relationships in organizing the work. It gives the construction worker a measure of control over the work and a sense of his own importance and involvement in creating the product.

Controlling the work process is a key element in construction behavior and lays the basis for the large measure of job satisfaction that construction workers enjoy. Since the craftsworker is permitted to work out the methods for accomplishing his work tasks, he and she controls the pace of the work as well as the solving of work assignments. This enhances the role and prestige of the tradesman and tradeswoman, which may be raised or lowered by the behavior of the individual journeyperson, but remains basically high. Construction workers behave on the job as independent units capable of carrying out their tasks with only general communications as to the work that needs to be accomplished, leaving all the steps necessary to carry out the tasks to the ability and ingenuity of the construction worker.

As part of the craft nature of the industry, the traditional work ethic is still strong in construction. The behavioral patterns of construction workers include getting to work on time, following instructions and orders, cooperating with other crafts, having pride in workmanship, being honest about one's work, caring for tools and equipment, and being willing to perform difficult or dangerous work. This is an ideal set of cultural norms, never fully lived up to. But the fact that it is the norm affects the consciousness and behavior of construction workers who do, in the main, strive to live up to it.

Not only are work task activities conducted on a personal basis, but recruitment to the industry is also carried out through family and friendship relationships. The most frequent and surest way to get into construction is to know someone in the industry. Both the data on the industry and my personal experiences, past and present, attest to the fact that father-son, brother combinations, and friendship networks are still prevalent in the industry. The personal basis of recruitment reinforces and supports the personalized nature of the work process itself. With no established social networks, blacks, Hispanics, and women find it difficult to break into the industry (Silver, 1986, p. 117), although based on the figures cited in the text, Hispanics have been the most successful in entering the industry.

One of the cultural characteristics of construction workers is their love of the outdoors, which includes sports, hunting, fishing, and camping. They also enjoy kidding and horseplay, both on and off the job. This serves to create group cohesion and familiarity, reinforcing the personalized nature of their work relationships. The men know each other well enough to refer to each other's personal and private lives. Because they are close socially they are willing and able to exchange insults in a friendly, kidding manner that only they, as insiders, are allowed to indulge in.

INDEPENDENCE AND AUTONOMY

Construction workers usually are not part of the type of bureaucratic administration that exists in most large industrial and business organizations in the United States. This is due to the technological and organizational nature of the construction industry where the craftsworker has a large measure of control over the work process. The result is a pattern of behavior among construction workers that stresses autonomy and independence.

Ownership of the tools to carry out production is rare among any group of workers in our society. Construction is the one major industry where this situation exists. Union agreements and custom spell out which tools are provided by the craftsworker and which are furnished by the contractor. Most hand tools are owned by the tradesperson and most power tools and heavy equipment are the property of the contractor. Ownership of tools gives the construction craftsworker the alternative of going into his own business. This increases his independence and autonomy, since the contractor is not only dependent on the craftsman's labor, but also on the craftsman's proprietorship of the tools necessary for production. Alienation of workers from their product still exists since construction workers do not own the product they produce, but they are not alienated from the means of production since they generally have the wherewithal to produce. This is not true for the heavy and highway portion of the industry, where cranes, backhoes, graders, blacktop machines, trenchers, and trucks are necessary to carry out the work. But it is true for carpenters, masons, plumbers, steamfitters, tile cutters, painters, concrete finishers, roofers, millwork carpenters, and others who rely on hand tools. If power equipment is needed, it can be rented. Since these workers have the tools as well as the skills, they can put themselves to work independently of their employers if they so choose. Of the 1.92 million establishments in construction in 1992, 70 percent were independent, self-employed contractors with no payroll. Of course, the 30 percent with payrolls accounted for 93 percent of the dollar value in construction. The construction industry has the highest percentage of self-employed as a percentage of its workforce, than all nonagricultural industries (Construction Chart Book, 1998, charts 2 and 21).

Workers' autonomy is a significant element in the culture of construction workers. Conflicts arise when management encroaches upon this autonomy. A competent journeyman knows his talents are sought after by contractors, so he is not afraid to quit a job if he does not like the way things are run. This makes him feel independent even in the face of the insecurity in the construction field. The independence of construction workers is supported by the unions which control the work rules, the training of apprentices, and entry into the industry. Even among nonunion construction workers there is a sense of independence since they know that management cannot carry out the work without them and cannot easily replace a good tradesman. Since supervisory personnel belong to the union where work is carried on with union employees, contractor management finds it difficult to exercise autocratic power over the workers through their supervisors. Management is ultimately dependent on the craftsworker's responsibility to his work, which reinforces the independence of craftsmen.

Every trade in construction is considered important. No building can be completed without the contribution of every trade. This results in a kind of democracy on a construction project, with each craft enjoying its place in the sun. This democracy extends the sense of autonomy and prestige for each trade, since every tradesman knows that his contribution counts for something in the total construction process.

The hiring and firing process in construction is reflective of the autonomy enjoyed by the men. Construction workers are hired directly for a project, sometimes on the project without the involvement of management. Employment is based on personal contacts. Workers feel a sense of obligation to those who hire them. Since construction workers secure their jobs mostly through personal contacts with superintendents or through the union hiring hall, they feel less tied to their employers and more to each other, thus giving them a collective sense of independence in relation to the contractor.

Autonomy and independence among construction workers are enhanced by the worker's right to refuse to work in inclement weather or unsafe conditions. Workers, not management, make the decisions whether or not to work when such conditions prevail. This right is backed by the union agreement, and in the case of safety, by federal regulations. This situation is in contrast to factory rules where refusal to work is usually a cause for dismissal. The fact that construction workers can refuse to work, with just cause, provides them with an additional sense of power and its consequent feeling of autonomy.

JOB SATISFACTION

The main patterns of organization, behavior, and culture in the construction industry has led to a large degree of job satisfaction among construction workers. This has been manifested to me through conversations with construction workers, through my friendships of many years with men I've known in many parts of the country, and through such objective criteria like low levels of absenteeism, lateness, or job grievances. There are still strikes in the construction industry, but they usually occur when the contract expires and the issues involve wage increases, benefits, and work rules. Some young construction workers express a desire to get out of the industry to go back to school or relocate to another part of the country. But almost all men that have been in the industry for a number of years are satisfied with their wages, the work they do, and the work environment.

The measurement and analysis of job satisfaction has resulted in the compilation of a long and complicated research literature. A number of factors identified by researchers as correlating with job satisfaction can be used to ascertain if they are present among construction workers.

One of the critical factors in job satisfaction is type of management and supervision. This has been cited in many studies of job satisfaction among all types of workers. An examination of supervision among construction workers reveals that most of the positive elements in management associated with leading to worker job satisfaction are present in the construction industry. These are:

1. Supervisors treat their subordinates as human beings rather than cogs in a production machine.
2. Supervisors generally do not behave in an authoritarian manner. Most good supers realize they must treat the tradesworker with respect if they are to get anything out of them. There are a thousand ways that the journeymen can undermine and defeat an authoritarian superintendent.
3. Superintendents are often employee-oriented. This occurs because many of them carry union cards or because most good superintendents have come up through the ranks and were once journeymen before they became supers or foremen.
4. Due to their origins, superintendents and foremen consider themselves part of the work group.
5. Superintendents and foremen are often friends or relatives of the men they lead on the construction site. They also socialize with the men they supervise.

Many studies on worker satisfaction cite participation in decision making and control over the work process as important factors in worker satisfaction. This is especially true today when more and more industrial and business organizations are learning that setting up worker circles and decentralizing decision making on the shop floor are necessary and responsible for increasing worker satisfaction and worker-induced increases in productivity. Every crew on the construction site makes decisions about how to fulfill their work assignments. I've seen many examples over the years of workers "dogging it," that is, just standing around when the foreman is not there, or guys dressing early in the afternoon before quitting time, or guys extending the coffee breaks. But no construction worker will last on any job or with any company, if he consistently fails to complete his job assignments when the super or the foreman expects him to. When I make my rounds on the jobs that I presently manage I find the men consistently working conscientiously, or even intently, at their tasks. They may take a break to figure out their next move, or to socialize or kid, but they know what their responsibilities are regarding the work. Last week, I was on one of my jobs and observed two men carrying 20-foot lengths of rebars, one on each end, and placing them in a foundation wall being readied for a concrete pour. I went into a meeting and emerged two hours later and saw the same two men still carrying those bars on their shoulders and placing them in the foundation. It was a 95 degree day and they were still walking at a steady pace and were able to greet me with a cheerful, "How's it going?" They knew what they had to do and they knew that the next operation, pouring the foundation wall, depended on them getting their task done. This autonomy in the work process increases job satisfaction for construction workers because they know they have a recognized role and responsibility in that process.

Studies among female construction workers have shown that when women work in teams and interact with other women on the job, their job satisfaction goes up. As shown in Chapter 9, one of their major complaints was that on the jobs where they worked there were no other women to team up with, and that when the men isolated them, they had no one to socialize with, which is why job satisfaction is low when workers must work alone. Workers cite congenial peer relationships as an important part of a good job. Construction workers are fortunate that their work usually leads to the use of teams and crews to perform the tasks. Human sociability is an intrinsic part of the work environment on construction projects, which function like mini-communities during the life of the building project. Integrated work groups bind construction men together in their work assignments. Their tasks require cooperation between trades and within crews. This atmosphere generates feelings of job satisfaction that flows from the knowledge that one is an accepted member of a social group.

An extension of the concept of integrated work groups is the notion of an occupational community. Whether or not construction workers actually do constitute an occupational community needs more research. I have only shown that construction workers exhibit some of the characteristics of occupational communities—the mutual sharing of their work and nonwork lives; the development of self-images and value systems based on their occupations; and the development of a sense of prestige from belonging to an identifiable occupational group.

Not all aspects of construction work are satisfying. A major source of dissatisfaction is the high rate of unemployment in the industry that lowers the annual wages of those in the field and fills workers with insecurity about their prospects for the year. A frequent quote heard on many construction projects from workers is, "Hey, I'm doing okay but I'm working my way out of a job." Another source of dissatisfaction is bad weather that is unpleasant to work in and leads to temporary layoffs. Danger is not really a source of dissatisfaction. It is accepted as part of the industry, and construction workers get satisfaction from overcoming dangerous and hazardous work. The positive elements that favor job satisfaction outweigh the negative ones associated with dissatisfaction. In general, construction workers enjoy a high degree of job satisfaction that is reflected in their attitudes, behavior, and willingness to stay in the industry for a long period of their working lives.

A FINAL COMMENT

Construction, like all other aspects of our society and like life in general, is certainly subject to change. During my 42 years in the industry I have seen many changes in products, lifting equipment, and management techniques like CPM, but mainly I have seen continuities, and despite the changes the structure of the industry has remained basically the same. The industry is localized in each area of the country where it has its own core of construction workers and contractors; the craftsperson still retains control over the work process; the work is still carried on through the extensive use of subcontractors, who outnumber general contractors; and the management style on the construction site is still personal, informal, and nonbureaucratic. Since 1956, a number of large construction firms have appeared in the industry which have a yearly volume of construction exceeding $1 billion. But there are still over 600,000 construction contractors and construction is still a highly competitive industry (U.S. Bureau of the Census, 1997, p. 544).

The emergence of large construction firms has been accompanied by the introduction of new management methods and styles. It remains to be seen whether these large firms and their new methods of management will drastically alter the nature of construction work. Will management be able to take full control over the work process from the construction craftsman? Will general contractors be able to encompass within their organizations all of the trades and thus eliminate the subcontracting system? Will bureaucratic management be able to work out in advance all the moves on the construction project, thus eliminating the talents of supers, foremen, and journeymen? Will bureaucratic management and a rational, impersonal style of management replace the strong personalized leadership and crucial role of human relationships in the construction work process?

The answer to all of the above questions is negative.

Why negative? Because it won't work. Burawoy (1979, p. 242) said, "Attempts to introduce a centralized managerial authority in construction are known to be ineffective."

One reason why the continuation of construction as a decentralized, personalized and worker-oriented industry at the present time is so important, is that it fits in with the latest thinking about how work should be organized. It is ironic that something that has been part of the past and the traditions of construction work should now be found to fit in with new thinking on the part of those who manage our corporations and our industrial and commercial organizations.

I have drawn the conclusion that a restructuring of the construction industry that does away with decentralized decision making, craft control of the work process, handicraft technology, and nonbureaucratic management will not make much headway at the present time or in the immediate future. Perhaps this is a good thing. Perhaps it is also a good thing that we still have some places in U.S. society where workers control their own work, enjoy the satisfaction of camaraderie with their workmates, and take pride in seeing the physical embodiments of their labor.

APPENDIX

Table A.1
Model of the Construction Industry

Industry Characters	Social Organization	Worker Behavior Patterns
Uncertainty	Flexible	·Acceptance of insecurity ·Crisis orientation ·Nonrepetitive work tasks
Hand tool technology	Decentralized decision making	·Independence ·Control over the work ·Autonomy ·Ownership of tools ·Loose supervision
Informal work system	Variable rules and regulations	·Face-to-face relationships ·Shifting roles and goals ·Kinship networks ·Friendship networks ·Informal hiring
Subcontracting	Diffusion of administration	·Democracy among trades ·Cooperation of tradesmen
Localized industry	Networks of firms, crafts, and suppliers	·Integrated social groups ·Merging work and nonwork activities

Table A.2
Characteristics of an Occupational Community

Attributes	Application to the Construction Industry
1. Sense of Group Identity	Construction workers identify by crafts and skills.
2. Lifelong commitment	Lengthy training fosters lasting commitment to construction. Job satisfaction encourages commitment.
3. Common values	Values construction workers share: • Independence and autonomy • Control over the work process • Deep involvement with work skills and knowledge • High economic rewards and prestige • Ownership of tools and pride in craft
4. Common definitions	Craft unions detail roles and rights of journeyworkers. Socialization defines roles of journeyworkers. Building Trade Councils define craft jurisdictions.
5. Common language	Each craft has its technical language. Each craft has its jargon for tools, methods, practices, and materials.
6. Community power	Unions bring members up on charges for anti-union acts. Prestige among fellow journeymen based on behavior and skill.
7. Social boundaries	Localized construction community composed of: •Contractor Associations •Workers' Union and Central Trade Councils •Joint Apprenticeship Councils •Architects and Engineers Professional Societies •Networks of Suppliers and Equipment Renters
8. Control over recruitment	Apprenticeship training controlled by unions. Recruitment based on family and friendship contacts. Training schools run by craft unions. On public works, recruitment affected by affirmative action programs.

Source: Adapted from William J. Goode, "Community Within a Community," *American Sociological Review,* 22 (1957), pp. 194–200.

BIBLIOGRAPHY

"Accident Record in Construction." *Engineering News-Record* (November 15, 1979).

AFL-CIO Building and Construction Trades Department. *The Builders* (Washington, DC, 1983).

Allen, Steven G. "Much Ado About Davis-Bacon: A Critical Review and New Evidence." *Journal of Law and Economics*, 16, no. 3 (1983), 707–736.

————. "Why Construction Industry Productivity Is Declining." *Review of Economics and Statistics*, 67, no. 4 (1985), 661–669.

————. *Unionized Construction Workers Are More Productive* (Washington, DC: Center to Protect Workers' Rights, 1997).

Applebaum, Herbert. "Construction Management: Traditional versus Bureaucratic Methods." *Anthropological Quarterly*, 55, no. 4 (October 1982), 224–234.

Arendt, Hannah. *The Human Condition* (Chicago: University of Chicago Press, 1958).

Arneson, Eric. "Up From Exclusion: Black and White Workers, Race, and the State of Labor History." *Reviews in American History*, 26, no. 1 (March 1998).

Baumgartel, H. "Leadership Motivations and Attitudes in Research Laboratories." *Journal of Social Issues*, 12, no. 2 (1956), 24–31.

Becker, Howard S., and J. W. Carper. "Elements of Identification with an Occupation." *American Sociological Review*, 21, (1956), 341–348.

Bergmann, Barbara B. *In Defense of Affirmative Action* (New York: Basic Books, 1996).

Best, Norman E. *A Celebration of Work* (Lincoln: University of Nebraska Press, 1990).

Blauner, Robert. *Alienation and Freedom in American Industry* (Chicago: University of Chicago Press, 1964).

————. "Work Satisfaction and Industrial Trends in Modern Society" In *Class, Status, and Power*, edited by Reinhard Bendix and Seymour M. Lipset (New York: The Free Press, 1966).

Blum, Fred H. *Toward a Democratic Work Process* (New York: Harper, 1953).

Borjas, George J. "Job Satisfaction, Wages and Unions." *Journal of Human Resources*, 14, no. 1 (1979), 21–40.

Bourdon, Clinton C., and Raymond E. Levitt. *Union and Open Shop Construction* (Lexington, MA: Lexington Books, 1980).

Brayfield, A. H., and H. F. Rothe. "An Index of Job Satisfaction." *Journal of Applied Psychology*, 35 (1951), 307–311.

Brooks, Thomas R. "Job Satisfaction: An Elusive Goal." *The American Federationist*, 79, no. 10 (1979), 1–7.

Bruyn, Severyn T. *The Human Perspective in Sociology* (Englewood Cliffs, NJ: Prentice-Hall, 1966).

Buffalo News (April 29, 1978).

Burawoy, Michael. *Manufacturing Consent* (Chicago: University of Chicago Press, 1979).

"Call Off the Underground Menace." *Construction Equipment* (July 1977), 27.

Cantril, Hadley. *Public Opinion, 1935–1946* (Princeton, NJ: Princeton University Press, 1951).

Caplow, Theodore. *The Sociology of Work* (New York: McGraw-Hill, 1954).

Cassimatis, Peter J. *Economics of the Construction Industry, Studies in Business Economics No. 111* (Washington, DC: The National Industrial Conference Board, 1969).

Chapple, Eliot D. "Applied Anthropology in Industry." In *Anthropology Today*, edited by A. L. Kroeber (Chicago: University of Chicago Press, 1953).

Cherry, Mike. *On High Steel* (New York: Quadrangle Press, 1974).

Chicago Women in Trades. *Breaking New Ground: Worksite 2000* (Chicago: Chicago Women in Trades, 1992).

Chinoy, Ely. *Automobile Workers and the American Dream* (Garden City, NY: Doubleday, 1955).

Civil Engineering (April 1979), 63–68.

Colean, Miles L., and Robinson Newcomb. *Stabilizing Construction* (New York: McGraw-Hill, 1952).

Construction Chart Book. *The U.S. Construction Industry and Its Workers* (Washington, DC: The Center To Protect Workers' Rights, 1998).

"Construction Employment—Bad News Today and Tomorrow." *Construction Equipment* (August 1977), 11.

"Construction Volume." *Engineering News-Record* (April 14, 1977), 67.

Cottrell, Fred W. "Death by Dieselization." *American Sociological Review*, 16 (1951).

Cremeans, John E. "Productivity in the Construction Industry." *Construction Review* (May–June 1981), 4–6.

Crenshaw, Kimberle Williams. "Color Blindness, History and the Law." In *The House That Race Built: Black Americans, U.S. Terrain*, edited by Wahneema Lubiana (New York: Pantheon Books, 1997).

Crozier, Michel. *The World of the Office Worker* (Chicago: University of Chicago Press, 1971).

Curle, Adam. "Incentive to Work: An Anthropological Appraisal." *Human Relations*, 2 (1949), 41–47.

Drucker, Peter. *The New Society* (New York: Harper, 1950).

Durkheim, Emile. *The Division of Labor in Society* (New York: The Free Press, 1949).

Edley, Christopher, Jr. *Not All Black and White, Affirmative Action, Race, and American Values* (New York: Hill and Wang, 1996).

Eisenberg, Susan. *We'll Call You if We Need You: Experiences of Women Working Construction* (Ithaca, NY: ILR Press, 1998).

"Employment Picture—1977." *Construction Equipment* (July 1977), 22.

Enchautegui, Maria E., Michael Fix, Pamela Loprest, Sarah von der Lippe, and Douglas Wissoker. *Do Minority-Owned Businesses Get a Fair Share of Government Contracts?* (Washington, DC: The Urban Institute, 1996).

Finkel, Gerald. *The Economics of the Construction Industry* (New York: M. E. Sharpe, 1997).

Fleishman, E. A., and H. E. Burtt. *Leadership and Supervision in Industry* (Columbus: Ohio State University Bureau of Educational Research, 1965).

Fleishman, E. A., and E. F. Harris. "Patterns of Leadership Behavior Related to Employee Grievance and Turnover." *Personnel Psychology*, 15 (1962), 43–46.

Foner, Philip S., and Ronald L. Lewis, eds. *Black Workers: A Documentary History from Colonial Times to the Present* (Philadelphia: Temple University Press, 1989).

Foster, Charles. *Building With Men* (London: Tavistock, 1969).

French, J. R. P., Jr., J. Israel, and D. As. "An Experiment on Participation in a Norwegian Factory." *Human Relations*, 13 (1960), 3–19.

Friedmann, E. A., and R. J. Havighurst. *The Meaning of Work and Retirement* (Chicago: University of Chicago Press, 1954).

Fromm, Erich. *Marx's Concept of Man* (New York: Frederick Ungar, 1961).

Gerstl, J. E. "Determinants of Occupational Community in High Status Occupations." *Sociology Quarterly*, 2 (1961), 37–48.

Goldthorpe, John H., David Lockwood, Frank Bechhofer, and Jennifer Platt. *The Affluent Worker: Industrial Attitudes and Behavior* (London: Cambridge University Press, 1968).

Goode, William J. "Community Within a Community," *American Sociological Review*, 22 (1957), 194–200.

———. "The Protection of the Inept." *American Sociological Review*, 32 (1967), 5–19.

Gouldner, Alvin W. *Patterns of Industrial Bureaucracy* (New York: The Free Press, 1954).

Gouldner, H. P. "The Norm of Reciprocity: A Preliminary Statement." *American Sociological Review*, 25 (1960), 161–178.

Graves, Bennie. "Particularism, Exchange, and Organizational Efficiency: A Case Study of a Construction Industry." *Social Forces*, 49 (1970), 72–81.

———. "Conflict and Work Force Stability in Pipeline Construction." *Urban Life and Culture*, 2, no. 4 (1974), 415–431.

Haas, Jack. "A Study of High Steel Ironworkers' Reactions to Fear and Danger." *Sociology of Work and Occupations*, 4, no. 2 (1977), 147–171.

Haber, William, and Harold J. Levinson. *Labor Relations and Productivity in the Building Trades*. University of Michigan Bureau of Industrial Relations (Ann Arbor: University of Michigan Press, 1956).

Hanson, Sandra L., Jack K. Martin, and Steven A. Tuch. "Economic Sector and Job Satisfaction." *Work and Occupations*, 14, no. 2 (May 1987), 286–305.

Hayes, Carleton J. *A Political and Cultural History of Modern Europe* (New York: Macmillan, 1946).

Heidegger, Martin. *Poetry, Language, Thought* (New York, Harper & Row, 1971).

Heilbroner, Robert L. *The Economic Problem* (Englewood Cliffs, NJ: Prentice-Hall, 1970).

Herzberg, Frederick, Bernard Mausner, and Barbara Snyderman. *The Motivation to Work* (New York: Wiley, 1967).

Herzberg, Frederick, et al. *Job Attitudes* (Pittsburgh: Psychological Service of Pittsburgh, 1957).

H.E.W. Report. *Work in America* (Cambridge, MA: MIT Press, 1975).

Highway and Heavy Construction. Editorial (March 1978).

Highway and Heavy Construction. Editorial (March 1996).

Hill, Herbert. "The Equal Employment Opportunity Commission: Twenty Years Later." *The Journal of Intergroup Relations*, 11 (Winter 1983), 45–72.

———. "Black Labor and Affirmative Action: An Historical Perspective." In *The Question of Discrimination, Racial Inequality in the U.S. Labor Market* (Middletown: Wesleyan University Press, 1989).

Hoppock, Robert. *Job Satisfaction* (New York: Harper, 1935).

H.U.D. Report. *Action Against Seasonal Unemployment in the Construction Industry* (Washington, DC: U.S. Government Printing Office, 1973).

Hughes, Everett C. *Men and Their Work* (New York: The Free Press, 1959).

———. "The Study of Occupations." In *Sociology Today*, edited by Robert Merton, Leonard Broom, and Leonard Cottrell (New York: Basic Books, 1959).

———. *The Sociological Eye: Selected Papers* (Hawthorne, NY: Aldine, 1971).

Hurlbert, Jeanne S. "Social Networks, Social Circles, and Job Satisfaction." *Work and Occupations*, 18, no. 4 (November 1991), 415–430.

International Labor Organization. *Construction Skills* (Geneva, Switzerland: CIRF Publications, 1969).

Issues and Opportunities Report (newsletter), 1, no. 3 (1998).

Jacobson, E. *Foreman-Steward Participation Practices and Worker Attitudes in a Unionized Factory* (Ann Arbor: University of Michigan Press, 1951).

Jones, Jacqueline. *American Work, Four Centuries of Black and White Labor* (New York: W. W. Norton, 1998).

Joyce, John T. "Construction Unions in the Seventies." *American Federationist*, 80 (1973), 9–15.

Kasl, Stanislav V. "Work and Mental Health." In *Work and the Quality of Life*, edited by James O'Toole (Cambridge, MA: The MIT Press, 1974).

Katz, D., G. Gurin, and L. G. Floor. *Productivity, Supervision and Morale Among Railroad Workers*. Survey Research Center, Institute for Social Research (Ann Arbor: University of Michigan Press, 1951).

Katz, D., N. Maccaby, and N. C. Morse. *Productivity, Supervision and Morale in an Office Situation*. Survey Research Center, Institute for Social Research (Ann Arbor: University of Michigan Press, 1950).

Kay, E., J. R. P. French, and H. H. Meyer. *Behavioral Research Services Report, No. EBR-11* (New York: The General Electric Co., 1962).

Kerr, W. A. "On the Validity and Reliability of the Job Satisfaction Index." *Journal of Applied Psychology*, 32, (1958), 275–281.

Kluckhohn, Florence. "The Participant-Observer Technique in Small Communities." *American Journal of Sociology*, 46, (1940), 331–343.

Knowdell, Richard L. "The 10 New Rules for Strategizing Your Career." *Futurist*, 32, no. 5 (June–July, 1998), 19–24.

Kusmer, Kenneth L. *A Ghetto Takes Shape: Black Cleveland, 1870–1930* (Urbana: University of Illinois Press, 1976).

LeMasters, E. E. *Blue-Collar Aristocrats* (Madison: University of Wisconsin Press, 1975).

Leonard, Jonathan S. "Employment and Occupational Advance under Affirmative Action." *Review of Economics and Statistics*, 66 (1984), 377–385.

———. "The Impact of Affirmative Action Regulation and Equal Employment Law on Black Employment." *Journal of Economic Perspectives*, 4, no. 4 (Fall 1990), 47–63.

Levison, Andrew. *The Working Class Majority* (New York: Penguin Books, 1974).

Likert, R. *New Patterns of Management* (New York: McGraw-Hill, 1961).

Lipset, S. M., M. Trow, and J. Coleman. *Union Democracy* (New York: The Free Press, 1956).

"Listening to Contractors." *Architectural Record* (February 1998), 54–57.

Locke, John. *Two Treatises of Government* (Cambridge, UK: Cambridge University Press, 1967).

Lopreato, Joseph. *Italian Americans* (New York: Random House, 1970).

Mattila, John M., and Erwin A. Gaumnitz. "An Econometric Analysis of Construction." *Bureau of Business Research and Service, Wisconsin Commerce Reports* (Madison: University of Wisconsin Press, 1955).

Mills, C. Wright. *White Collar* (New York: Oxford University Press, 1953).

Mills, Daniel Q. *Industrial Relations and Manpower in Construction* (Cambridge, MA: The MIT Press, 1972).

Mills, Quinn. *Staying Afloat in the Construction Industry* (Washington, DC: BNI Publications, 1966).

Mills, Ted. "Altering the Social Structure in Coal Mining." *Monthly Labor Review*, 99 (10), (1976), 3–10.

Monthly Labor Review, 94 (July 1971), 7.

Moreno, J. L. *Who Shall Survive?* (Washington, DC: Nervous and Mental Disease Publishing Co., 1937).

Morse, Nancy E., and E. Reimer. "The Experimental Change of a Major Organizational Variable." *Journal of Abnormal Social Psychology*, 52, (1956), 120–129.

Mottaz, Clifford J. "Age and Work Satisfaction." *Work and Occupations*, 14, no. 3, (August 1987), 387–409.

Myers, R. R. "Interpersonal Relations in the Building Industry" *Human Organization*, 5 (1946), 1–7.

Norr, J. L., and L. I. Norr. "Work Organization in Modern Fishing." *Human Organization* 37, no. 2 (1978), 163–171.

Northrup, Herbert R. "Salting the Contractors' Labor Force: Construction Unions Organizing with NLRB Assistance." *Journal of Labor Research*, 14, no. 4 (1993), 469–492.

O'Brien, James J., and Robert G. Zilly. *Contractor's Management Handbook* (New York: McGraw-Hill, 1971).

Orton, E. S. "Change in the Skill Differential: Union Wages in Construction, 1907–1971." *Industrial and Labor Relations Review*, (October 30, 1976), 6–24.

Otterbein, Keith F. *Comparative Cultural Analysis* (New York: Holt, Rinehart and Winston, 1977).

Park, Robert. "Human Nature, Attitudes and Mores." In *The Self in Social Interaction*, edited by C. Gordon and K. J. Gergen (New York: Wiley, 1968).

Philips, Peter, Garth Mangum, Norm Waitzman, and Anne Yeagle. *Losing Ground: Lessons from the Repeal of Nine "Little Davis-Bacon" Acts* (Salt Lake City: University of Utah Department of Economics, 1995).

Pilcher, William W. *The Portland Longshoremen* (New York: Holt, Rinehart and Winston, 1972).

Radcliffe-Brown, A. R. *Structure and Function in Primitive Society* (Glencoe, IL: The Free Press, 1952).

Reskin, Barbara F., and Patricia A. Roos. *Job Queues, Gender Queues, Explaining Women's Inroads into Male Occupations* (Philadelphia: Temple University Press, 1990).

Riemer, Jeffrey W. *On Building Buildings*. Ph.D. dissertation (University of New Hampshire, 1975).

————. *Hard Hats: The Work World of Construction Workers* (Beverly Hills: Sage Publications, 1979).

Rifkin, Jeremy. *The End of Work* (New York: G. P. Putnam, 1995).

Roediger, David. "White Workers, New Democrats, and Affirmative Action." In *The House that Race Built: Black Americans, U.S. Terrain,* edited by Wahneema Lubiano (New York: Pantheon Books, 1997).

Roethlisberger, F. J., and W. J. Dickson. *Management and the Worker* (Cambridge, MA: Harvard University Press, 1939).

Ross, I. C., and A. Zander. "Need Satisfaction and Employee Turnover." *Personnel Psychology*, 10 (1957), 327–338.

Ruegg, Rosalie T., and Harold E. Marshall. *Building Economics Theory and Practice* (New York: Van Nostrand Reinhold, 1990).

"Safety Net Result: Money Spent, Lives Saved." *Engineering News-Record* (July 18, 1976), 16.

Schneider, Scott, and Pam Susi. *Ergonomics and Construction: A Review of Potential Hazards in New Construction* (Washington, DC: Occupational Health Foundation, 1994).

Schroedel, Jean R. *Alone in a Crowd: Women in the Trades Tell Their Stories* (Philadelphia: Temple University Press, 1985).

Scott, Rachel. *Muscle and Blood* (New York: Dutton, 1974).

"Seasonal Unemployment Remains a Labor Problem." *Engineering News-Record* (November 7, 1997), 3.

Seidman, Joel, Jack London, Bernard Karsh, and Daisy L. Tagliacozzo. *The Worker Views His Union* (Chicago: University of Chicago Press, 1958).

Sheehan, George A. *Dr. Sheehan on Running* (Mountain View: World Publications, 1975).

Silver, Marc L. *Under Construction, Work and Alienation in the Building Trades* (Albany, NY: SUNY, 1986).

Slichter, Sumner H., J. J. Healy, and E. R. Livernash. *The Impact of Collective Bargaining on Management* (Washington, D.C.: Brookings Institute, 1960).

Smith, Patricia C. "Strategy for the Development of a General Theory of Job Satisfaction." *Cornell Studies of Job Satisfaction* (Ithaca, NY: Cornell University Press, 1963).

Sobel, Lester A. *Quotas & Affirmative Action* (New York: Facts on File, 1980).

Spero, Sterling D., and Abram L. Harris. *The Black Worker* (New York: Columbia University Press, 1931).

Spier, John. *Elements of Job Satisfaction in the Railroad Operating Crafts* (Berkeley: University of California Press, 1959).

Steiger, Thomas L. *Skill as an Ideological Discourse: Justifying Pay, Power and Privilege.* Unpublished paper (Terre Haute: Indiana State University, 1977).

Steiger, Thomas L., and William Form. "The Labor Process in Construction." *Work and Occupations*, 18, no. 3 (August 1991), 251–270.

Stinchcombe, Arthur. "Bureaucratic and Craft Administration of Production: A Comparative Study." *Administrative Science Quarterly*, 4 (1959), 168–187.

————. *Information and Organizations* (Berkeley: University of California Press, 1990).

Strauss, George. "Controls by the Membership in Building Trades Unions." *American Journal of Sociology*, 61 (May 1956), 527–535.

————. "Unions in the Building Trades: A Case Study." *The University of Buffalo Studies*, 24 no. 2 (1958), 61–159.

————. "Professionalism and Occupational Associations," *Industrial Relations*, 2, no. 2 (1963), 7–31.

————. *Union Policies Toward the Admission of Apprentices.* Reprint No. 357 (Berkeley: University of California Press, 1971).

Taylor, Frederick W. *The Principles of Scientific Management* (New York: Harper, 1911).

Terkel, Studs. *Working* (New York: Pantheon Books, 1972).

Tolbert, Pamela S., and Phyllis Moen. "Men's and Women's Definition of 'Good' Jobs." *Work and Occupations*, 25, no. 2 (May 1998), 168–194.

Tomaskovic-Devey, Donald. *Gender and Racial Inequality at Work* (Ithaca, NY: ILR Press, 1993).

Trice, Harrison M. *Occupational Subcultures in the Workplace* (Ithaca, NY: ILR Press, 1993).

Trist, E. L., and K. W. Bamforth. "Some Social Psychological Consequences of the Longwall Method of Coal-Getting." *Human Relations*, 4 (1951), 3–38.

"Unions Finance Construction." *Newark Star-Ledger* (October 2, 1998), 41–42.

University of Michigan Survey Research Center. *Survey of Working Conditions* (Ann Arbor: University of Michigan Press, 1971).

U.S. Bureau of the Census. *Census of Construction Industries* (Washington, DC: U.S. Government Printing Office, 1967, 1976).

U.S. Bureau of the Census. *Statistical Abstract* (Washington, DC: U. S. Government Printing Office, 1992).

U.S. Bureau of the Census. *Statistical Abstract* (Washington, DC: U.S. Government Printing Office, 1994).

U.S. Bureau of the Census. *Statistical Abstract* (Washington, DC: U.S. Government Printing Office, 1996).

U.S. Bureau of the Census. *Statistical Abstract* (Washington, DC: U.S. Government Printing Office, 1997).

U.S. Bureau of Labor Statistics. *Monthly Labor Review* (September 1967).

U.S. Bureau of Labor Statistics. *Compensation in the Construction Industry*, Bulletin no. 1656 (Washington, DC: U.S. Government Printing Office, 1970).

U.S. Bureau of Labor Statistics. *Seasonality and Manpower in Construction*, Bulletin no. 1641 (Washington, DC: U.S. Government Printing Office, 1970).

U.S. Bureau of Labor Statistics. *Current Population Survey* (Washington, DC: U.S. Government Printing Office, 1996).

U.S. Bureau of Labor Statistics. *Career Guide to Industries* (Washington, DC: U.S. Government Printing Office, 1998).

U.S. Department of Commerce. *General Social and Economic Characteristics: Final Report* (Washington, DC: U.S. Government Printing Office, 1970).

U.S. Department of Commerce. *Construction Review* (Washington, DC: U.S. Government Printing Office, 1976).

U.S. Department of Commerce. *Construction Review.* Quarterly Industry Report (Washington, DC: U.S. Government Printing Office, 1997).

U.S. Department of Labor. *Apprenticeship: Past and Present* (Washington, DC: U.S. Government Printing Office, 1969).

U.S. Department of Labor. *Equal Employment Opportunity, Title 41, Part 60, of the Code of Federal Regulations.* Employment Standards Administration, Office of Federal Contract Compliance Programs (Washington, DC: U.S. Government Printing Office, 1978).

U.S. Department of Labor. *Pamphlet OFCCP 7, OFCCP at a Glance.* Employment Standards Administration (Washington, DC: U.S. Government Printing Office, 1994).

U.S. Department of Labor. *Government Contractors, Affirmative Action Requirements, Executive Order 11246, Final Rule.* Employment Standards Administration, Office of Federal Contract Compliance Programs (Washington, DC: U.S. Government Printing Office, 1997).

U.S. Department of Labor. *Occupational Outlook Handbook.* Bureau of Labor Statistics (Washington, DC: U.S. Government Printing Office, 1996–1997).

U.S. Department of Labor. *Career Guide to Industries, Bulletin 2503* (Washington, DC: U.S. Government Printing Office, 1998).

Van Zelst, Raymond H. "Empathy Test Scores of Union Leaders." *Journal of Applied Psychology,* 36 (1952), 293–295.

———. "Sociometrically Selected Work Teams," *Personal Psychology,* 5 (1952), 175–186.

———. "Validation of a Sociometric Regrouping Procedure," *Journal of Abnormal Social Psychology,* 47 (1952), 299–301.

Waldinger, Roger. *Still the Promised City* (Cambridge, MA: Harvard University Press, 1996).

Walker, C. R., and R. H. Guest. *Man on the Assembly Line* (Cambridge, MA: Harvard University Press, 1952).

Walker, Charles. *Modern Technology and Civilization* (New York: McGraw-Hill, 1962).

Wallick, Franklin. *The American Worker: An Endangered Species* (New York: Ballantine Books, 1972).

Wallman, Sandra. *Social Anthropology of Work* (London: Academic Press, 1979).

Weitz, J., and R. C. Nuckols. "The Validity of Direct and Indirect Questions in Measuring Job Satisfaction," *Personal Psychology,* 6 (1953), 487–494.

Weschler, I. R., and R. E. Bernberg. "Indirect Methods of Attitude Measurement." *International Journal of Opinion Attitude Research,* 4 (1950), 209–228.

Western New York. (July 1977).

Whyte, William F. *Men at Work* (Westport, CT: Greenwood Press, 1974).

Wickert, F. R. "Turnover and Employees' Feelings of Ego-Involvement in the Day-to-Day Operations of a Company." *Personnel Psychology,* 4 (1951), 185–197.

Wilson, William Julius. *The Truly Disadvantaged* (Chicago: University of Chicago Press, 1987).

Woldman, Elizabeth. *Employment Status of School Age Youth.* Report no. 11. U.S. Bureau of Labor Statistics (Washington, DC: U.S. Government Printing Office, 1968).

Index

About the Author

HERBERT APPLEBAUM is employed in the construction industry and is the author of eight previous books, including most recently, *The American Work Ethic and the Changing Work Force: An Historical Perspective* (Greenwood, 1998).

ISBN 0-313-30937-X

90000>

EAN

9 780313 309373

HARDCOVER BAR CODE